creative ESSENTIALS

LUCY V. HAY

WRITING AND SELLING THRILLER SCREENPLAYS

FROM TV PILOT TO FEATURE FILM

creative ESSENTIALS

This new edition first published in 2023 by Kamera Books,
an imprint of Oldcastle Books
Harpenden, Herts, UK

www.kamerabooks.com

Series Editor: Hannah Patterson

A CIP catalogue record for this book is available from the British Library.

978-0-85730-552-7 (Paperback)
978-1-84243-972-2 (eBook)

2 4 6 8 10 9 7 5 3 1

Typeset in 9pt ITC Franklin Gothic Standard
by Avocet Typeset, Bideford, Devon, EX39 2BP
Printed and bound by CPI Group (UK) Ltd, Croydon, CR0 4YY

CONTENTS

FOREWORD

Thriller: a genre that comes in all shapes and sizes, from low-budget, contained tiny indie productions to massive multimillion blockbusters; from epic high-octane sci-fi or fantasy TV series, to low-key cerebral murder mysteries. Thrillers straddle every imaginable genre, creating sub- and cross-genres of their own, embracing elements like vast science-fiction and fantasy worlds or period settings; female protagonists; ensemble casts and non-linear structures. In short, there's nothing thrillers can't do, plus they perform consistently well in the marketplace, making them a good bet for producers and/or screenwriters wanting to make a splash.

Ten years after the first edition of this book, the thriller landscape looks rather different nowadays. I've been a script reader and script editor for just over 20 years, and I'd venture to say there's been more change in the past five to six years than the fifteen that preceded them. The advent of streaming technology, plus audiences' desire to 'binge' content, not to mention the rise of the 'four-quadrant audience' – that's 'old, young, male, female' – has meant significant changes to how the industry does business. This also means what producers and agents are looking for in the spec pile has had to change too!

A decade ago, feature-length screenplays had the most currency in the industry: TV people would tend to read spec features, whereas film people would not tend to read spec TV pilots. In the 2020s it is the opposite: producers are likely to ask writers if their movie ideas could be limited series (aka serials). You will find out why in the course of this book, plus there is a new breakdown on what goes into writing serials, plus how the TV landscape has changed in the Netflix era.

First up, be warned: *Writing & Selling Thriller Screenplays* is NOT a 'how to screenwrite' book. I am making the assumption you know how to format your spec screenplay (courier 12 point, normal margins if you don't); and that you know the basics of writing craft. This book concentrates on more advanced elements of the craft, such as plotting archetypes, character tropes and genre conventions; it will also go into detail about such advanced career strategies as transmedia and film finance.

Divided into three parts, the book first gives a brief history of the thriller genre and the characters that frequently appear in them, both in produced content and the spec pile. All my case studies are both old and new, iconic and hidden gem, feature-length (aka movie) and television this time around. I have attempted to ensure most of the movies and TV series mentioned are easy to access: you should be able to find them (or trailers/clips of them) on platforms such as (but not limited to) Netflix, Amazon Prime, Disney+, BFIplayer or YouTube though this will depend on territory and where you are in the world. Inevitably, I can only scratch the surface of such a broad genre in terms of examining produced movies; this means the focus of the book concentrates on the Hollywood model of the thriller genre, so the majority of films I discuss are British and American. If you're a big fan of European, Eastern or art-house cinema, you may be disappointed, but given the 'hugeness' of the thriller genre I had to make a decision on what would mean the most to the most amount of people, especially when so many native English speakers appear to hate subtitles.

By the way: very often writers will read case studies of produced content but not bother watching (or rewatching) the produced versions. This is a mistake. To get the most out of this book – and screenwriting education in general for that matter – it's a good idea to compare and contrast your own thoughts on the craft with the produced versions for consolidation purposes. It's also a great idea to IMMERSE yourself in the thriller genre, so you can understand what's come before and how you can write 'the same… but different' (or even 'bust' the genre – you can't do any of this intuitively, it requires study). This also means there will be spoilers AND LOTS OF THEM, so be warned. There will also be some swearing – B2W is known as 'sweary writing tips' on social media after all! You will also find a list of resources at the back of this book to help you with your own thriller endeavours.

Lastly, I would like to thank you for buying this book, especially if you are a 'Bang2writer' who forms part of the B2W community online. Your participation is greatly appreciated and I love to see and speak to you all – yes, even the 'Dudeflakes' who handily step onto my grill! Seriously, none of this would be possible without you all and I am grateful to each and every last one of you. See you online very soon.

Lucy V. Hay, February 2023

PART **ONE**

WHAT IS A **THRILLER**?

'People keep asking me if I'm back and I haven't really had an answer, but now? Yeah: I'm thinking I'm back.'

Keanu Reeves as John Wick, written by Derek Kolstad

DEFINITION OF THRILLER

Thriller has to be the most misunderstood genre in the spec pile. Despite getting the hang of horror, being clued-up on comedy and down on drama, screenwriters don't always seem to understand that their thriller screenplays need to thrill. Such a small thing, yet it means everything. I've read hundreds, probably thousands, of screenplays that have sought to call themselves 'thrillers', yet very few bear any kind of resemblance to the thrillers I see at the cinema or via streaming services. Yet thrillers being 'thrilling' is something we all demand at a grassroots level, as noted in this straightforward (albeit rather non-illuminating) dictionary definition:

Thriller *(noun)*

1. *A novel, play or movie with an exciting plot, typically involving crime or espionage.*
2. *A person, thing or experience that thrills.*

Thriller is an incredibly broad genre, so attempting a thriller screenplay for the first time – or, indeed, rewriting one – may seem like a daunting task to screenwriters. The problem is immediately apparent: what is deemed 'thrilling' to one person may make another claw his/her eyes out with boredom. Looking to produced movies in isolation may not help either, since everyone has different views on what makes a 'good' film (never mind what makes thrillers 'thrilling'!) and this includes the actual people who write and make them. Similarly, while thrillers have so many subgenres and cross-genres, not to mention various common elements, they nevertheless have lots to set them apart from one another (more about that in a minute).

So how can we look at the thriller genre, when it is so broad and complex? Jon Spaihts, one of the writers of *Prometheus* (2012), whose spec thriller *Shadow 19* sold to Warner Bros in 2006, tweeted this excellent and concise summary of how thrillers work:

> *'In thrillers the hero is reactive; a firefighter. The villain is the fire. The villain's plan is in some ways the soul of your story.'*

As a script editor and reader, I couldn't agree more. Putting the villain or antagonist in the driving seat is what sets thrillers apart from all other genres, including horror. Making your protagonist/s work to foil the antagonist's 'plan' (or similar) is the foundation of your story; all other elements are then piled on top of it, including subgenre, characters and even how the plot is executed, as illustrated by this very good Wikipedia entry on the thriller genre:

> *'The aim for thrillers is to keep the audience alert and on the edge of their seats. The protagonist in these films is set against a problem – an escape, a mission, or a mystery. No matter what subgenre a thriller film falls into, it will emphasise the danger the protagonist faces. The tension with the main problem is built on throughout the film and leads to a highly stressful climax. The cover-up of important information from the viewer and fight and chase scenes are common methods in all of the thriller subgenres, although each subgenre has its own unique characteristics and methods.'*

So whether your protagonist is female and fighting home invasion (as in *Panic Room*, 2002); or a male protagonist attempting to expose his mafioso bosses (*The Firm*, 1993); or a child, tortured by visions of dead people (*The Sixth Sense*, 1999); or an ensemble cast of doctors fighting disease (*Contagion*, 2011), your thriller screenplay must ensure that your protagonist overcomes all the obstacles put in their way by the antagonist/s, not to mention the situation at hand.

START AS YOU MEAN TO GO ON

> *'Make sure you know the world you are in. Study the form, so you know each and every nuance of the language available to you. You can only do this by observing, in detail, how others have used it in the past. You cannot hope to know a genre, let alone make it your own, without sleeping with it regularly. Be promiscuous and bed every damn title on the shelf.'*
>
> **– Gub Neal, producer** (@GubNeal)

Before we really put the thriller genre under the microscope, stop! Forget all you know – or think you know – about thrillers. Forget about those cool set pieces you want to write in the second act; forget about your brooding heroes or your haunted heroines. Forget about 'refragmenting the narrative' or 'vertical writing' or 'rising action' or whatever the cool screenwriting buzz phrases of the moment are. Think instead about your story's identity.

Arguably the biggest issue I see in thriller screenplays is that they don't 'feel' like thrillers in the first instance. The reasons for this can be varied and complex but, generally speaking, the writer has neglected to set the tone and the rules of the story world we are dealing with. More often than not, the writer believes erroneously that we must be introduced to the characters first, THEN the story. They'll frequently attempt this via dream sequences, flashbacks and early morning/getting ready for the day montages (all three if the reader's *really* lucky!).

First things first then, research is key. Many writers mistakenly believe they must avoid watching or reading in their chosen genre, in case of being adversely influenced and accidentally copying what has gone before. This opposite is true: if you want to write a thriller screenplay, you need to watch and read a LOT of thrillers! All the thrillers mentioned or broken down in this book are easy to source on this basis; they are frequently for mass audiences and part of various streaming subscriptions, or available for rent at low cost. (Some you may have seen already, though I urge you to watch them again with a notebook or worksheet in hand this time, rather than relying on memory, especially if you watched it many years ago. Stories can be surprising when revisited for work!).

As a first exercise then, consider the following questions about how produced thrillers start out when watching your favourites as research:

- How does it begin? (Situation and first image we see)
- Is there a prologue? Is there a big chunk of exposition to understand the story world?
- Does the story smash straight into the problem at hand, or is it 'slow burn'?
- How do the characters interact? Are they happy and oblivious, or stressed out and anxious? Somewhere in-between?
- What is the 'feel' of the piece: is it unstable, threatening from the outset? Or are we plunged from a happy home to a living nightmare somehow? Something else?
- What is the tone and story world we're entering? How do we know?

Regarding the last question: tone is everything in the thriller. Defined in the dictionary as *'the general character or attitude of a place, piece of writing, situation, etc.'* tone helps us understand how a story world and the characters within it work. It is worth remembering thrillers are less about the human element of the day-to-day minutiae of life and more about 'bigger', high concept threats. There are also conventions (aka tropes) to the thriller that target audiences literally sign up for, such as the ticking clock or deadlines (and which I will go into in further chapters of this book).

Studying the genre is the ONLY way to ensure you don't accidentally fall into cheesy or stale ideas, tropes, characters or plots. It will also help you understand who your target audience is, what they expect from your 'type' of thriller and how to subvert those expectations so your story and characters feel fresh and relatable. The first thing we can do is ask, 'Why this story?'.

WHY THIS STORY?

> *'Why this thriller NOW? Try to plunge a big tap root into a current issue, concern, anxiety or the zeitgeist ether. If you tweak a raw nerve with your storytelling you start with the engine running.'*
>
> **– Barbara Machin, producer, screenwriter and show runner**

At the turn of the noughties, the spec pile was full of very worthy, very personal dramas. Nowadays, genre is the name of the game. Thriller is rising to the top of the spec pile on account of its versatility, both for low-budget filmmakers and audiences. Low-budget filmmakers now tend to shoot on digital (thus keeping costs down) and movies made for a few hundred thousand pounds can now look like they've had a million spent on them if made 'right'.

Indie producers have learnt a few tricks from Hollywood in selling their movies to the public, too: just like their Tinseltown counterparts, they want marketable scripts with a strong hook and commercial premise to attract big-name actors with, which means they can then sell their films to distributors easily. With the advent of social media and streaming platforms like Netflix and Amazon Prime, audiences are voting with their feet and getting behind indie films more than ever. This means your low-budget thriller screenplay has more chance than ever to pick up a deal, get made and distributed to audiences across the globe.

Similarly, even a big-budget, epic, blockbuster-style spec thriller screenplay can open doors for a spec screenwriter. Though the latter has little chance of being made if you are a complete unknown, stranger things have happened and, at the very least, some scriptwriting contests – particularly American ones – appear to love them. In addition, agents and producers have been known to check out these scripts as samples as they consider the writers for 'writer for hire' work.

What's more, there's been a significant shift in the last decade since I wrote the first edition of this book. In 2013, feature-length spec screenplays had the most currency: industry pros working in television tended to read features as well, whereas film pros didn't tend to read spec TV pilots. The reason for this was because television was expensive and writers without credits found it notoriously difficult to get their shows greenlit for a very, very limited number of slots.

However, it's a different story in the 2020s because of one major change in the past decade: streaming. Tony Jordan, CEO of Red Planet Productions and producer of such classic British TV such as *Life on Mars* and *Death In Paradise* explains why:

'Streamers have made an impact, definitely,' Tony says, 'in order to match the budgets streamers have, broadcasters have to come together.'

This influx of money has brought significant change to the television landscape across the board and means spec TV pilots are much more in demand than they were a decade ago. When I was growing up in the 1990s, the general consensus was that TV was thought of as the 'inferior cousin'. This meant stars would move *from* television to movies, but now it feels like it's the other way around.

'Talent on TV is off the scale now,' Tony confirms, 'actors and stars who were doing films before are now interested. They want to investigate characters over ten hours; they also know they can reach a worldwide audience.'

Tony makes a great point here about worldwide audiences. One of the reasons movies were always seen as so prestigious in the past was because they were sold in multiple territories to multiple audiences who would all go and see them at the same place: the cinema.

Whilst TV series were also sold in different territories, what that meant would depend on which channel and how they scheduled it. A series might be bought for a major channel – such as BBC1 – but could be dumped in the graveyard slot past midnight. Or a channel could buy a show and schedule it on a prime-time slot like 6pm, but its smaller audience share might mean fewer see it there!

Yet in the streaming era, schedules no longer have the impact they once had. Whilst some thriller series – such as Amazon Prime's *Picard* (2019–2022) or *The Boys* (2019–2022) are updated weekly on Fridays during their season runs, the vast majority drop their entire series all at once to capitalise on audience's love of bingeing.

This is all good news for Tony. 'This also creates more freedom for writers... If I wrote a pilot fifteen years ago, I could go to the BBC, ITV, maybe Sky with it. Now I have fifty choices.'

Having a potential cornucopia of places to go with your pilot does not mean all the industry doors are suddenly thrown open, however.

'All this competition is worse for mediocre writers,' Tony says, 'you have to respect the craft and work hard. You can't phone it in and expect to get ahead.'

Of course, it's not all good news. In the post-Covid landscape, streamers have to compete with one another as costs of living go up and people look to keep subscription costs down. At the time of writing this book, multiple media commentators have warned of an incoming 'age of austerity' where there won't be quite as much money to go around in TV production, though what this will mean remains to be seen.

COMMON THRILLER REHASHES IN THE SPEC PILE

> *'I think the fundamentals of success have remained constant. Writers must apply themselves towards developing their ideas into scripts. Irrespective of whether those scripts get produced, writing them is the only way you'll become practised in the craft of creating compelling character arcs and thrilling stories.'*
>
> **– Jed Mercurio, producer & showrunner** (@Jed_Mercurio)

So, what does 'phone it in' mean? Though there are, of course, lots of ways for thriller screenplays to play out, I generally get one of the following when it comes to thriller spec TV pilots and feature-length screenplays:

- A time-traveller and a ragtag group of his or her friends end up in various historical time periods and cause havoc wherever they end up. (If this sounds like *Doctor Who* to you, that's because it is!)
- A male antagonist vs a male protagonist; a 'small-scale' situation (i.e. a man searching for his missing wife, in whose disappearance

he is a suspect); a non-linear storyline. (Writers seeking to make substitutions here will usually have a female protagonist vs a male antagonist, usually a psychopathic doctor or scientist; our protagonist will be searching for her girlfriend, who will frequently be trapped by said psychopathic doctor in a hospital *for some reason*).

- A special unit is employed to look into supernatural or alien events – yes, just like *The X Files*. This is not necessarily a problem IF the writer comes up with a new slant of some kind, but they rarely do.
- A gang of criminal friends who are working for a Mr Big character; one of the gang wants to leave 'the life' and the rest of his friends then have to kill him, on the orders of Mr Big. (Sometimes writers will attempt to subvert this story, in the style of *Sexy Beast* [2000], by including dream sequences or extensive flashbacks or other non-linear devices, but hardly ever by focusing on female gangsters or characters of different ethnic minorities, which I always find interesting).
- A woman moves into a haunted house, usually after the death of her own child. She will see ghosts, dead people, blood coming up the plughole, etc, but of course her husband doesn't and wants to commit her to the funny farm until the resolution, where he sees the spirits at work *for some reason*. (In recent years, scribes have swapped the gender roles, so it's the man haunted by the dead child, to the chagrin of the oblivious wife instead).
- A group of super-humans come together because of some catalyst event and find themselves up against a villain who wants to destroy the world or universe as we know it. (Yup, a rehash of *X Men* or *Avengers*!).

There is, of course, no reason for any of the above not to work: I've read some excellent screenplays that follow one of these six storylines or their variations. However, when trying to stand out from the crowd, it's far easier to do so when your spec thriller screenplay is easily differentiated, using a story the average reader has not seen a million times before. Thinking, 'Why this story?', rather than going with your first idea blindly, empowers you as a writer to find out if your story really is the best it can be or whether you're jumping into ground many, many others have tilled previously.

BEGINNING, MIDDLE, END

> *'Keep the script lean and pacey, don't get bogged down with unnecessary set up, scene description and (especially) exposition. Structure the action around exciting set-pieces; don't let the story slow to a grind with introspective character studies or indulgent dialogue scenes.'*
>
> **– Danny Stack, script editor & writer/director** (@DannyStack_)

Structure. An element of screenwriting that never fails to have people gnashing their teeth with frustration and rage. All manner of accusations are levelled at it, from the notion it's horribly formulaic, through to its even being responsible for killing one's creativity. Generally, I tend to think of structure as the three acts described by Aristotle in *Poetics*, simply because it makes the most sense to me and because the industry (as I've experienced in meetings and similar) tends to talk about 'acts'.

Before I go further, however, it should be noted I am not a purist. I believe whatever works for the individual screenwriter is valid, be it three acts, five acts, Syd Field's Paradigm, John Truby's 22 Steps, Chris Soth's Mini-Movie Method, Blake Snyder's Save The Cat! Approach, or something else. As far as I'm concerned, all a story really needs is a beginning, middle and end (and not necessarily in that order). I'm a passionate believer in the notion of story counting above all else, which is why I always stop short of 'page counting' for turning points, etc, preferring instead to rely on 'intuitive script editing', i.e. does a particular moment in the story 'feel' as if it is in the 'right' place?

So, those disclaimers aside, put bluntly, I see thriller structure broken down basically as follows:

- **ACT ONE – SET UP:** Protagonist presented with problem by the antagonist; the protagonist *needs* to solve it (s/he *can't* just walk away).
- **ACT TWO – CONFLICT:** Protagonist is presented with variety of obstacles by the antagonist…
- **MIDPOINT:** Things get worse/eye of the storm (as appropriate).
- **ACT TWO – CONFLICT:** Those obstacles keep coming and the protagonist must keep overcoming them, even though each obstacle is more difficult than the last.
- **ACT THREE – RESOLUTION:** Looks like all is lost for the protagonist… It looks like the antagonist is going to win… And *then* the protagonist turns it around *in some way* and solves the problem (or not, as the case may be).

Structure is not a 'quick fix' cure, and nor should it be. However, I *do* think it works as a good model to place our spec thriller screenplays against, to establish whether they work or not (plus what that means and why). As with anything else, it will depend on the story you're telling. That said, there are particular templates, conventions or expectations audiences have of plot generally and thriller is no different in this regard.

THE MONOMYTH VERSUS THE HERO'S JOURNEY

One such structural template that does turn up again and again in the thriller is The Hero's Journey. Most writers have heard of this, but not everyone knows it's a reiteration of a previous work, *The Hero With A Thousand Faces* (1949) by Joseph Campbell. In the book Campbell discusses his theory of the journey of the archetypal hero which he termed *The Monomyth*.

Campbell argued all mythological narratives followed a very similar structure. The most obvious here would be Homer's *Odyssey*. Homer's epic poem details Odysseus' 10-year struggle to return home after the Trojan War (yes, the one with the wooden horse that took down

Troy). While Odysseus battles mythical creatures and faces the wrath of the gods, his wife Penelope and his son Telemachus stave off suitors vying for Penelope's hand and Ithaca's throne long enough for Odysseus to return.

The Monomyth is in seventeen stages and breaks down as follows, according to Campbell:

Departure:

1. **The Call To Adventure.** This is the inciting incident that draws our hero into the story for some reason. Remember, we don't watch movies or TV shows 'about characters'; we watch movies and TV shows *'about characters who DO SOMETHING for SOME REASON.'* In the case of the thriller, a protagonist will most often be in 'the wrong place, wrong time' and be dragged into the antagonist's 'evil plan'.

2. **Refusal of the Call.** Very few protagonists want to engage at first across all genres, but this is especially true in the thriller genre. Remember, thrillers are antagonist-led and your protagonist is most likely in the 'wrong place, wrong time'.

3. **Meeting the mentor.** Most thrillers have a character who shows the protagonist the ropes in some way. This might be an overt mentor like Morpheus in *The Matrix* or it may be a 'stealth mentor' who seems like they're on the other side, or who even helps by accident when they're trying to get in the way.

4. **Crossing The First Threshold.** I like to think of this one as being around plot point one in the traditional Three Act Structure, though sometimes it can be pulled back to around page 10 (aka minute ten) or left under later. It depends on the story being told. However it's worth remembering there's no time to waste in thriller.

5. **Belly of the whale.** Campbell is referencing the bible story of Jonah and The Whale here. If you're not a practising Christian, you may never have heard of this story. Put simply, Jonah didn't want to do what God instructed him to do – and had to learn his lesson by being swallowed by a whale. In the same way, in this

part of the story, the thriller hero passes from the ordinary world into his or her (or their) adventure whether they like it or not.

Initiation:

6. **The Road of Trials.** This is where the REAL obstacles begin. Remember, thrillers need to escalate, so think of your hero as climbing walls, each one bigger than the last towards that ultimate showdown.

7. **The Meeting With The Goddess.** This is where the Monomyth really starts to show its age. On the road, the hero may meet a powerful female figure who will help him somehow. The goddess may be a mystical or supernatural being or she may be an ordinary woman with whom the hero gains support. Obviously this is a step that can be used, but is not strictly necessary in modern screenwriting.

8. **The Woman As Temptress.** Aaaaand here we go again! The Hero is cast as automatically male again and of course, jezebels and sirens tempt him and try to distract him, or get in his way (ack).

9. **Atonement With The Father/The Abyss.** Here so-called 'Daddy issues' come into play. The (male) hero must realise he is just like Dear Ol' Dad. Whilst some thrillers deal with this notion, it's probably not necessary. (Intriguingly in modern produced thrillers, female leads are more likely to have 'Daddy issues' than their male counterparts which I always find interesting).

10. **Apotheosis.** This is a super-fancy word that means 'exaltation to divine rank; deification.' In other words, this is the stage where the hero starts to fight back and even potentially win. His success makes him potentially 'god-like' according to The Monomyth.

11. **The ultimate boon.** This is the reward or thing the hero went on the quest to get. It might be metaphysical like 'peace', 'enlightenment' or 'love', but in modern thrillers is very likely to be a specific artefact like the ark in *Raiders of the Lost Ark* (1981) or The 'Kragle' in *The Lego Movie* (2014), which must be reunited with 'the piece of resistance' by 'The Special' before evil

President Business (Will Ferrell) sticks everybody and everything down forever.

Return:

12. **Refusal of Return** – This is where modern thriller screenwriting starts to deviate from The Monomyth. Whilst this is the first step of the return stage, the hero is initially reluctant to return to their mundane life. It could be argued this element is more use in thriller movie sequels or further seasons of TV series, eg. in the case of a series like *Ozark* (2017–2022), the Byrdes have opportunity to cut their losses and escape, but they refuse to. As Wendy Byrde (Laura Linney) always insists 'Don't you quit on me now.'
13. **Magic Flight** – Though the hero has answered their call and completed the reason for their journey, they are still chased by others. Here feels like a retread of step 2 on this list – 'refusal of the call'.
14. **Rescue From Without** – We're back with the mentor again from step 3. Another retread.
15. **Crossing the Return Threshold** – This one is tough to place in modern screenwriting, though it could be argued this is 'the last hurrah'. In past thrillers of the 1980s and 1990s, sometimes the antagonist looks like he has been vanquished, only to return for a last go at victory but that's not so common now.
16. **Master of Two Worlds** – Since the hero has been on the journey, they need to learn to balance their mundane life and the world they experienced on the journey. Again, this doesn't seem especially relevant to thrillers.
17. **Freedom to Live** – The hero acclimates back into their mundane life and lives peacefully. Thrillers are never meant to be peaceful, so this must be the ending of the story.

As we can see then, whilst The Monomyth can be useful, it's rather dated and more than a little sexist in the way it's described. What's more, not all of its stages really 'fit' with thrillers or even modern screenwriting as a whole, especially steps 12-17 which feel like a bunch of retreads.

Let's contrast all The Monomyth against Christopher Vogler's version. Working as an Exec for Disney, Fox and Warner Bros, Vogler was very inspired by Campbell. Vogler used Campbell's work to create a 7-page company memo for Hollywood screenwriters, *A Practical Guide to The Hero with a Thousand Faces.*

This became *The Writer's Journey: Mythic Structure for Storytellers and Screenwriters*, which is frequently referred to as just *The Hero's Journey*. It breaks down as follows, into just twelve sections to Campbell's seventeen:

Departure

1. Ordinary world
2. Call to adventure
3. Refusal of the call
4. Meeting with the mentor
5. Crossing the first threshold

Initiation

6. Tests, allies and enemies
7. Approach to the inmost cave
8. The ordeal
9. Reward

Return

10. The road back
11. The resurrection
12. Return with the elixir

As we can see, Vogler does away with all the bits of Campbell's work that take 'too long' at the ending or seem to suggest ideas that feels like a retread. 'Resurrection' and 'Return with the elixir' are the only two that are hugely different in terms of language, but even so it's obvious what Vogler is getting at: the hero returns, victorious.

He also removes the religious allegory and the latent sexism that suggests women aren't heroes or are wily jezebels that get in men's way. He also streamlines many of the stages so it feels much more vital and smooth.

There's a strong chance you feel very familiar with The Hero's Journey, even if this is the very first time you've seen it written down. This is because it's acted as a template for nearly every thriller or action-adventure blockbuster movie for the past four decades. Chances are you can think of your favourite thriller and see immediately how it corresponds with the stages laid out by Vogler.

'THE SAME... BUT DIFFERENT'

Writers frequently hear the phrase, 'the same... but different', but just as often misunderstand what it means: they either go too 'samey' with their concepts, imitating those produced movies they've seen, or they go too different, meaning their specs are a difficult sell. As with most things in scriptwriting (or, indeed, life), 'the same... but different' is about balance.

Consider two thrillers which are obviously similar: *Die Hard* (1988), in which a bloody, daring siege takes place in a towering building; and *Con Air* (1997), in which prisoners perform an equally bloody and daring coup on their guards, this time on board an airplane. In both, only one man can stop the criminals, holding everyone, literally, to ransom. But crucially, John McClane in *Die Hard* and Cameron Poe in *Con Air* are two quite different men. Perhaps just as importantly though, Hans Gruber and Cyrus the Virus are two very different antagonists. And, what's more, the secondary characters and their individual role functions are very different in each film. So, whilst we might have the same spirit and tone in both films (larger than life, with comedic and action elements), we nevertheless have wildly different characters and settings (building versus a plane).

So, if you want to attempt 'the same... but different', take a good look at what has gone before. Work out what you want to emulate and how, whilst still ensuring your script has its own original take on the story. It is difficult to get right, but, if you can, this will really help your spec thriller's chances in the marketplace in the long run. (For more on 'the same... but different', check out Part Two of this book under 'genre busting', and find out what you can really do in this respect to get attention for your thriller screenplay).

ON 'RISK-AVERSE' HOLLYWOOD

Lots of writers like to pontificate online about how Hollywood is 'risk-averse' and should be 'braver' in funding more original projects. Yet Hollywood is not a patron of the arts, plus no one makes money from throwing it into the void on a hunch (hell, you can lose money even when you've done your homework *and* crunched the numbers!).

This is why sequels, reboots, remakes and franchises are favoured over new projects because, like it or not, audiences literally favour them too. It's a sad fact that even an underperforming franchise film tends to do better at the box office than an original film.

In the first two years of 2020s alone we have had the following thriller remakes, reboots and franchise movies (and this list only scratches the surface!):

- *Bad Boys For Life* (2020)
- *Wonder Woman 1984* (2020)
- *The Witches* (2020)
- *Mulan* (2020)
- *Fast & Furious Part 9* (2021)
- *No Time To Die* (2021)
- *Ghostbusters: Afterlife* (2021)
- *Dune* (2021)
- *Venom: Let There Be Carnage* (2021)
- *The King's Man* (2021)
- *The Suicide Squad* (2021)
- *Spider-Man: No Way Home* (2021)
- *Morbius* (2022)
- *Doctor Strange in the Multiverse of Madness* (2022)
- *The Batman* (2022)

- *Top Gun: Maverick* (2022)
- *Jurassic World: Dominion* (2022)

All of these movies made a big splash with audiences, either via their wallets, the chatter online, or both. Audiences lavished praise on them or excoriated them, saying they were the 'best' or 'worst' movies ever made. A couple of them were the focus of boycotts. Many of them received (grudging) praise from critics and a couple were critical darlings, receiving awards nominations.

Most importantly, all of them made money. Some were record-breakers. If the films underperformed in theatres, they still carried enough weight to attract a secondary audience via 'home premieres' on streaming services which charge extra for subscribers to see it 'earlier' than regular subscribers.

Whether we personally like such movies or characters is immaterial. Millions of people do, so that is their value. We can fight this – and lose – or we can accept that until people vote with their wallets and go to more original movies as standard, remakes and reboots are here to stay.

CINEMA VERSUS STREAMING

'The Death of Cinema' has been announced many times in the past 40 years. VHS, satellite television, video games and smartphones have all made a serious dent, with many independent cinemas closing in small towns and only huge, centralised multiscreen chain Odeons surviving in many places.

With the advent of streaming, we are seeing something similar occur in real time. Even streamers like Netflix, Amazon and Apple TV+ which seek added prestige for their movies via awards like the Oscars need only place their films in a handful of cinemas to become eligible (and who knows how long that stipulation will continue?).

In the past ten years studios have become complicit in killing off cinemas, launching their own platforms such as Disney+, Warner Bros or HBO Max. This means studios will be less inclined to give box office dollars to cinemas now that they have their own streaming platforms. The Covid pandemic accelerated this, showing multiplatform releases were possible and in some cases, even preferred by certain demographics.

'Why go and see *Death on the Nile* when it's available to stream?' says Steve La Rue, a development executive who has worked for Paramount, NBC/Universal and Twentieth Century Fox, 'No babysitter needed, no parking hassles, no Covid concerns.'

The core demographic of young males aged 15-25 years is still prized by cinemas, but the last decade has made some significant changes here too. A-list directors like Christopher Nolan or Michael Bay can still demand cinema releases for their films – but crucially, only if their movies make money.

Nolan's hotly anticipated 2020 thriller *Tenet* was nevertheless considered as a 'box office flop', as was Bay's 2022 chase thriller *Ambulance,* despite being his best film in decades. What this means for their future releases remains unclear at the time of writing this book.

It is worth mentioning too Netflix recorded an epic loss of one million subscribers in 2022. As a market disruptor such a loss was considered 'inevitable' by media experts, especially as competition in the streaming space with multiple channels – both paid-for and free – grows. Rising cost of living was blamed for people tightening their belts and cutting back on subscription services. Other commentators suggested a number of other issues Netflix might be suffering, such as Netflix being too free and easy on favourite limited series cancellations; or platforming controversial comedians such as Dave Chappelle and Ricky Gervais; or their movie content being rather lacklustre in contrast to other streamers such as Amazon Prime, whose film Originals tend to receive more critical acclaim.

So it's important to note no one really knows for definite, not even Oscar-winners like the writer-director Guillermo del Toro! Speaking to SlashFilm.com in 2022, he said:

> *'There are many answers to what the future is. The one I know is not what we have right now. It is not sustainable. In so many ways, what we have belongs to an older structure.'* Del Toro referenced the abrupt, 1920s transition from silent films to talkies. *'That's*

how profound the change is. We are finding that it is more than the delivery system that is changing. It's the relationship to the audience that is shifting. Do we hold it, or do we seek and be adventurous?'

If the lack of answers and forward-thinking on this issue is affecting A-listers like del Toro, then it will be an issue for people further down the food chain. That's why I think it's worth considering alternative routes to get industry pros' attention, rather than 'just' write spec screenplays and cross our fingers.

CINEMA IS DEAD... AGAIN?

Now the older members of Generation Z (aka those born between approximately 1997 and 2010) are coming of age, it's predicted cinema may have its biggest challenge yet.

'For young females, streaming is the destination,' says Steve La Rue, 'Cinemas are still important, but only for four-quadrant movies like *Spider-Man: No Way Home*. The headline of the next ten years will be "survival of the fittest."'

It's clear there are going to be even more marked changes in the decades ahead. With studios effectively betting against themselves by creating their own streaming platforms and offering 'home premieres', it seems like cinema-going might finally be in real danger, especially when we consider many low-budget films have already effectively been 'locked out' of theatrical releases by rising distribution costs.

That said, cinemas have found lots of inventive ways to stay current in the past four decades. There's 'event cinema' which shows livestreams and recordings of West End productions. There's also re-releases of fan favourites at certain times of year: I finally saw both *Home Alone* and *Die Hard* on the big screen last Christmas which was a real treat, since I'd only watched them on VHS or TV. There's also film festivals like Frightfest and of course, the big four-quadrant blockbusters that become an event too, such as *Top Gun: Maverick* and *Jurassic World: Dominion* both demonstrated in 2022.

So for everyone sounding the alarm, it's not over... yet. It will be interesting to see what happens next. For now, we are in a period of transition.

THE ROUTE TO YOUR AUDIENCE

'Give the audience your plants to allow them that sense of fear... They must fear, anticipate, worry about the protagonist.'

– **Daniel Martin Eckhart, writer** (@dmeckhart)

Audiences know what they want, so as writers we need to give it to them. This is not to say we should 'dumb down'; far from it. It is possible to convey any manner of complex and interesting messages and themes within the perimeters of what audiences want... which is to be *entertained*, first and foremost. Forget this at your peril. It's not rocket science. Yet the average spec thriller screenplay is not entertaining, because it has forgotten the notion of whom it's actually FOR.

Like or loathe them, some of the most successful filmmakers of the last 30 or 40 years have made thrillers, many of them in the action subgenre: George Lucas; Steven Spielberg; Tony Scott; James Cameron; Quentin Tarantino; JJ Abrams; Christopher Nolan; Michael Bay. (Yes, even Michael Bay. Deal with it.) The reason these guys are so successful is because, though they often make testosterone-soaked sausage-fests, they provide what audiences want. In these cases, audiences want brooding heroes; epic arenas; huge fights, explosions and high-octane CGI-based sequences. The potential audience knows exactly what it's going to get when it sees those filmmakers' names attached to various films.

This is why people go in droves to see them. It is no accident blockbuster movies are often thrillers, comprising of action and adventure. That feted 'four-quadrant' audience – male, female, young, old – absolutely love to watch movies with larger-than-life characters and situations. At the time of writing this book, the top 10 highest grossing movies of all time (according to Box Office Mojo) were:

1. *Avatar* (2009)
2. *Avengers: Endgame* (2019)
3. *Titanic* (1997)
4. *Star Wars: The Force Awakens* (2015)
5. *Avengers: Infinity War* (2018)
6. *Spider-Man: No Way Home* (2021)
7. *Jurassic World* (2015)
8. *The Lion King* (2019)
9. *Marvel's The Avengers* (2012)
10. *Furious 7* (2015)

The past decade has been BIG news for thrillers. Nearly all the movies on the highest-grossing list are part of franchises, sometimes reboots or remakes as well. Eight out of ten of the movies are for the four-quadrant audience: families are able to enjoy them together, which means even once the theatrical release is over, they can stream them together.

All of the movies on the list are rated 12 (aka PG-13 in the USA). With the exception of *Jurassic World* and *Furious 7*, all of them are available on Disney+. *Jurassic World* is considerably more bombastic than its predecessors in the *Jurassic Park* franchise. Owen (Chris Pratt) is every bit the swashbuckling hero, rather than the 'thinking man's' protagonist Alan Grant (Sam Neill) or stooge antagonist Doctor Ian Malcolm (Jeff Goldblum). In contrast Claire (Bryce Dallas Howard) is an 'upgrade' on the sidelined female characters of the originals like Ellie Sattler (Laura Dern). Even so, the Indominus Rex presents a credible monster threat, with many close-ups of people getting chomped that may scare younger children.

Whilst *Furious 7 and Titanic* are both rated 12 too, they have considerably more adult content in them than any of the other movies. In *Furious 7's* case there is nudity, extended fight scenes, some considerable swearing and tobacco use.

The only one predating 2009 is *Titanic* (1997). Love or hate it, *Titanic* was a cultural phenomenon in the 1990s and has passed into cinema history as a cult favourite, plus its writer-director is James Cameron who is also responsible for *Avatar* (not to mention other thriller behemoths like *Terminator 2: Judgment Day* and *Aliens)*. A mixed genre piece of both romance and thriller, there is a sex scene as well as considerable peril, plus it's a true story (which may make some viewers upset at the thought of those things really happening). *Titanic* still benefits from Cameron's expert take on thriller tropes, especially once the movie becomes a story of survival. Who can forget the hair-raising moment Rose and Jack hang on to *the outside* of the ship as it breaks in half and bobs upright, sending those still on the deck plummeting to their deaths?

Overall, writers can be assured the modern audience of all ages LOVE thrillers. There's also a surprising diversity in what is 'allowed' in a blockbuster thriller aimed at a four-quadrant audience. As long as it's exciting and racy but not too over-the-top, families will watch as well as individuals without children.

Now I'm not advocating we all write thrillers about giant killer sharks, dinosaurs, drag racing, shipwrecks, aliens or robots (though go ahead, if you want to). Rather I am suggesting we learn a lesson from the Spielbergs and Camerons and Nolans in terms of *entertainment*. Be honest about *what* you write, *who* you want to appeal to and *how* you are going to appeal to that potential audience. It's no good to say, 'Well, it's great writing, it will appeal to everyone' or 'I see the trailer in my head, it's gonna be awesome'. That way disappointment lies – for you, because it will never get 'off the page'. You need to figure out exactly how you are going to entertain your audience, and you can't do that without working out who they are first. In order to do so, I recommend thinking about the following:

- **What is my audience's demographic?** Be specific, but not too specific. It's fine if you're going primarily for a specific age group or gender but say stuff like 'only white people will be interested' and suddenly you seem like an over-privileged idiot.

- **How can I open this up?** Not so long ago the supposed core demo of cinema-going people was 15–25-year-old males. Whilst studios still like this demographic, in the 2020s the aforementioned 'four-quadrant audience' is much more highly prized. It's not hard to see why: everyone loves a good yarn, well told. So if you can come up with a great story, with great characters, you have every chance of tapping into a MASS audience. Despite being 'old' movies now, the likes of *Jurassic Park* (1993) and *Avatar* (2009) do extremely well with audiences year on year, *not* because they are full of special effects but because people can relate to the stories, the characters, the messages behind them (whether we, as writers, agree with those messages or not). In the case of *Jurassic Park*, it's also rather funny, in terms of both comedy dialogue and moments. There's all manner of things you can do as a writer to 'open up' your audience and include as many people as possible, so never underestimate this.

- **Why would they watch this movie?** This is where you get really specific. It's not good enough to say, 'It's really exciting.' What has gone before? What is 'the same... but different' about it? How does it break new ground? How is this a new take on what we have seen already? What might your audience have seen before, which may make them want to watch your movie?

Last of all, never ever undervalue your audience, think they're stupid or that you need to spoonfeed them. Modern audiences are smart; they are more media-literate than ever before and can decode stuff instantly. This is why you need to 'hit the ground running'.

HITTING THE GROUND RUNNING

'Open with something provocative, unusual, visual and dynamic.'

– Ed Hughes, Linda Seifert Management (@LindaSeifert)

A few decades ago, even Hollywood movies had 'slow-burn' techniques, but today modern audiences demand that stories 'hit the ground running'. Where once audiences were happy to wait for the protagonist and the situation in hand to be introduced over the course of ten or even fifteen minutes, we now slam into the action within two or three, meaning screenwriters must adjust their techniques accordingly. Many thrillers even begin with a shocking or intriguing catalyst in the first minute, out of sync time-wise with the rest of the story, that then requires the audience to 'rewind' to days, or a few hours, earlier. (Interestingly, this, too, is now beginning to feel rather old hat, leading me to wonder if more slow-burning techniques may return, for want of a change?)

However you choose to open your thriller screenplay, it's crucial to remember that character and story must be introduced hand in hand, which is possible even with slow-burn techniques. As mentioned previously, spec screenwriters often believe we must be introduced to the characters first, THEN the story. As a result, the reader (and thus the audience) is left waiting for the story to start. In this media-literate age, when audiences can pick up even the most scant of information and decode it instantly, being made to wait even just five minutes can spell disaster for your spec screenplay's chances in the marketplace. Common mistakes from writers trying (and failing) to 'hit the ground running' include montages to attempt to set the tone; disjointed prologues that take too long to connect to events *in* the situation at hand; and flashbacks to unrelated events that are somehow 'character-building' for the protagonist, particularly if she is female. It is worth noting that female protagonists in spec thriller screenplays are commonly rape and child abuse survivors, and/or fighting depression or other mental illnesses. Beware of piling such pasts/backstories on your characters (*not* because issues of rape, abuse or mental illness, etc, are not serious or worth talking about). However, by making such backstories supposedly 'character building', you risk trivialising them and thus isolating your audience. Your audience will also have specific expectations of your thriller, which you need to bear in mind too.

TROPES & GENRE CONVENTIONS

When I was researching my 2017 book *Writing Diverse Characters For Fiction, TV or Film* it became obvious to me there's a lot of confusion over what tropes really are. This was largely because the internet –

particularly Twitter – uses the word 'tropes' to mean 'I don't like this'. I even read blogs and whole threads about how tropes were supposedly responsible for 'ruining' movies, TV and storytelling in general!

A trope is simply a 'recurring idea or motif' in a story that may or may not form part of genre conventions. Genre conventions are those elements (such as topics, tropes, characters, situations and plot beats) that are common in specific genres. Put simply, genre conventions are those recognisable things that 'make' a genre.

This means that tropes are NOT responsible for 'ruining' anything – writers literally need them to write stories!

For example, common tropes in the thriller genre include (but are not limited to):

- The lone protagonist 'up against it'
- Detectives (police or amateur) who must solve a mystery
- Escape plans – most often literal
- Mind games such as manipulation or coercion
- High octane set pieces
- Reliance on plot-driven storytelling
- Life or death stakes

Just as most musical composition needs chords, stories need tropes. They form a framework for people to understand the story. It's no good to reinvent the wheel when people actively WANT these things from your thriller!

But when is a trope not a trope? When it becomes a CLICHÉ: these are those moments where characters or plotlines are far too obvious, cheesy, stale or even offensive. We can guard against this by studying the craft and paying attention to sites such as www.tvtropes.org or www.tropedia.fandom.com which describe common and uncommon tropes, how they work and where they can be seen. Reading blogs and threads by marginalised people, plus paying for notes from paid-for script readers and sensitivity consultants can also help guard against cliché, but it should be stressed none of these are a magic bullet. There will always be someone who hates on your writing, no matter how much due diligence you do. You have to get okay with criticism, whether it's warranted or not. It's the nature of the job.

HORROR VERSUS THRILLER

Many writers and filmmakers mistakenly believe horror and thriller to be more or less the 'same' – leading many to label their scripts and pitches 'Horror/thriller'. Whilst the two genres DO share some similar or even the same attributes, there are significant differences to place them apart (otherwise they wouldn't be different genres!).

Whilst thrillers and horrors may 'cross over' in terms of tropes, topics, characters, situations a lot, HOW they do this will differ. So let's break this down in a very obvious way.

As mentioned at the beginning of this book, thrillers need to be EXCITING. Everything the story does will be built around with this goal in mind. This is why chase sequences, stunts, explosions and other set pieces are so important in this genre – and why most blockbuster movies are thrillers. Even when thrillers are more cerebral (such as crime mysteries/whodunnits), excitement is still the core dynamic.

In addition, thrillers are usually 'kicked off' via a catalyst provided by the ANTAGONIST, not the protagonist – a key element to remember, because thrillers is the one genre that does this. This also means the audience are asked to put themselves in the place of the protagonist and relate to what they are going through at the hands of the antagonist.

In contrast, horror is supposed to SCARE us. Some writers believe this relates to gore but I don't think it's as simple as that (especially when thrillers are more gory than ever in the 2020s!). I don't think it's necessarily topics either: serial killers can be found in both thrillers and horrors; so can ghosts, aliens, haunted houses, exorcisms and so on.

So whilst some audience members might also be excited by being scared, that's not the primary reason we're watching. There's a kind of voyeurism to Horror we don't get in thriller: we are usually not asked to relate to the protagonist going through the horrifying things (hence the popular notion of hiding your face behind a cushion when you get 'too' scared by what's on screen).

What's more, unlike thriller, horror protagonists usually make active decisions to go into the 'lion's den': they move into the haunted house; they adopt the possessed child; they land on the forbidden planet. In short, they go where they are not supposed to be and/or do what they are not supposed to do. This is a huge difference when we compare to the thriller protagonist who usually gets caught in the antagonist's 'spider web' against their will.

However there is one genre convention that both thriller and horror share, which is the prime cause of confusion over the genres – 'flight versus fight'. More, next.

DRAMATIC CONTEXT – FLIGHT VERSUS FIGHT

'Think about putting us in the moment with the main character(s), so that we can react as they react... If we're way ahead of the characters, it gets dull. The second half of that, of course, is that if we're in the moment with the characters the pressure is on for them to react convincingly – and not be stupider than the audience.'

– Scott Mullen, screenwriter

Another thing that marks out the thriller is its dramatic context (though, unhelpfully, horror is very similar, hence the confusion with some writers). You've heard the saying, 'Two sides to every story'? This is most true in thrillers, which typically ask their audiences to invest in two aspects of the protagonist's struggle throughout the narrative:

- **Flight (non-engagement).** This is where the protagonist chooses NOT to engage with the situation at hand and attempts to outrun the problem (often literally).
- **Fight (engagement).** The second half is where the protagonist must engage with the situation (or all is lost, again often literally) and, unsurprisingly, FIGHT or engage with the antagonist directly in some way.

Frequently the dramatic context of 'flight' will be the first half, or even three quarters, of the story, with 'fight' taking up the resolution (though, again, it obviously depends on the individual story and its execution). This transition is usually clearly marked for the audience, either in a given scene or moment, and most notably in the 'prepare to fight' montage that is so popular, particularly in action thrillers and classic creature thrillers like *Aliens* (1986) and *Predator* (1987).

MYSTERY AND THRILLER

> *'Remember, audiences LOVE mystery. They love to watch and connect A-2-B, to figure it out as it's happening, but, mostly, they love to be surprised with a clever story, something they never saw coming but in retrospect was obvious.'*
>
> **– Chris Jones, writer/director (@livingspiritpix)**

In the 2020s, mystery has cemented itself as a go-to device in thriller screenplays. This means modern television seeks out content that has mystery at its heart. This is again most obvious in crime series, especially police procedurals on television. However mystery thriller movies (of varied types, not just detective thrillers) also exist and can be a significant draw in the 2020s too.

Thanks to the popularity of serials in the streaming era, mystery presents the ultimate in 'bingeworthy' content for audiences. Mysteries typically have a big reveal at the end of the story, hence their colloquial name 'Whodunnits'.

Mysteries tend to be cerebral on this basis. One of the reasons mystery is so popular in the streaming era is because it involves the audience in the story. Figuring out who is 'Behind It All' can be satisfying whether we're right OR wrong. Of course, not all thrillers require mystery to qualify as a thriller, but it's rare for mysteries to have zero thriller conventions at all. (For example, it's common for characters who have figured out who is Behind It All to then be threatened with death by the antagonist in the showdown of Act 3).

There's a number of genre conventions mysteries require to qualify as mysteries. They may not use all of them, but they typically use at least 1-3 of the following:

- **Red herrings are misleading or outright false clues.** It is a common literary device used in mysteries that can lead the detectives (and thus the audience) down a false path or otherwise distract them from what's really going on. (Why 'red herring'? Because apparently herrings go red when smoked, but more importantly: a 1686 gentleman's magazine suggested confusing foxhounds on a rival hunt by dragging a dead cat or red herring across their trail!)
- **'The Agatha Christie Rule'**. Agatha Christie is largely thought to be the queen of mystery; she is still the bestselling author of all time with an amazing two billion sales to her name. Many academics have broken down and decoded her novels to try and work out her success. One element that has been proven over and over is the fact the culprit is always introduced and mentioned within the first 25 per cent of Christie's stories. Her influence has led to scores of writers following this 'rule' in their own mysteries, so their mystery antagonists are 'hiding in plain sight' too.
- **Working theories.** Most detective characters (whether actual police or not) will indulge in working theories to try and make sense of the mystery. Often these working theories are incorrect or way off-base (as in 'the version' in the *CSI* franchise). We still need them to help advance the story.
- **The Patsy or Wrong Suspect.** Sometimes someone is caught and charged almost immediately for a crime. In the case of the Patsy, it's a frame-up: someone has ensured that person is wrongfully charged or convicted somehow *on purpose*. In the case of the Wrong Suspect, there's no frame-up involved. Instead that suspect is the unfortunate victim of being in the wrong place at the wrong time, with evidence pointing to them *despite* their innocence. This may be as a result of police ineptitude, or it may be through a series of events that would fox even the straightest arrow police detective. Whatever the case, a detective must stand up against

the system and prove these characters' innocence, or a miscarriage of justice will occur. Shows such as *Bosch* (Amazon Prime, 2015–2021) often have storylines like this. This is because the show's protagonist Detective Hieronymus 'Harry' Bosch refuses to be morally compromised, unlike every other character around him as the series continues.

- **Stooge Antagonists.** A 'stooge' is a subordinate who is employed or forced to do another's dirty work, either overtly or covertly; alternatively they may do the antagonist's job by being obnoxious and diverting attention away from the Real Baddie by accident. In the case of conspiracy thrillers in particular, that stooge antagonist will be the first person the detective character looks for – think The One-Armed Man from *The Fugitive* (1993) here. Richard Kimble (Harrison Ford) is desperate to prove his innocence and avoid the death penalty by proving such a man exists... When he eventually finds him, he realises The One-Armed Man aka Sykes (Andreas Katsulas) is on the payroll of a pharmaceutical company, headed up by his friend Doctor Charles Nichols (Jeroen Krabbé). Kimble realises he has been a patsy, his wife murdered to cover up Nichols' faulty research into a powerful drug.
- **The Big Reveal.** Arguably the only trope that MUST be included for a mystery, The Big Reveal is as its name suggests: the perpetrator is revealed and the 'whodunnit' is solved.

THE WHYDUNNIT

In contrast to the whodunnit, the 'Whydunnit' reveals the perpetrator from the offset (if only to the audience)... and that BIG REVEAL at the end will cover *why* they did whatever it was they did. 'Whydunnits' have gained in popularity in recent decades, though they are yet to eclipse the popularity of the classic 'Whodunnit'.

A recent example of the Whydunnit would be 2017 Netflix serial *The Sinner*, starring Bill Pullman. Pullman stars as Detective Harry Ambrose who investigates crimes committed by unlikely culprits and attempts to uncover their motivations.

In the first season, Jessica Biel plays Cora, a seemingly ordinary wife and mother who stabs a man to death on a crowded beach. This inciting incident matches its shock value with intrigue, making the audience ask WHY she has done such an appalling act. Is it the result of some hidden trauma? Even Cora herself doesn't seem to know.

One of the downsides of the Whydunnit is the rest of the story may not be as intriguing or shocking as that first inciting incident. It takes extraordinary craft on the writer's part to keep the audience hooked from episode to episode.

So if you can't decide between a Whodunnit or a Whydunnit, I'd always recommend the former over the latter. But of course, it's up to you as the writer!

TYPES OF THRILLER

'Audiences show up for story, not for big themes or great characters. But it's the big themes and characters that send them away happy.'

– Stephen Gallagher, screenwriter & show runner (@brooligan)

Writers often attempt to write thrillers without having watched all the thrillers they can get their hands on that resemble the story they are attempting. This is foolhardy. Knowing what has gone before in produced content is absolutely key in writing your low-budget thriller spec or your blockbuster script sample. If nothing else, questions you may be asked by producers, execs and agents when pitching your thriller may include: 'What film is your screenplay most like?' or 'What's different about your screenplay to (this produced movie)?' What's more, if you don't know what's gone before, how are you going to create a new take on the genre? You simply must identify where your story *is* in the thriller genre and how it works in comparison.

The following is by no means an exhaustive list; many of the movies mentioned may exist on two, three or even more sub/cross-genres, and new ways of looking at thrillers are happening all the time. The focus of this book concerns the Hollywood model of genre films with a strong hook and high-concept story (and which have made significant inroads into British filmmaking, especially post-2000 with the advent of digital). It's also worth considering how films from other cultures impact on our own storytelling. Eastern and European cinema has created some of the most iconic thrillers, for example, and colleagues working for American production companies tell me they have been instructed to look farther afield to these films, and to stop mining the same old tired Hollywood tropes. But for starters, in no particular order, check these out:

- **THE ACTION THRILLER.** Action thrillers are the epitome of 'thrilling', so it's not hard to see why people immediately think of them when asked to consider what makes a good thriller. Huge set pieces abound in this subgenre: car chases, explosions, daredevil stunts and meticulous fight choreography all figure for the ultimate thriller experience. Enigmatic male heroes dominate this section of thrillers: Bourne and Bond are the most obvious, not to mention superheroes like Batman, Superman, Spider-Man, Iron Man et al (though their films may also stray into action-adventure territory, too). Muscle-bound stars like Stallone and Schwarzenegger made their names on action thrillers, as did martial arts icons like Jason Statham or Jet Li. Then there are the (usually white) actors with whom we associate the cool, comic quips, like Bruce Willis in the *Die Hard* franchise; Harrison Ford in the *Indiana Jones* series; or Mel Gibson in the *Lethal Weapon* movies; also the likes of Will Smith in films such as *Bad Boys 1* and *2* or Shia LaBeouf in the *Transformers* series, who is markedly younger than your average hero (though arguably only because the heroes of the 1980s are now old enough to be grandads). Occasionally we're treated to three-dimensional female protagonists, such as Evelyn in *Salt* (2010) or *Haywire*'s Mallory (2011). Action thrillers are frequently 'spy thrillers' in this day and age, though, in the past, spy thrillers were often psychological and/or crime thrillers.
- **THE PSYCHOLOGICAL THRILLER.** Psychological thrillers are those that depend – unsurprisingly – on the psychological, rather than epic set pieces or violence, to thrill the viewer. Psychological thrillers frequently explore themes of identity and loss, plunging

protagonists into battles of wits or journeys where they must discover who they really are, often utilising a big 'reveal' at the end. For an extended period in produced movies, both the antagonist and protagonist *were* the same person as in *Fight Club* (1999), *Identity* (2003) and *The Ward* (2010), though this is considered a little old now. The psychological lends itself to any number of scenarios and the savvy spec screenwriter would do well to figure out what's the next big thing here.

- **THE CRIME THRILLER.** While action thrillers are often epic, sweeping, Hollywood blockbuster affairs, crime thrillers are often low-budget, indie and psychological. Mostly associated with the detective character, like Leonard Shelby in *Memento* (2000), crime thrillers also include 'normal' people who may be tempted by crime, such as in *Shallow Grave* (1994) or *A Simple Plan* (1998). Enigmatic couples may also play a part in this section of thriller, as in the title couple of *Bonnie and Clyde* (1967); Kit and Holly in *Badlands* (1973); Clarence and Alabama in *True Romance* (1993); and Mickey and Mallory in *Natural Born Killers* (1994). Of course, the 'Serial Killer thriller' also falls under 'Crime' but is so frequently a subject matter that it deserves a section of its own.
- **THE SERIAL KILLER THRILLER.** Often taking the thriller genre towards horror, the serial killer thriller frequently places an unwitting protagonist or group of characters against a larger-than-life, bloodthirsty killer, as in the *Saw* franchise, or group of killers, as seen in *Severance* (2006). Arguably, what separates horror from thriller in this instance is how the killer is represented: is he a 'whole' person, complete with a personality/POV of his own? Or a monstrous 'Other' type, faceless and inscrutable, almost supernatural in his ability to track the characters down and kill them, one by one? If the former, I would venture your script is more of a thriller than a horror, especially if there is a 'race against time' to stop him from committing his horrific crimes. Most famous serial killer thriller movies include all the incarnations of Dr Hannibal Lecter, from *Manhunter* (1986) to *The Silence of the Lambs* (1991), *Hannibal* (2001), *Red Dragon* (2002) and *Hannibal Rising* (2007), though of course there are countless other serial

killer thrillers, including an all-time favourite of mine (and countless others), *Psycho* (1960). Hard to believe it's over 50 years old!

- **THE CREATURE THRILLER**. Often closely linked to action thrillers and just as often straying into horror territory, creatures called forth by this section are frequently 'other worldly' in the literal sense (aliens and extraterrestrials) or supernatural (vampires, ghosts and other spooky stuff). Both *Aliens* (1986) and *Predator* (1987) are the height of creature thrillers, rather than horrors. Though both movies contain horrifying elements (who can forget the cocooned colonist – *'K-Kill me...'* – or the dead soldiers, flayed alive?), both set about *thrilling* their audience primarily, rather than *horrifying* them. Consider *Alien* (1979) and *Aliens*. We now live in an age where even '15' and sometimes '12A' certificates carry quite an obscene amount of violence or gore, so *Alien* may seem quite quaint to us now. But, when it was made, over 40 years ago, people had never seen anything like it before. The sight of the chestburster, not to mention the creature it grows into, quite positively *horrified* a 1970s audience. Similarly, the other set pieces of the first movie, such as Brett getting killed in the cargo hold, Dallas getting despatched in the vent, or Lambert and Parker's double demise, are all on a similar level in terms of violence, set against moments of quiet that are both suspenseful and nerve-wracking as we wait for the beast to strike next. In comparison, then, *Aliens* is a white-knuckle thrill ride from the off, first with Ripley's dream-sequence chestburst, through to the 'drop' on to the planet, not to mention the surprise of the infamous 'nest' and Ripley's driving of the armoured personnel carrier to rescue the surviving marines. From there, each set piece gets bigger and bigger, until we're confronted with the Alien Queen in all her glory. Yet it doesn't stop there, for Ripley ends up fighting the Alien Queen hand to hand, Ripley in the robotic loader. This succession upwards towards the climax of the resolution marks *Aliens* out as a thriller, whereas *Alien* was very definitely a horror. *Predator* follows much the same path, so, by the time Dutch reaches the resolution – more or less the sole survivor – we know the only thing left is for him to confront the creature via hand-to-hand combat, which, of course, he does... though, unlike Ripley, who forces the creature out of the airlock a second time, Dutch must use his wits, not brute force, to vanquish the beast.

- **THE CONSPIRACY THRILLER.** More psychologically driven than the action thriller, an isolated protagonist usually must go up against a higher power (usually the government or the police) in these thrillers, usually to save his own life and potentially others' (and it usually is a man at the heart of the narrative, though occasionally a female protagonist pops up, like Darby Shaw in *The Pelican Brief*, 1993). Conspiracy theory thrillers are frequently heavy on plot and include complicated blink-and-you-miss-it moments, though this rarely matters, since what the audience is really invested in is obvious: will our hero, a) get away with his life, and b) expose the evil people who are Behind It All? Conspiracy movies sometimes utilise the twist ending (like in *No Way Out*, 1987) and frequently end with our hero in some 'faraway' place, enjoying his newfound anonymity after being Public Enemy Number One (as in *The Bourne Identity*, 2002 or *Safe House*, 2012). Other movies in this vein include *The Fugitive* (1993), *Conspiracy Theory* (1997) and *Enemy of the State* (1998).
- **THE MOB THRILLER.** Often slick and cool and distinctly American in tone, mob thrillers are frequently high-budget affairs. The higher power our protagonist must go up against is either literally the Mafia (as in *The Godfather* franchise or *Goodfellas*, 1990) or is acting *like* them. Crucially our (usually male) protagonist is often an insider, or an outsider brought in willingly, rather than unwittingly (unlike the conspiracy theory thriller). The mob thriller frequently kills off its protagonist literally (as in *Scarface*, 1983 or *The Departed*, 2006) or ensures he cannot return to his former life. Women can play an important role in mob thrillers and not always as mere decoration, creating real problems for the protagonist, such as Tony's younger sister, Gina, in *Scarface* (1983). Though mob thrillers do not have to be 'rise and fall' stories, they frequently are.

- **THE GANGSTER THRILLER.** In contrast, gangster thrillers are much more 'British': usually lower budget and grittier, complete with rapid-fire dialogue and foul language, with usually few female characters of any substance. Gangster thrillers often start with a willing protagonist, who at first rejoices in his new wealth and life of crime, with the dramatic context in the first half of the screenplay charting his rise up the ranks. The second half of the story then frequently details our protagonist's fall from grace *for some reason*, often because he wants to leave the life to enjoy retirement or because he has become an unwilling double agent for the police or a rival gangster. Typical gangster movies include *Hard Men* (1996), *Lock, Stock & Two Smoking Barrels* (1998) and *Sexy Beast* (2000).
- **THE HITMAN/ASSASSIN THRILLER.** Often very little will separate the protagonist and antagonist of such thrillers, except which side they're on. It's nearly always hitmen or male assassins (often linking back to the action thriller AND the conspiracy thriller), though occasionally we get female assassins, undoubtedly inspired by Luc Besson's *La Femme Nikita* (1990, remade in the US as *The Assassin* in 1993). Comedy occasionally makes an appearance, such as in *Mr and Mrs Smith* (2005). Hitmen thrillers are frequently slicker, more stylised or, conversely, more realistic (especially when it comes to graphic depictions of violence) than gangster thrillers, which is why it's always surprised me there haven't been that many British hitman thrillers and why I was happy to get involved in *Assassin* (2015), which features a *Drive*-type lone protagonist and not one, but two savvy female characters as well as the usual count of mafiosos and hard men.
- **THE HEIST THRILLER.** Heists form a significant part of the thriller genre, often using comedy as in *The Italian Job* (1969) or the *Ocean* franchise; hardcore violence as in *Reservoir Dogs* (1992); and/or double-cross like in *Man on a Ledge* (2012). Teams and conspirators are frequently male-only and cross over into gangster territory, though from time to time women will figure in heists, or even lead them, like Martine in *The Bank Job* (2008), though crucially she is not the protagonist.

- **THE URBAN THRILLER**. Frequently part of the gangster, heist and/or spy thriller or similar, these can be sprawling epics or tiny, gritty productions. Sometimes thrillers will take place in an urban dystopia, usually featuring characters from different ethnic or low-economic backgrounds. *Attack the Block* (2011) is a great example of a thriller that draws on obvious science-fiction classics like *Terminator* (1984) and *Tremors* (1990), but is both urban and distinctly 'British'. We can also see thriller tropes at work in the Netflix 2019 reboot of *Top Boy* (see the case study in Chapter Two).
- **THE WAR/WESTERN THRILLER**. These stories frequently place an external conflict at the helm, most often World War 1 or 2, or a conflict regarding control of a town at the beginning of the New World in America (sometimes Australia or New Zealand as in *The Proposition*, 2005 or *The Stolen*, 2017). The usually male protagonist will be fighting this external conflict either overtly or covertly, whilst also attempting to solve a personal issue of some kind, most often an escape or quest in the case of war movies, or vengeance for the death of a loved one in the case of westerns. War thrillers are frequently staid and sombre affairs, with little room for comedy, in direct contrast to the western, which often makes comedy a feature. War thrillers are nearly always male-dominated, but westerns have memorably placed women at the helm of some stories, including *The Quick and the Dead* (1995) and the Coen Brothers' remake of *True Grit* (2010). Sometimes we are treated to modern westerns, though they are frequently combined with other genres, such as *Near Dark* (a western and vampire thriller, 1987) or *Drive* (a western and crime thriller, 2011).
- **THE STALKER THRILLER**. Stories where someone malevolently obsesses over our protagonist have established a small, yet nevertheless significant, corner of the thriller market. Antagonists are frequently female in this subgenre, with the protagonist often another woman, such as in *Single White Female* and *The Hand That Rocks the Cradle* (both 1992). When the protagonist is male, his stalker is often a woman with whom he has broken off a relationship, an action she is unable to accept, such as Alex in *Fatal Attraction* (1987). Often themes of 'outsiders' are explored

in the stalker thriller, as in *One Hour Photo* (2002). Inevitably, the stalker thriller will often stray into serial killer thriller territory, such as in *The Watcher* (2000).

- **THE DISASTER THRILLER.** Disaster thrillers draw on the 'worst-case scenario' on a huge, sometimes even global, scale, bringing forth meteorites crashing to Earth (*Armageddon* and *Deep Impact*, both 1998); cataclysmic effects of climate change (*The Day After Tomorrow*, 2004); and even the world stopping spinning (*The Core*, 2003). These modern disaster thrillers owe much to their predecessors in the 1970s such as *The Poseidon Adventure* (1972) or *The Towering Inferno* (1974), which in turn borrow from disaster movies of the 1950s.

- **THE SUPERNATURAL THRILLER.** Life or death stakes (even when someone is already dead!) figure prominently in the supernatural thriller. A quest for the truth or demonstration of what faith means usually drives the protagonist, with unseen, antagonistic forces attempting to get in his/her way. Supernatural thrillers may bring forth notions of reincarnation, guardian angels or an afterlife, but infrequently lend themselves to religious themes like those in *Stigmata* (1999), which more often appear in supernatural horror, particularly possession movies. As with most thriller films, male protagonists feature heavily, though female protagonists appear almost as often, especially post-1999, with *What Lies Beneath* (2000), *The Grudge* (2004) and *The Awakening* (2011), as well as the aforementioned *Stigmata*, to name but a few.

- **THE WOMAN IN PERIL THRILLER.** The one area of thriller that always puts women at the forefront of the story, with the threat nearly always being typically 'male'. Home invasion, domestic violence and kidnapping are staples of the women in peril subgenre; a female protagonist must realise she can only rely on herself to rid herself of the antagonist, once and for all. The best women in peril thrillers have her do this via her wits, like Amber's double cross in *Deviation* (2012), rather than undermining her with extreme fantasy violence. 'Woman in peril' infrequently combines with other genres, though, when it does, it's often memorable, as in *The Shining* (WiP with psychological/supernatural, 1980) and *The Terminator* (WiP with sci-fi, 1984).

- **THE REVENGE THRILLER**. The desire for revenge when someone wrongs you is universal, so it's not hard to see why revenge thrillers are so popular. Returning from near-death experiences, or even from the grave itself (as in *The Crow*, 1994), our hero (sometimes heroine) will show the bad guys to 'do as you would be done by', and then some! Frequently, themes of loss, redemption and catharsis are called forth by the revenge thriller, letting the audience live vicariously through the protagonist's actions: he or she is doing what we wish we could do, were there no sanctions like the law.

- **THE CONTAINED THRILLER**. Americans call these films 'man-in-a-box' thrillers, since they are frequently limited to one or few locations and are particularly desirable for the indie filmmaker, though they are really difficult to get right. The contained thriller was in big demand when Chris Sparling's *Buried* (2010) sold and everyone wanted the next one, though we'd actually seen examples of the contained thriller many times before, most obviously with *Phone Booth* (2002), but even as far back as 1954 with *Rear Window*. Frequently contained thrillers will be hostage or fugitive scenarios, such as the aforementioned *Panic Room* and *Deviation*, but also genre-busting takes on this story such as *Desperate Measures* (1998), where protagonist Connor must not only pursue, but protect, antagonist McCabe, the only person able to save the first man's sick son, via bone marrow transplant.

- **THE NON-LINEAR/MULTIPLE POV THRILLER**. Non-linear and multiple-viewpoint thrillers will manipulate time and/or characters in giving an account of what happens in the story. Timeframes may shift or events change as in *Twelve Monkeys* (1995) or *The Butterfly Effect* (2004). Or we may see the same event from different people's points of view at the same moment, as in *Pulp Fiction* (1994) or *Vantage Point* (2008).

- **THE SCIENCE FICTION THRILLER**. Perhaps one of the most diverse of thriller subgenres: protagonists may be confronted with a mystery to solve, such as Detective Spooner in *I, Robot* (2004); or the protagonist must overcome a higher power, such as the machines in the *Matrix* trilogy; or perhaps complicated themes of what 'makes' a human being are explored, as in *Blade Runner* (1982) and *Impostor* (2001). Frequently, science fiction will explore the notion of 'reality' itself and people's perceptions of it, most notably in the aforementioned *Matrix* trilogy, but also in lesser known sci-fi thrillers like *The Thirteenth Floor* (1999) and *The Final Cut* (2004).

- **CLASSICS**. And now for those thrillers considered so good they transcend time. During my research for this book, these movies were recommended countless times by colleagues, whether they were script readers, agents, execs, directors or producers:

  - *Rear Window* (1954)
  - *Vertigo* (1958)
  - *North by Northwest* (1959)
  - *Psycho* (1960)
  - *The Manchurian Candidate* (1962)
  - *The Ipcress File* (1965)
  - *Duel* (1971)
  - *The French Connection* (1971)
  - *The Poseidon Adventure* (1972)
  - *Don't Look Now* (1973)
  - *Chinatown* (1974)
  - *Jaws* (1975)
  - *Witness* (1985)
  - *Manhunter* (1986)
  - *No Way Out* (1987)
  - *The Silence of the Lambs* (1991)
  - *Pulp Fiction* (1994)
  - *Heat* (1995)
  - *Memento* (2000)

Of course, some have had their time and now feel a little dated to us – I'm thinking *Manhunter* in particular on this – but it's still worth checking out all the classics recommended here if you want your thriller screenplay to feel fresh, relevant and ultimately desirable to people in the industry, who will naturally have their own favourites in the genre. We all do!

THE COMEDY THRILLER

One of the most attractive elements of the thriller is the fact it can be mixed with most genres. This means it becomes a very attractive vehicle for bankable talent and character actors, lone protagonist stories and ensembles, movies or television, for audiences of all ages. Thriller's versatility is quite literally its superpower!

Comedy and thriller have been effective bedfellows since time immemorial, but especially since the 1980s. Most blockbuster movies have some kind of comic element, whether that's part of the story overall and/or a dedicated character (aka 'comic relief') whose job it is to drop quips as stuff explodes and aliens invade. Some stars even build their entire careers on this: A-listers like Arnold Schwarzenegger, Will Smith, Dwayne Johnson and Chris Hemsworth are as well known for their comic timing as they are their physical prowess.

In recent years, this has also made its way into television as well. An Amazon Prime show like *Sneaky Pete* (2015–2019), created by David Shore and Bryan Cranston (yes, *Breaking Bad's* Bryan Cranston) delivered a seemingly 'unlikely' combination of humour and extremely gory violence via judicious use of thriller tropes. Its protagonist is 'Pete' aka Marius Josipović (Giovanni Ribisi), a released convict who adopts the identity of his cell mate, Pete Murphy, to avoid his past life and 'lay low' after prison.

Pete hasn't seen his family for over 20 years since he was a child, so when Marius rocks up at the family farm, they're delighted to see him and have no reason to suspect he's not who he says he is. Of course, it's not as simple as that and Marius soon finds himself wrapped up in the family's own secrets and lies, not to mention various vendettas and problems of their own. The series sparkles with both hilarious and absurd exchanges, but more importantly the plotting is tight, pushing the story forward and revealing character in every scene. Bryan Cranston puts in a compelling performance as crime don Vince (whom Marius is trying desperately to avoid). The violence is extreme and enough to make even the most hardened thriller fan shudder, so be aware of this if you're of a delicate disposition!

Another thriller TV series that makes excellent use of humour to keep its target audience engaged is *Justified* (2010–2015). Starring Timothy Olyphant as the iconic US Marshal Raylan Givens, it is based on the 2001 Elmore Leonard short story *Fire in the Hole*. Leonard also executive-produced the series until his death in 2013.

Raylan thought he'd escaped his roots in Kentucky, only to be slammed back into his past. The cowboy lawman is backed up brilliantly by colleagues Tim, Rachel and Art who all despair of Raylan's methods yet facilitate him because it takes the heat off them. Also, unusually for a maverick Raylan does have to face consequences.

Raylan and main antagonist Boyd Crowder (Walton Goggins) are doppelgängers: they grew up and 'dug coal together' but have gone in vastly different directions. Even so, Raylan is not the 100% hero he thinks he is, just as Boyd is not the 100% villain he thinks he is, too. This is underlined by their shared ex Ava (Joelle Carter).

Justified was a series on the cusp of the transition between returning drama series and serial. Unlike other favourite shows of the same era like *Sons of Anarchy* (2008–2014), *Justified* has not dated in quite the same way. Its commentary on society and class, disability and mental illness (especially veterans), gender and race are still relatable.

The reason why some series date quicker than others is not entirely clear; it's more a case of 'you know it when you see it'. I would argue it's a case of staying relevant. Whilst comedy can date a story quickly, if it's skilful and well-observed (and refers to issues 'bigger' than the time it's made) then it can still be considered 'on point' even decades later. It doesn't matter to us writing spec screenplays anyway – we have to get produced before we can worry about whether our stories are going to date quickly!

Brooklyn Nine-Nine (2013–2022)

If TV thrillers can include humour and gory violence then, other unlikely combinations can also work well. Whilst sitcom is not known for using thriller tropes, that doesn't mean there are none in existence.

Running for eight seasons, *Brooklyn Nine-Nine* was a sitcom starring a diverse ensemble case in the fictional 99th precinct in Brooklyn, New York. Following the fates of protagonist and maverick cop Jake Peralta (Andy Samberg) versus 'robotic' antagonist Captain Raymond Holt (Andre Braugher), Peralta and Holt are joined by a variety of differentiated and archetypal characters, including 'mother hen' and care-giver Sergeant Terry Jeffords (Terry Crews); the outlaw and mentor Detective Rosa Diaz (Stephanie Beatriz); love interest/creator Amy Santiago (Melissa Fumero); BFF and lover-not-a-fighter Charles Boyle (Joe Lo Truglio); and sage/stealth mentor with an attitude problem Gina Linetti (Chelsea Peretti); plus bottom-feeders Hitchcock and Scully (Dirk Blocker and Joel McKinnon). They're also joined by a variety of 'antagonists of the week' including Holt's nemesis Madeline Wuntch (Kyra Sedgwick); Major Crimes' Keith 'The Vulture' Pembroke (Dean Winters); and loose cannon Adrian Pimento (Jason Mantzoukas) who might be the squad's friend, but always throws a spanner in the works somehow.

Unusually for a workplace sitcom, *Brooklyn Nine-Nine* mixes comedic and thriller tropes, often making fun of iconic thriller movies such as *Die Hard* and *Lethal Weapon*. Jake styles himself on John McClane so much he quotes action movies constantly and attempts set piece feats straight out of the movies: jumping off roofs, sliding across car bonnets and zip-lining through windows into criminal hideouts.

Part of the fun is Jake often creates more issues for the squad with this obsession, plus he is about as far from McClane as you can imagine. He is neither tough nor uncompromising, but crucially he is not bad at his job either. He is what might have once been described as a 'new man': he listens to his co-workers, holds progressive views and accepts he has much to learn from marginalised people.

It's very common in the 2020s for online commentators to lament 'wokism' as the supposed 'death of comedy' (and stories generally). *Brooklyn Nine-Nine* illustrates what a nonsense this is, pairing 'woke' diverse comedy with near-to-the-knuckle sexualised running gags (a fan favourite being 'title of your sex tape'); puerile humour such as fart jokes; plus even lofty references to Shakespeare, Plato and foreign films.

The reason *Brooklyn Nine-Nine* works is not just because it's funny, but because it knows the thriller inside out. Whether Jake is screwing up an interrogation, getting framed for a bank heist, or rounding up escaped convicts, its target audience can feel the familiarity of the tropes from movies that came before it, such as the aforementioned *Die Hard* and *Lethal Weapon*, but also others such as *Suicide Squad* (2016) or *The Fugitive* (1993). It is the 'same... but different' – the difference being, this time it's played for laughs.

Bosch (2015–2021)

Produced TV cop dramas frequently use thriller tropes to make audiences invest in the character's need to solve the case. Mystery is incredibly important to the cop drama if it doesn't have another element (such as comedy or action) to distract the audience. This might sound obvious (because it is!), but the multiple cop drama spec scripts that end up on my desk rarely have mystery in them.

Running for seven series, *Bosch* is based on the Michael Connelly novels and is frequently credited as being the first Amazon Original on the streaming service. (In real terms it was probably its first most popular, since political drama *Alpha House* pre-dated Bosch by two years).

One of my Bang2writers left a comment under my Instagram review of *Bosch* claiming the series is 'the serious version of Brooklyn Nine-Nine! I hadn't made that connection, but once I read that comment I couldn't NOT see it!

The two series are very similar indeed: like Jake Peralta, Detective Harry Bosch (Titus Welliver) is a classic Maverick cop, but with a twist. He is unusual because he always places his moral compass at the centre of everything he does. He forces the others around him to do the same... No mean feat when most people on the force are weighing everything up and making various compromises both good and bad to get ahead.

Also like Jake, Harry is surrounded by a diverse cast of highly differentiated archetypal characters. Women are frequently hung out to dry even by other women, as we see with Lieutenant Grace Billets (Amy Aquino), an out gay woman at work. She has to consistently defend herself against power plays that take advantage of her sexuality. Equally Honey 'Money' Chandler (Mimi Rogers) is a defence lawyer who is both antagonist or ally to Bosch, dependent on what is happening. Bosch also finds himself up against ex-wife Eleanor (Sarah Clarke) and daughter Maddie (Madison Lintz) on a similar basis.

Harry is uncompromising and respectful of the law without being 'by the book'. In fact, nearly all the other characters will find themselves compromised in some way... but not him. This rigid worldview inevitably leads him into trouble with perps, superiors and his loved ones.

Now the differences: unlike *Brooklyn Nine-Nine* which concentrates on the characters' relationships and detectives solve crimes in a blink ('Oh by the way I solved the case!') *Bosch* places the mystery at the heart of every episode via deft use of serialised storytelling.

Every case hits the ground running at breakneck speed and viewers are expected to keep up. Naturalised dialogue, the Hollywood setting and the dark, film noir style tropes – jazz music, femme fatales and Hitchcockian 'unstable space' – means anything can happen and frequently does. Again, *Bosch* knows exactly what it is and what came before it, bringing forth 'the same... but different' with it.

The Rookie (2018–2022)

So the pendulum swings from a police thriller played for laughs to one that's uber-serious to another that's the perfect blend of both: *The Rookie*, starring Nathan Fillion as John Nolan, an everyman who starts over in his forties and pursues his dream of joining the LAPD as the oldest rookie they've ever had.

Blending *B99*'s comedy with *Bosch*'s hardline view of the police, this series is an effortless blend of comedic moments and thriller tropes, but not action thriller style. As modern audiences demand (especially in the post-BLM protests era), the police are not automatic heroes like John McClane. In fact, they don't even get the benefit of the doubt, even when they're trying to help!

Like *B99* and *Bosch*, Nolan is surrounded by a diverse cast of secondary characters. Lucy Chen (Melissa O'Neil) and Jackson West (Titus Makin) are Nolan's fellow rookies. Lucy is an insightful and kind psychology major whose parents don't support her being in the police. Her training officer Tim Bradford (Eric Winter) was in the military and comes across as a tough, rogue cop... but underneath it all, he plays by the rules and has a bleeding heart.

Jackson is the 'golden boy' of the academy, plus he has big shoes to fill (his father's, who is none other than the head of Internal Affairs). He's also gay yet this is played out in a low-key way with no fanfare which is great.

Nolan himself is not the maverick in this story; his training officer Nyla Harper (Mekia Cox) is instead, plus she is a lone wolf, brave and uncompromising, especially as her undercover persona 'Crystal'. Scratch the surface and she is nurturing to her daughter and friends, presenting a layered and nuanced character.

My favourites though are Angela Lopez (Alyssa Diaz) and her significant other Wesley Evers (Shawn Ashmore). Cops and defence attorneys infamously don't see eye-to-eye and inevitably they often end up arguing on opposite sides. This doesn't stop Angela and Wesley being madly in love.

The Rookie shows that it can cover similar ground as its predecessors; like *Brooklyn Nine-Nine* and *Bosch* before it, the show differentiates itself from what has gone before. This is why writers attempting a new show in popular arenas such as the police simply MUST know not only what is the 'same... but different' about their concept, but they must deliver something modern audiences want from a cop drama, which are currently:

- A diverse cast of characters (not just gender, but race and LGBT status too)
- Strong relationships amongst the characters (for good or ill)
- Layers and nuance for the characters
- Examination of difficult issues in the plot (with no easy answers)
- Consistent tone (or 'feel' of the piece)

- Thriller tropes mixed with human drama

So if you find yourself pitching a TV series that has MANY predecessors like the cop drama, be sure you know exactly what's the 'same... but different' about yours. Producers WILL ask!

HOW POLICE PROCEDURALS HAVE CHANGED

Looking back as little as ten to fifteen years, we can see returning drama series such as *Castle*, *The Mentalist*, and *Person of Interest* (to name but a few!) laying the groundwork to make the jump from returning drama series to the serialised storytelling that has become the norm in the streaming era.

In all the series mentioned, the story hinges on a show-stopping and 'larger than life' male character who is motivated to do something extraordinary while helping law enforcement agencies, either overtly or covertly.

Castle (2009–2016)

In *Castle*, Nathan Fillion plays Rick Castle, a bestselling mystery novelist who helps the New York police department solve cases after a copycat murderer uses his novels as inspiration. The show combines thriller and Comedy elements to bring forth a slick and fun ride for viewers that's not remotely plausible but fun regardless. Rick is a ladies' man and irresponsible with it until he meets Detective Kate Beckett played by Stana Katic. Like many female protagonists of the era Beckett is badass and somewhat of an ice maiden, though as Castle and Beckett's arcs grew, so did their characters and they became much more layered and nuanced.

They're also joined by a diverse cast of characters, with some interesting commentary on gender and race at a time this was not the 'norm'. I particularly loved Rick's mother Martha (played to perfection by Susan Sullivan). Martha is a faded Broadway star who is somewhat of a flirt and rather mercenary with it: she had to be, bringing Castle up on her own and ensuring he had all the things she didn't, such as a private education. It was refreshing to see an older mother character who is allowed to be sexual without being a 'Lady Macbeth'.

Castle ran from 2009 to 2016 and illustrates the 'crossover' of returning drama becoming more serialised as streaming became mainstream. The first series in 2009 was just ten episodes and its format very obvious: there was a case of the week which needed resolving. As the series continued, larger serial arcs were introduced, such as the conspiracy surrounding Beckett's mother's murder.

What was most interesting to me was how difficult *Castle*'s mystery element was to predict, even as a script reader who writes crime mystery novels herself! Nine times out of ten I can work out far in advance who the perpetrator is (not because the series is underwritten, but because I live and breathe crime mystery daily). *Castle* is one of the few mysteries I have watched that consistently beat me on this. I believe the reason for this is because of how skilful the writers were at 'bait and switch' not only on main suspects, but red herrings too.

Person of Interest (2011–2016)

Person of Interest ran from 2011 to 2016 and starred Jim Caviezel as John Reese, a former Special Forces soldier who is living rough on the streets of New York and presumed dead by his previous employers. He is approached by Harold Finch (Michael Emerson), a reclusive billionaire software genius who has created what he only calls 'The Machine' for the US government after September 11th 2001. The Machine monitors all electronic communications and video surveillance feeds in order to predict further terrorist atrocities… but there's a catch. This 'all-seeing eye' predicts everyday crimes too against individuals but discards them. Unable to ignore his conscience, Finch recruits Reese to try and stop those crimes against individuals from occurring.

As with *Castle*, we can see change-in-action from returning drama to more serialised storytelling as the series goes on. What's particularly interesting then about *Person of Interest* is the fact it pairs mystery with science fiction.

We don't see the pairing of sci-fi and mystery often on screen and script readers see it even less in the spec pile. The reasons are obvious: science fiction requires a lot of worldbuilding and exposition; so does mystery. It's very, very difficult to pull off both within the same story world.

In contrast to the intricate mysteries of *Castle* however, *Person of Interest* pays lip service to mystery, rather than showcasing anything too involved (especially in earlier seasons). This makes sense because of the unusual pairing of sci-fi and crime mystery. If the writers had gone 'too deep' into mystery, it may have felt like overkill in a sci-fi world.

The Mentalist (2009–2015)

In *The Mentalist*, former fake 'psychic' Patrick Jane (Simon Baker) works towards redemption as a consultant with The California Bureau of Investigation (CBI). Like *Castle*, the show combines thriller and comedy tropes. Unlike Castle who utilises his friendship with the mayor of New York to strong-arm Beckett into letting him shadow her for book research in the first series, Patrick's motivation is much, much darker. He helps the CBI with their cases in the hope one of them leads him to his nemesis, the serial killer Red John who murdered his wife and child. The show reflects this darkness too; it is considerably gorier and threatening, with many killings enacted on screen, whereas Castle usually arrived on the scene to find the bodies already murdered.

Running from 2009 to 2015, *The Mentalist* is particularly unusual because it was a returning-drama-series-cum-serial hybrid from the offset. Setting up Jane's long-term mission from episode one to find and kill Red John, its Dramatic Question is obvious and drives the series: 'Who is Red John?' In getting there, we are treated to a 'case of the week' that was resolved as was the expectation of the time. However Jane's mission to kill Red John is never far from the surface and everything returns to that, via both flashbacks and stuff playing out in 'present time'.

The Mentalist stands up incredibly well in modern times and has dated very little across the board. This is because of its commitment to characterisation which can act as the gold standard for writers even ten to fifteen years on. The show illustrates how it is possible to use a tried-and-tested motivation like revenge for a leading male character, but bring something new to the mix.

Patrick is a sociopath, but amiable with it; it's clear he won't be swayed from his path. When Patrick is given the opportunity to kill Red John (or the serial killer's allies – the conspiracy is far-reaching), he has no qualms about doing so, too.

More interesting however is Patrick's personal journey from his days on the carnival circuit with his abusive father, not to mention his own regrets he placed his own family in harm's way due to sheer arrogance by baiting Red John live on TV. Across the series we watch him travel from the edge of existence as a mentally ill, suicidal and guilt-struck loner to a friend and ally of the other characters in the show.

It would have been easy to make the story all about Jane's quest for vengeance and underwrite the secondary characters, but the show sidesteps this temptation with aplomb. Patrick works on a diverse team with 'boss' Teresa Lisbon (Robin Tunney), who is a blue-collar street-smart woman who had to raise her brothers when her mother died and her father was an alcoholic. This was and still is unusual when female high-flier characters are frequently more privileged, even now in the 2020s.

Next there's Patrick's colleague Wayne Rigsby (Owain Yeoman). Emotionally literate male characters like Rigsby are still at a premium, but he's no 'wimp': he is also a typically macho action hero, his signature move being diving off balconies in pursuit of suspects. Then there's Grace Van Pelt (Amanda Righetti): she looks like a model, plus she presents on the surface as everyone's expectation of beautiful women: she seems idealistic and princess-like, keen to see the best in people. Scratch that gorgeous surface and a will of steel is revealed, not to mention shocking anger not afforded to many female lead characters before OR since. She is also not above using her feminine wiles to manipulate and trap suspects.

My favourite however has to be Kimball Cho (Tim Kang). East Asian characters of any gender are often missing from stories altogether, but here the show places him front and centre. He is a brilliant interrogator, deadpan and witty with it. One of his lines is a legendary .gif that still does the rounds amongst the show's fans on Twitter, Facebook and Tumblr over ten years after the episode first aired:

SUSPECT: *I can make one phone call and your career is toast.*

KIMBALL CHO: *That's impressive. The best I can get with one call is a pizza.*

What's more Kimball is masculine, an ex-gang member and his girlfriend is a sex worker (no de-sexed 'model minority' stereotypes here!). Cho is a hero, no question – and it's just a shame there are still so few East Asian characters like him in the 2020s.

DRAMA VERSUS THRILLER

> *'Imagine the writing and the selling as thrillers in their own right – take your self and your script down dark alleys, see it crash and burn but somehow pick itself up and keep fighting, eventually – despite impossible odds – to win.'*
>
> **– Dominic Minghella, producer and show runner** (@DMinghella)

Many writers struggle with the difference between drama and thriller. As a result, many write spec screenplays that don't make use of enough thriller tropes such as the deadline/race against time, 'flight to fight' or even tension. This means these writers' attempts at thriller essentially become gritty dramas with a fair amount of running about in!

Yet comparing dramas and thrillers can be very illuminating. Consider a British crime drama like *Top Boy* (2011–2013), created by Ronan Bennett and set in the fictional Summerhouse estate in the London borough of Hackney. The story focuses on two drug dealers Dushane Hill (Ashley Walters) and Gerard 'Sully' Sullivan (Kane Robinson). Whilst the series has always involved crime, HOW they present it has changed over its four seasons as it moved from the UK's Channel 4 to Netflix, a global platform that has different requirements.

Top Boy (2011–2013) As Drama

Originally a mini-series of just four episodes each, *Top Boy's* first two seasons were broadcast on Channel 4 here in the UK. Considered an authentic yet gritty look at the dark side of London, the original series focused very much on the struggles of individuals who go up against Dushane and Sully or get caught in the crossfire. This meant *Top Boy* in its original incarnation was more gritty realist 'kitchen sink' drama than crime thriller.

When Channel 4 cancelled *Top Boy* in 2013, that seemed to be it. Then in 2017 Canadian rapper Drake announced Netflix would do a 'soft reboot' of the series. Ten new episodes were ordered, with Walters and Robinson reprising their roles, as well as Bennett and most of the original production team.

The new version of *Top Boy* premiered on Netflix in 2019, with the original C4 series added to the platform as *Top Boy: Summerhouse*. So why the change between the two?

In one sense, nothing has changed. The Netflix version of *Top Boy* is true to its roots. Individual struggles are still part of the story as they were in *Summerhouse*: gentrification, immigration and poverty all loom large, as do other equality issues, especially for black and gay people as well as women.

The police and other authority figures are treated with suspicion at best: the message is systems cannot be trusted, because if they could? People wouldn't have to live like that in the first place. As a teen mother forced to live on the fringes myself, it's this I love most about *Top Boy* because it has so much emotional truth.

However that drama element and emotional heart is no longer the driving force plot-wise of *Top Boy* as it was in the previous two series.

Top Boy (2019–2023) As Thriller

Netflix's *Top Boy* in s3 and s4 (sometimes referred to as s1 and s2, depending where you look!) place many more thriller tropes at the heart of the story. Rather than focus on the disenfranchisement such young people have to face, it instead places 'The Road' at the heart of the plot. This means dodgy dealings, betrayals and murder are the main event.

The new version also goes way beyond the boundaries of the Summerhouse estate. In fact, we join Dushane in s3 in Jamaica; Sully is back in Blighty, in jail. Both are seemingly all washed up and have been replaced on The Road back in Hackney by newcomer, Jamie. Of course Dushane is dragged back to London, plus Sully is released from prison.

This spells trouble for the Top Boy who took their place, Jamie (Micheal Ward) whose territory is being encroached. Even worse, he is the father figure and sole provider for his two brothers Aaron and Stefan after the death of their parents.

Full-scale gang war erupts. Jamie is forced to reconsider his position as he is dethroned as Top Boy in the estate when he is besieged by underhand dealings, ambushes and killings.

Everything revolves around usurping the Top Boy. By the end of s3, Jamie is left with nowhere to go – literally! Dushane has retaken his place as the kingpin and offers Jamie only two options: jail, or to work for him. With Aaron and Stefan to provide for, Jamie grudgingly accepts Dushane's offer.

He's not the only one who is disgruntled: Sully is suspicious of Jamie and wants him dead. Dushane does not listen to his friend, sure Jamie can take over The Road from them one day. In addition, Dushane wants to deal with middle-class hipster types with a view to going legit eventually. Dushane has a ten-year plan and Sully is NOT happy about it.

In s4, even more thriller tropes are piled on. The story world becomes even more global, taking in Spain and Morocco, as well as more product. Dushane is forced to deal with cartel and foreign gangs, as well as dirty police officers. Still sure Jamie is his protégé, Dushane sends him abroad, unaware Jamie is thinking about grabbing the power back for himself.

When Jamie seemingly isn't able to negotiate a percentage properly (he is too busy planning his own next move), Dushane sends Sully. Ever faithful, Sully makes Dushane's point known: he murders the dirty police officer. Problem solved. Though he doesn't know for sure about Jamie's plot with another character Lizzie (Lisa Dwan) behind Dushane's back, he guesses enough to get suspicious.

Meanwhile other story strands in s4 revolve around Lauryn (Saffron Hocking), the sister of Jaq (Jasmine Jobson, who is Dushane's right-hand woman on The Road). In s3 Lauryn was sent away in disgrace for a discretion that almost got Sully killed; now she is pregnant to Curtis (Howard Charles), a gangster in Liverpool. He and his sister Vee (Ava Brennan) are essentially holding Lauryn hostage via coercive control. She is not even able to use the phone or go to the toilet alone.

Lauryn fears for her life once the baby is born. During snatched moments, Jaq promises to get her out but Dushane is not interested in helping. This leads to Lauryn having to take matters into her own hands. In a nerve-wracking escape, she manages to leave Curtis and Vee in a shopping centre, taking a taxi back to London.

When Curtis and Vee inevitably track her back to Jaq's, Dushane and Sully somewhat grudgingly step up. They warn off Curtis who appears to take heed, only to shoot up Dushane's girlfriend Shelley's nail salon. Enough is enough and Dushane plans an ambush to take Curtis out for good.

Understanding she needs to redeem herself for her actions in the previous season, plus she needs Curtis out of her life for good, Lauryn lures him instead to Jaq's. Promising she will return to Liverpool with him, she pulls a knife from her bag and stabs him to death. Dushane, Jaq and Sully arrive to discover Curtis bleeding out on the carpet. They dispose of the body and his car, with Sully phoning Vee to tell her that her brother will never be returning.

Meanwhile, Dushane is dealing with the death of his mother and her belief Summerhouse was a community, not the 'shithole' he thought it was. He had been pumping money into gentrification of the area, thinking he was doing a good thing as well as moving towards legitimate business like he planned. His girlfriend Shelley makes him realise how he has been lying to himself.

Discovering Jamie's plot with Lizzie, Dushane plays a card that will get him what he wants: he tells fellow investor and Lizzie's husband Jeffrey (Shaun Dingwall) that he will have to kill his wife. Jeffrey is appalled, telling him he will do whatever he wants. Dushane says he wants the gentrification of Summerhouse to be suspended.

Jamie has been given an ultimatum too: after discovering best friend Kit was behind the death of one of Dushane's 'youts' Attica, he must kill Kit or kill himself. After initially planning to run away with Kit, Jamie eventually realises he cannot take Aaron and Stefan on the lam. With a heavy heart he kills his best friend and informs Dushane.

It seems everything has come up roses for Dushane and his crew: he informs Sully Jamie came through and they can trust him again. Sick of Jamie's underhand dealings, Sully is either not convinced or jealous (or both) and goes to Jamie's home, shooting him in the chest and head in front of Aaron and Stefan in a shock cliffhanger.

The new *Top Boy* is about power plays and making your way to the top by whatever means necessary. It's a 'dog eat dog' world where only the strongest and most cunning survive. Put simply, it's a thriller through and through.

OTHER COMMON ISSUES IN SPEC THRILLER SCREENPLAYS

> *'Most thriller spec scripts are simply not thrilling or scary or engaging enough. Too often first-time writers (and some more experienced writers) are too confident that their great plot will carry the day. But we don't care about the characters. The readers need to become emotionally involved in genre. When writing a thriller remember that the plot should come out of who the characters are.'*
>
> – **Stephen Volk, screenwriter & novelist** (@SteveVolkWriter)

Despite the plethora of produced content, not to mention screenwriting information at writers' fingertips, thrillers still remain one of the most misunderstood and ill-executed genres in the spec pile. Often this is due to the writer's inexperience in actual writing, but even seasoned screenwriters can fall into one of the following writing traps:

- **They don't know the difference between horror and thriller.** Many writers claim there is not much difference between these two genres, but from my experience of reading both thriller and horror screenplays, and watching thriller and horror movies, I would venture there is a difference, albeit a very subtle one. Put simply, horror places, unsurprisingly, the emphasis on *horrifying* its audience, in comparison to a thriller that wants to thrill or, rather, *excite*. Remember that all-important notion of tone, here.

TIP: ***Thriller may have horrifying elements and horror may have thrilling elements, but this does not mean the two genres are interchangeable at will. Remember* Alien vs Aliens.**

- **Their supernatural thriller is really a supernatural horror.** The supernatural thriller is a subgenre of thriller that tends to go in and out of fashion. It was most popular around the turn of the millennium in the English-speaking world. There are elements other than just the paranormal that mark it out from other stories. Generally speaking, a protagonist is haunted *for some reason* and that character must seek out why, as demonstrated most famously by *The Sixth Sense*, but also in *Stir of Echoes* (1999), *Stigmata* (1999), *Dragonfly* (2002) and *White Noise* (2005), to mention just a few. What drives supernatural thrillers is a quest for the 'truth' (sometimes a demonstration of faith) and solving of a mystery, often to allow a supernatural force to be 'at peace' at last. Supernatural thrillers will frequently include twist endings or ambiguous storytelling to achieve this. In comparison, then, movies about actual haunting (including possession movies, whether human or a house) are usually horrors in which protagonists must 'vanquish the beast' and emerge victorious, even if that victory means death. Consider Blumhouse Horror movies like the *Paranormal Activity* (2007–2021), *Insidious* (2010–2018) or *Sinister* (2012–2015) franchises. In each of these, the characters have no mystery to solve *per se*; though characters may or may not find out what motivates the ghosts, it's nevertheless accepted ghosts or other supernatural creatures exist. Instead, the story focuses on dealing with them (or not, as the case may be).

TIP: ***If using the paranormal in your spec thriller screenplay, remember the notion of the quest for 'truth' and mystery over the more typical horror elements of demonic possession and haunting.***

- **Their protagonist appears too late.** Many classic thrillers, whilst undoubtedly thrilling at the time, now feel dated and slow, despite their excellent storytelling. One problem that rears its head over and over again with the spec thrillers I see is that the protagonist is introduced far too late, which often interferes with that other important notion of 'hitting the ground running'. When tackled about this, writers will frequently cite John Book's appearance in *Witness* as being approximately 15 minutes into the film. However, it's important to remember that *Witness* came out over 25 years ago; which other films have done this in the last two or three years? Audiences move on in terms of what they find acceptable and, at the moment, especially in thrillers, they like to be introduced to the protagonist immediately, so readers usually want to see a protagonist on page one of a screenplay, or at least very close to page one. If the protagonist is not there by then, there has to be a really good story-based reason: for example, in a TV crime series where we need to see the crime occur first as it is the catalyst for what comes next.

TIP: ***It's really important to ensure your screenplay feels current, so know what conventions are considered 'old hat'.***

- **Their thriller is too slow... or simply too arty.** Sometimes, a writer will look to films that are simply too dated (even though they might be classics) for a modern audience. If we look to films that have been remade (ignoring the inevitable howls of 'It's not as good as the original!'), we can see immediately that certain elements need updating, structure being the most obvious. Similarly (and rightly or wrongly), though there are always exceptions, it would appear art-house is generally a step too far for English-speaking audiences, at least in terms of commercial return, if not critical acclaim (hence me not including it in the rundown of thriller subgenres and cross-genres). That said, a well-thought-out art thriller can occasionally work really well as a sample script and get a scriptwriter work on others' films.

TIP: ***Don't merely mimic your old favourites, and avoid art-house, especially if you want the best shot of being produced in the UK or America.***

- **Their non-linear thriller doesn't work.** Every time a well-received non-linear thriller does well at the box office, there is a rash of copies in the spec pile. In comparison to that produced thriller, however, most of these copies do not work. This is usually because the writer in question has not 'restructured their structure' or, in other words, worked out how the non-linearity works *for* the story. Linda Aronson, author of *The 21st Century Screenwriter* and expert on non-linearity, summed up this issue for me:

  'Non-linear screenplay structures lend themselves to thriller writing because good non-linear structures always create a mystery that the flashbacks or time jumps answer, bit by bit. Bad non-linear films are usually dreary or actively painful precisely because they don't set up a mystery. They don't start on a moment of real crisis for the most interesting character, that is, a moment of real emotional or physical danger.'

Linda's notion of starting at the 'worst possible point' is absolutely key in engaging the reader in your non-linear structure. What's more, a non-linear storyline has a 'throughline', which the scriptwriter must follow so the reader (and thus the audience) can follow the story. This might be by having the main plot go backwards ('Find John G'), with the subplot going forwards ('Remember Sammy Jankis') as in *Memento* (2000). Alternatively, produced thrillers may 'reset' to a particular point, such as returning to the bed in *Premonition* (2007) or the bombing in *Vantage Point* (2008). Or, we may return to the past that forms its own storyline if 'added together' as in *The Crow* (1993) and *The Bourne Supremacy* (2004).

TIP: ***Make sure you restructure your story accordingly if using non-linearity and that readers can follow your 'throughline'.***

- **Their thriller meanders.** Perhaps the greatest crime of all, because it means tension lapses – the single most important element of a thriller. This is why the notion of deadline is so important here. Making your protagonist do something *by a certain time* at the behest of the antagonist (or to thwart them) is usually the best shorthand to ensure tension is kept up throughout the narrative and that it builds to a satisfying climax. This is why deadlines in thrillers rarely exceed approximately a week and are usually far less, sometimes as little as a few hours, or even in real time, such as *Nick of Time* (1995).

TIP: ***Introducing a deadline can help give the story that 'race against time' feel so necessary in thrillers – and make sure every single scene works towards that deadline.***

SUMMING UP...

- The antagonist tends to drive the thriller narrative, with the protagonist forced to play *their* game, at least in the first instance.
- Even if not writing a blockbuster, there's plenty to learn from big-budget, high-concept thrillers – especially in terms of thriller conventions and tropes.
- Tone is all-important in setting up the world of the story and its rules.
- Characters and story must be introduced 'hand in hand'.
- It's key to consider who your audience is, as is opening it up and making your screenplay as accessible as possible, via any story-telling device you want.
- 'Hitting the ground running' is important, even with slow-burn techniques.
- Mystery can be a very important part of the thriller, especially in spec television pilots. Know the difference between a 'whodunnit' and a 'whydunnit'.

- Dramatic context needs to follow the 'flight vs fight' phenomenon.
- You need to know what's gone before of the types of thriller you want to write, plus how audience preferences have changed in order to stay relevant.
- Knowing what type of thriller you're writing is paramount; watch as many as possible, especially in the subgenre you're writing, but all the classics too.
- The difference between thriller and horror is a subtle one.
- Knowing the usual pitfalls of spec thrillers is important in avoiding them, especially when attempting a non-linear thriller screenplay.
- The deadline is one of the most crucial elements of the thriller genre.

CHARACTERISATION IN THRILLERS

THE LONE PROTAGONIST VERSUS THE GROUP

'Use silence to milk the drama and create tension. Thrillers stop being thrilling when characters talk too much.'

– **Pilar Alessandra, script consultant** (@onthepage)

So, typically, as Spaihts suggests in his tweet back in Chapter One, thriller movies tend to feature a lone protagonist, up against a lone antagonist (or, if not *actually* alone him/herself, the antagonist is the 'recognisable face' of the antagonistic force in the situation at hand, i.e. The Mob or The Government). If we compare this notion to horror, we can immediately see where one of the biggest differences between thriller and horror occurs at surface level. Traditionally – and taking its lead from *Alien* in 1979 – horrors will place a group of characters in front of the audience, often with a so-called 'false leader' whom we assume will survive at least until the beginning of the resolution, but is killed relatively early on (in *Alien*'s case, Dallas). Within this group, then, is a 'quiet protagonist' (like Ripley) who, throughout the course of the narrative, will emerge as the real leader as the others die/are indisposed. Now compare Ripley in *Alien* to Ripley in *Aliens*: in the second film, she is marked out from the start as the lone protagonist, not just because it is a sequel, but because it is a thriller, rather than a horror.

That said, there is absolutely no reason why a thriller movie cannot have a group of characters, nor horror a lone protagonist. In the past decade, we've seen a reversal of expectations in thriller movies on this basis. In the 2020s, the Marvel Cinematic Universe has placed an ensemble of characters front and centre, most notably in the *Avengers* movies (2012–2019). Growing from five main protagonist characters in the first movie – Iron Man, Thor, Hulk, Hawkeye and Black Widow – over the course of the narrative the group grew larger and larger. By 2019's *Avengers: Endgame* a huge plethora of characters faced down antagonist Thanos, most of them completing their own arc (small to large) in doing so.

In contrast, Blumhouse's work in the past decade in the Horror sphere shows how well they can present the lone protagonist in all manner of hideous yet relatable situations. Consider 2017's *Get Out*, an Oscar-winning horror that places protagonist Chris (Daniel Kaluuya) against the sinister and fetishistic Armitage family. What works so well about *Get Out* is the fact it doesn't fall back on expected tropes about racism: this is not a story about right-wing extremism like the KKK, but the harm white people can do when they consume black culture like locusts. Hauntingly, even though they are literal body-snatchers, the Armitages even think of themselves as being progressive. As patriarch Dean (Bradley Whitford) splutters with his dying breath: 'I would have voted for Obama for a third time if I could.'

In contrast to thriller movies, television is more likely to use an ensemble cast as standard. As mentioned in part one, incredibly varied TV thrillers such as *Top Boy*, *Brooklyn Nine-Nine* and *The Mentalist* may feature a protagonist and antagonist who just edge out 'above' the other characters. The role functions of the protagonist and antagonist may swap over dependent on what's going on in the season and frequently do. If there's a name for this phenomenon, I've never seen it, so I call these characters the 'umbrellas' which provides a visual of them 'sheltering' the other characters underneath in the ensemble. In *Top Boy* the umbrellas are Dushane and Sully; in *Brooklyn Nine-Nine*, it's Jake Peralta and Captain Raymond Holt; in *The Mentalist*, it's Patrick Jane and Special Agent Teresa Lisbon.

It's always worth remembering audiences are forever demanding new ways to engage with genre and characters. If thrillers nearly always utilise a lone protagonist, perhaps working with a group of characters (and the struggles for power that invariably come with this) might bring the industry attention your writing deserves? Of course, regardless of whether you choose a lone protagonist or group, your characters have to rock. Yet, as any script reader or viewer will attest, we are being assaulted on every level by clichéd characters, with boring and predictable motivations. So how to avoid this?

WHY THIS CHARACTER?

> *'Try to have as much tension flow as possible from character, not just from plot. It's easier to create tension with plot devices and twists, but the harder road is usually the most profitable.'*
>
> – **Stuart Hazeldine, writer/director** (@stuarthazeldine)

Many writers have told me over the years that originality is overrated and 'it's the execution that counts'. They have insisted no story or character can *truly* be the same and that I must be exaggerating when I say I'm seeing the same sorts of stories and characters in spec thriller screenplays (and, indeed, all genres). Make no mistake: I am not exaggerating. If you do not believe me, check out your nearest spec pile. You will not have to go very deep into it to discover many screenplays, particularly genre screenplays (but dramas, too), with similar and even *identical* premises, characters, motifs, motivations and more. You *need* to avoid the usual characters, performing the usual kinds of actions, arising from those usual motivations. I cannot stress this strongly enough. The odds are already against us as writers; do not lengthen them even more by being the same as countless others. Always go *against* expectation whenever you can. Never take the easy way.

But how to do this? Well, just as I encouraged you to think, 'Why this story?' in Chapter One, I also think it's worthwhile to consider, 'Why this character?' I believe a lot of screenwriters 'see' a character in their mind and form an attachment almost immediately, without thinking whether said character is best for the story, or indeed *what* their story is communicating with that particular character at the helm.

Too often, writers will simply recreate the protagonist we expect in a thriller: most often this will be a white male or female lead of approximately 25 to 40 years old, who is also straight and able-bodied. Yet as I already mentioned in Chapter One of this book, audiences respond to diversity favourably in the 2020s and may even demand it dependent on the story being told (despite all the 'go woke, go broke' nonsense parroted by sexists and racists on the dark corners of Reddit).

Of course, sometimes that 'usual' character really is the best character for the story, but considering 'why this character?' still helps make him or her that little bit more interesting than all the rest. For instance, Indiana Jones might be a white, heterosexual male in the usual age group, but he also has an irrational fear of snakes, so obviously he's going to come up against them in his adventures. Seeing him flap about, hysterical (when he's usually so capable), endears him to the audience. This, then, 'opens up' other unusual elements of his character, such as his pettiness in the first movie with Marion, who can look after herself. Similarly, his didactic belief that historical artefacts should be in museums and not the hands of greedy collectors leads him into a number of scenarios in which his life is in danger.

In addition, produced movie characters will frequently have typical and somewhat bland names, like John or Ellen, but names have power and connotations all their own. Choosing a name different from the norm can make all the difference – think Indiana Jones again. Different cultures and locations to the norm can also give your characters, and even your story, a whole new outlook: imagine your conspiracy theory thriller in Chinatown, instead of just 'London'; or your woman in peril thriller involving people from the Jewish community; or your gangster thriller in a middle-class area: what does it add to your story? Perhaps nothing directly, but it may provide a completely different backdrop or outlook for the protagonist to go up against the antagonist. As with everything in scriptwriting, it is a delicate balancing act, but characters different from the 'usual' (whatever that means) are a great way to help your spec stand out and gain champions for your writing.

As JK Amalou (@jkamalou), writer/director and producer of British thriller *Assassin* (2015) points out, being original – or at least *seeming* original – is key to creating perceived 'value' in your thriller screenplay: *'Mix the genre with another one. Create protagonists that we care about. Find never-seen-before takes on the genre conventions/ tropes: chases, murders, cat and mouse games (if you can't, bring these clichés into the story in an original, surprising manner). Use settings not seen before. Oh, and ALWAYS create a memorable villain.'*

WHAT IS A HERO?

Very often we use the words 'protagonist' and 'hero' interchangeably. This didn't really matter for an extended time because main characters were most often literal heroes in thrillers. However characterisation in the 2020s has changed considerably. Audiences demand much more nuance and layers as standard, which means protagonists do not always behave in heroic ways; in fact, sometimes they're literal *anti*heroes.

But what if we DO want to write an archetypal hero? As mentioned in Chapter One, the hero is an archetypal character described by Campbell and Vogler in *The Monomyth* and *The Hero's Journey* respectively. 'Archetype' is defined in the dictionary as:

'the original pattern or model from which all things of the same kind are copied or on which they are based; a model or first form; prototype.'

In Jungian psychology, Jung talks of archetypes as being inherited ideas and/or collective beliefs from society. This means everyone has a strong, shared idea of what being a hero really means (it also probably means you have a strong idea of what being a villain means, too).

Chances are you already think a hero is a real person or a fictional character who, in the face of danger, combats adversity through feats of ingenuity, courage, or strength. This is viewed as 'common sense'. After all, even small children will talk of 'goodies' and 'baddies'! Like other formerly gender-specific terms, 'hero' is often used to refer to any gender (though the actual word 'heroine' only refers to women).

I've been writing and researching The Hero's Journey for a long time now. I've published a huge number of articles on this plotting archetype, especially with reference to what it means for the characterisation of both male and female leads.

So imagine my surprise when female writers started telling B2W that The Hero's Journey is 'for men'!

I started to notice this pushback around the time I was writing and revising my third non-fiction book, *Writing Diverse Characters For Fiction, TV or Film* in 2017. It was only the odd comment here on a Facebook or Twitter thread, or question at a workshop, so I thought it was just one of those momentary things.

Yet as the years have progressed, I started seeing this claim more and more. I was already aware of various retellings of The Hero's Journey from the female POV (and there's a lot of them!), but I'd always rejected them as redundant. Why? Because I don't believe heroism is gendered. Nor is being a warrior, standing up for yourself, fighting obstacles or engaging with allies to get what you need (in fact, these are all things most women will report having to do in life or work!).

As someone with significant traumas in her life, I'd always taken great comfort in The Hero's Journey. It puzzled me greatly when other women claimed it was not 'for women'. This belief also accidentally plays straight into the hands of sexist men online that B2W calls 'Dudeflakes'. Like the Dudeflakes then, those women are likening heroism to be the ultimate in machismo, a MALE achievement. Yikes.

Now, if women want to complain about the sexist language in the Joseph Campbell's Monomyth that's a different thing. He really *does* say only men can be heroes and obviously, that is incorrect.

Historically, heroes are more often depicted as male in stories, then okay – but again: that's a different thing. Or maybe complain about the idea we use The Hero's Journey TOO MUCH in storytelling... sure. But again, this is not the same thing.

These are the facts:

1) Heroism is not gendered.
2) Women can be warriors (literal and metaphorical or both).

3) The Hero's Journey is literally gender-neutral (in contrast to The Monomyth).
4) The Hero's Journey can be incredibly meaningful to many women and relevant to their personal experiences.
5) Women CAN be heroes.

It's understandable that some women believe females in society are socialised differently to males, because they are. It's also true women tend to deal with adversity in different ways, tending to rely on brains over brawn. This is why female antagonists in our lives often indulge in power plays, from Queen Bees in the playground through to jobsworths at work or manipulative abusers in the home or family. Unlike male aggressors, female ones may not even lift a finger to deliver blows you never see coming (and may even have you doubting it happened at all, despite the psychological wound inflicted).

Yet as we can see from the breakdown in Chapter One, *The Hero's Journey* does not insist heroes must engage in huge feats of overt strength to be considered heroic in a thriller or action-adventure. Put simply, all our female heroes need is an arc, a foe and allies, just like their male counterparts. But what do we mean by 'arc'?

THE TRANSFORMATIVE ARC

The Hero's Journey is generally thought of as a transformative arc where our hero literally changes or 'levels up' via the events in the story. This is not rocket science, plus we can see it in action very easily because we are so familiar with it.

Often such heroes will start as someone 'weak' or 'helpless' who just wants a quiet life. Over the course of the story this hero will rise and face hardship and adversity, often overthrowing governments or whole galaxies in their bid to do what's right.

An obvious example here would be Luke Skywalker in the original *Star Wars* (1977) or his female counterpart Rey in *The Force Awakens* (2015). Both are orphans, living on desert planets at the beginning of their journeys. They both must face their Jedi destiny to take on the evil Galactic Empire and First Order respectively, headed up by Emperor Palpatine both times.

Both Luke and Rey must find mentors – Luke and Obi Wan Kenobi, Rey and Luke himself, as well as Leia – and they recruit allies along the way too such as Chewbacca, robots R2D2 and C3PO, plus ex-Stormtrooper Finn and fighter pilot Poe Dameron to name just a few.

The Transformative Arc has always been popular with audiences. For a long time, The Hero's Journey has been in evidence in most thrillers. We can see and recognise this plotting archetype easily, its familiarity feels recognisable and relatable, whether we are watching the downfall of evil empires like the *Star Wars* franchise; or just one character's fight against an abuser such as *Sleeping With the Enemy* (1991); a boy wizard's attempts to save his school and friends (*Harry Potter* franchise, 2001–2011); or a young girl's attempts to save her sister and take on a tyrannical ruler (*The Hunger Games* franchise, 2012–2014); or a chief's daughter who wants to save her home land from pestilence (*Moana,* 2016); or an Amazonian princess' travels where she helps the human world in times of war (*Wonder Woman*, 2017); or a young prince's realisation he must save his home country and share its gifts with the world (*Black Panther*, 2018).

No doubt you can name plenty more. The transformative arc via The Hero's Journey is so ubiquitous that many screenwriters believe protagonists MUST change… otherwise the characterisation is 'no good'. Certainly when I began writing about heroism and characters on www.bang2write.com, I got huge pushback for suggesting otherwise! It was believed as little as ten years ago that such heroes – again, often used as a straight synonym for 'protagonist' – needed to be 'educated' by what happened to them in the course of the story. If they weren't, they were considered 'two-dimensional' and lacking in nuance.

However, in recent years it has become much more obvious the appeal of both The Hero's Journey and The Transformative Arc has begun to wane with audiences. There have been a number of thrillers in recent years that have experimented with alternative plotting archetypes that are subtly different to The Hero's Journey and frequently do NOT necessarily have fundamental transformation (aka 'change') built in. Time to name a few.

THE FLAT ARC

So if the old model demands the protagonist is 'educated' by what happens to them in the course of the story, then in modern times the protagonist is the *educator*. This means the protagonist's arc is shorter and they create a 'ripple effect' for all the secondary characters (and sometimes the antagonist as well). In other words, they don't change but may cause the other characters to change. Sometimes this is referred to as 'the flat arc'.

Powerful 'flat arc' characters that appear in Hero's Journey stories include Katniss Everdeen (Jennifer Lawrence) from *The Hunger Games*. Whilst Katniss undergoes the hero's journey, she does NOT refuse the call: she jumps headlong into the arena in place of younger sister Primrose, because it's the right thing to do.

So Katniss has a sense of duty and sacrifice, but crucially she does not learn this in the arena, but in her home before the story even starts. This means she starts and ends as a highly capable young woman who put others ahead of themselves. Her selflessness is her sacrifice, but crucially it is hardwired into her personality. She starts and ends the story with it; she does not have to 'learn' it or fundamentally change who she is.

What's more, the flat arc is turning up more and more in movie franchises and long-running TV series. This is because it allows for more longevity. Think about it: if a character has to constantly change movie after movie, or TV season after TV season, their position quickly becomes untenable because their metaphysical journey stretches credulity as we begin to ask why such a character never learns 'enough' to walk away and/or avoid the central problem.

However, if the journey is NOT principally about change, then opportunities for new narratives involving that same character open up. In the case of Katniss Everdeen, she is forced back into the arena a second time in *Catching Fire* (2013). This is not her choice but the evil President Snow's, who decides all previous winners must face one another in 'The Quarter Quell' to celebrate 75 years of The Hunger Games. In other words, she is unable to 'refuse the call' again.

Crucially, Katniss is the same girl she was in the first movie. During the sequel she must face her fears and try and save Peeta, all over again. What's different is the fact she is now considered a real threat by President Snow (Donald Sutherland). Katniss' clever suicide pact with Peeta (Josh Hutcherson) in the arena in the first movie has inspired uprisings in many of the districts across Panem and he is desperate to put Katniss in her place, once and for all.

Of course this doesn't happen and Katniss manages to survive the arena and become the face of the resistance in parts three and four of the saga, *Mockingjay* (2014). Again, she has not changed: she is the same girl she has always been. She has low self-worth but a high sense of responsibility, meaning she feels obligated to go into battle – yet again – whether she likes it or not. Her arc may be flat, but it's still incredibly meaningful: Katniss is a true and selfless hero whose personal sacrifices never stop her doing what's right.

REBIRTH

Of course, just as characters in thrillers *can* have flat arcs in The Hero's Journey, they may have transformative arcs in other plotting archetypes. Let's look at some other intriguing changes to how we view heroes that have popped up more often in the last five to ten years.

In contrast to The Hero's Journey which asks heroes to go through a series of trials to defeat an antagonistic (often evil) force of some kind, the 'Rebirth' plotting archetype creates an event which forces the main character to change their ways and (most frequently) become a better person.

Carol Danvers aka 'Captain Marvel' (Brie Larson) became Marvel's first ever movie female protagonist in 2019. There's been a lot written online about how Carol Danvers 'doesn't' have an arc... But this betrays commentators' lack of understanding about different plotting archetypes.

What they really mean is *Captain Marvel* might have a transformative arc, but hers does NOT follow the classic 'Hero's Journey' template. Carol Danvers is a Kree warrior known as 'Vers', a member of Starforce with her mentor Yon-Rogg (Jude Law). Their shared nemesis is the Skrull race, who are a technologically-advanced, shape-shifting race of reptilian humanoids. They are able to replicate other lifeforms seamlessly right down to their DNA, and infiltrate planets without suspicion which makes them especially dangerous.

So as you can see, the lines are drawn between 'good and bad' very obviously at the beginning of this story, just like The Hero's Journey... but that is where the similarity ends. *Captain Marvel* is a 'rebirth' story, examining how a hero can be made from finding out the truth and making a stand for what's right.

This means that Carol will discover she is on the WRONG SIDE in the course of the story; everything she thought was real and true is not. It turns out the Kree are the *real* oppressors and the Skrull are just trying to fight against the genocide of their people.

What's more, it turns out Carol is not even Kree at all, but human. An accident means she absorbed the powers of the Tesseract (yes, the same one from *Avengers Assemble,* 2012) and developed superpowers. As a result Carol must go on a journey of both self-discovery and to protect the Skrull from the Kree.

There is a strong message in *Captain Marvel* about not believing everything you hear just because it comes from the people in charge. In an age of 'fake news', this is especially relevant to everyone in the audience regardless of gender. Characters must confront the truth, no matter how horrible, in order to become a 'better person' in Rebirth stories.

This Rebirth arc was incredibly meaningful to many women and girls in the audience. Throughout the story Carol is told repeatedly not to trust her emotions by male mentor Yonn-Rogg; he even says she cannot meet her true potential if she does not disregard them. This is something females in the real world are met with constantly. Throughout history 'hysterical' females have been disparaged at best and at worst, even medicated and locked away in institutions.

What's more, the Kree's Supreme Intelligence is presented as the patriarchal 'Elders' from many cultures including the Western World's. Carol is reminded again and again by those around her that she was 'made' by the Kree. Like so many abusive parents, the Kree threaten Carol with having everything taken away from her if she does not conform to their expectations: 'Without us, you are weak.'

That's why so many women and girls cheered when Carol defeats both Yonn-Rogg and the Krees' Supreme Intelligence *just by being herself*: 'I've been fighting with one arm tied behind my back. What happens when I am finally set free?'

It's also important to note that whilst Carol must realise she is on the wrong side, she doesn't change who she is *fundamentally*. She starts and ends as a capable female character: she is a pragmatic wisecracker who will do whatever it takes to do the right thing.

THE MIXED ARC

Perhaps what's most surprising about all the furore about 2019's online row about Captain Marvel 'not having an arc' is the fact Carol's was not the first time we saw the Rebirth archetype in the Marvel Cinematic Universe.

Iron Man (2008) kicked off the first phase of the Marvel Cinematic Universe. Starring Robert Downey Jr as the titular lead character, the movie begins in very obvious Hero's Journey territory. We join Stark in 'The Ordinary World', demonstrating his weapons in Afghanistan with his usual cool quips as they explode: 'That's how Dad did it. That's how America does it... and it's worked out pretty well so far.'

It's clear Tony believes creating and selling weapons keeps America 'safe', but within minutes his convoy has been ambushed (aka 'Call to adventure'). Injured and waking up in a literal cave, he discovers his life has been saved by fellow prisoner Yinsen (played by Shaun Toub), who has installed the 'arc reactor' that will become Tony's signature power source for his Iron Man suit.

To his confusion, his captors call Tony 'the greatest mass murderer in America', before demanding he build the Jericho rockets he had been demonstrating for US troops. As the Hero's Journey demands Tony refuses, but it's clear he has no choice in the matter.

Yinsen becomes both a mentor figure and ally to Tony as he *apparently* starts work on the rockets in that cave. Of course it's a double-cross and Tony actually creates a prototype for his suit and lights up all his captors, but not before Yinsen sacrifices himself in order to help Tony escape (as per the 'expendable hero' trope).

After despatching the enemy, Tony's reward is his freedom. He must literally take 'the road back' by trekking through the desert until he is rescued by his friend Colonel Rhodes (Terrence Howard).

Tony returns 'resurrected' to the USA as the prodigal son at a press conference, but not before stunning everyone by declaring Stark Industries will no longer be manufacturing weapons. Instead Tony believes the arc reactor in his chest to be the answer to an exciting new possibility for world peace.

Yet this is NOT the end of the movie. In fact, this playing out of The Hero's Journey accounts for only approximately forty minutes of a two-hour picture. Like Captain Marvel will in 2019, Tony realises he is on the 'wrong' side via the Rebirth archetype.

This means the film has a mixed arc in terms of blending the two plotting archetypes: I like to call it 'Hero's Rebirth'. Tony talks of the trauma of seeing young Americans killed by the very weapons he designed to protect them. He shuts down the weapons division without consulting the board of directors, or his main allies Rhodes, his assistant/love interest Pepper Potts (Gwyneth Paltrow) or his 'father figure' and business partner Obadiah Stane (Jeff Bridges).

Stark Industries goes into free fall but Tony is unconcerned. It is left to Obadiah to manage the fall-out, seemingly with good humour. Trusting him, Tony upgrades his arc reactor 'heart' with grudging help from Pepper and he starts building his Iron Man suit, v2. Meanwhile, Tony's captors search the desert for that prototype Iron Man suit he was forced to leave behind in his trek out of the desert.

As with most Rebirth stories, Tony's trust in Obadiah is misplaced. At the mid-point approximately 60 minutes in, Obadiah reveals he has locked Tony out of his own company, cementing him as the real villain of the story.

Tony vows to undo this, but not before creating the iconic suit in red and gold and flying off to Gulmira where he was initially held at the beginning of the movie. There he helps refugees overcome his captors, The Ten Rings. On his way back Tony creates problems for the United States Air Force, forcing Rhodes to cover for him: 'It was just a training exercise'!

Meanwhile Obadiah's treachery is discovered to be even worse: he colluded with The Ten Rings to kidnap Tony in the first place! He double-crosses the Rings' leader Omer when he offers him the prototype Iron Man suit, then returns to America and steals Tony's arc reactor right out of his chest.

Thankfully Pepper did not throw away the prototype Yinsen gave Tony as instructed, so he is able to save himself. This means that when Obadiah attempts to kill Pepper and agents of S.H.I.E.L.D at Stark Industries in his own version of the Iron Man suit, Tony arrives to save the day but not without Pepper's help.

The movie ends *not* with Tony confirming the calamity at Stark Industries was 'just a training exercise' – a running gag throughout the movie – but his new identity: 'I am Iron Man'.

This catchphrase echoes throughout the franchise, most poignantly as Tony's last words in *Avengers: Endgame* (2019) when he manipulates Thanos' 'Iron Gauntlet' which is made of the same nanotech as Tony's suit. By 'catching' the infinity stones, Tony transfers them to himself and snaps Thanos et al out of existence, but their raw power costs him his own life.

VOYAGE AND RETURN

So, if a protagonist can have...

- A transformative arc in the Hero's Journey
- A flat arc in the Hero's Journey
- A transformative arc in other plotting archetypes like 'Rebirth'
- A mixed arc where we see two plotting archetypes at work

... does that mean main characters can have flat arcs in plotting archetypes other than 'Rebirth'? Absolutely, yes!

Voyage and Return is super-similar to The Hero's Journey and especially relevant to thrillers as well. *The Seven Basic Plots* by Christopher Booker (2004) describes Voyage and Return as '*The protagonist goes to a strange land and, after overcoming the threats it poses to them, they return with experience.'*

Thrillers and action-adventures that follow this plotting archetype include (but are not limited to): *Back to The Future* (1985); *Toy Story* (1995); *The Lion, the Witch and the Wardrobe* (2005); Tim Burton's *Alice In Wonderland* (2010); *Gravity* (2013); *Dawn of the Planet of the Apes* (2014); *San Andreas* (2015); *Mad Max: Fury Road* (2015); and *The Adam Project* (2022).

Whilst similar, Voyage and Return is markedly different to The Hero's Journey. Whilst The Hero's Journey requires its protagonist to go up against evil forces as standard, there is no such requirement in Voyage and Return (though the characters may still do this, such as the children against the Snow Queen in Narnia, or Furiosa and the Wives against Immortan Joe in *Mad Max: Fury Road*).

It's just as likely the forces the characters are up against are natural (as in disaster movies like *San Andreas*, or the hostile vastness of space as in *Gravity*); or as the result of an accident (as in *Toy Story*, where Woody and Buzz get left behind at the gas station when they fall from the car); or a different culture (like *Dawn of the Planet of the Apes*); or as the result of curiosity, experiments or the world going to hell in a handbasket (as in *Alice in Wonderland, Back to the Future, or The Adam Project* respectively).

THE LONE PROTAGONIST BECOMES THE VOYAGER

So the lone protagonist is a popular trope in thriller and has frequently appeared as a warrior-in-the-making via The Hero's Journey over the past 40 years. This is most obvious in the blockbuster action or adventure thriller, but may appear in other types of thriller too.

What makes Voyage and Return feel so fresh in contrast to the Hero's Journey is simply the fact we haven't used it as much. Yet it's also appeared enough in movie history for us to feel familiar with it – the ultimate in 'pre-sold' storytelling!

In addition, the protagonists of Voyage and Return stories most often don't have to do any special training in order to deal with the situations they find themselves in (unlike The Hero's Journey, who trains with a mentor and/or allies).

Instead these characters dig deep with the attributes they already possess, or had been hiding about themselves up until that point. This makes very attractive characters for those in the audience who feel overlooked, underappreciated, or marginalised.

The Voyager is a protagonist who is **already capable.** S/he doesn't need to change or train, but solves a significant problem presented **with skills and attributes they already possess.**

Carol Danvers aka Captain Marvel is a Voyager. She does not have to change herself fundamentally in order to become a hero. In fact, she has to uncover who she was BEFORE the strange crash that haunts her dreams. This means she has to learn to trust herself and stop being hoodwinked by the corrupt values of the Kree.

Two iconic Voyager characters are not only fan favourites, they're loved by mass audiences even the best part of four decades later:

- **Ellen Ripley.** In *Aliens* (1986), we learn Ripley (Sigourney Weaver) promised her daughter Amanda she would be back from her work on the Nostromo in time for her eleventh birthday. After the events of *Alien* (1979), Ripley was lost in space in her cryo-sleep tube for 57 years: during that time, Amanda grew up, married and died. Though *Alien* is actually a horror, *Aliens* is a thriller, but like the movie before it, Ripley does not change everything about herself fundamentally in order to emerge victorious. In fact, she starts and ends the movie as a mother, taking on Newt as her substitute for Amanda.
- **John McClane.** In *Die Hard* (1988), we discover protagonist John McClane (Bruce Willis) is on his way from New York to Los Angeles because he is separated from his family. He is a blue collar guy who has some resentment against his wife Holly Gennaro McClane (Bonnie Bedelia) for taking a relatively high-powered white collar job in another state. That said, his resentment is not the result of sexism but the changing values of a marriage he hadn't planned for or foreseen (something most married people can relate to, especially if they have been together a long time). In the course

of the movie only John has the skills to save the people in the Nakatomi Plaza, but crucially Holly also provides some relief for the rest of the hostages due to her superior negotiation ability. Neither character change anything fundamentally about themselves during their respective ordeals, so it makes sense when John refers to his wife as 'Gennaro' to the press reporters at the end of the movie, only for Holly to correct him and call herself 'McClane'.

When I first started writing about Voyager characters, the pushback against the idea iconic characters like Ripley or McClane do not change was huge. The idea that 'good characters = change' was so ingrained that it was almost heresy to suppose otherwise.

Writers are now willing to consider different plotting archetypes, tropes and ideas when it comes to characterisation. This is just as well, because as illustrated audiences are very interested in the 'Voyager' character in modern movies.

The John Wick franchise (2014–2023)

Consider *John Wick* (2014) which I believe to be one of the most obvious modern Voyager characters. His past as an assassin literally buried, former Marine John (Keanu Reeves) is facing up to the death of his wife (we assume from cancer). When she dies, a puppy is delivered to his home as a last gift from her to help him grieve. John is keen to honour his wife by doing as she wishes. He has no plans to return to his old ways at this point.

This all changes when gangster playboy Iosef (Alfie Allen) sees John's car at a gas station and wants to buy it. He does not take kindly to being rebuffed. With friends, he breaks in to John's place that night to steal the car. Before they do this, they ambush John, beat him up and kill the puppy.

This marks a change in John. He has no need to consult any allies or mentors; he is a lone wolf. He literally digs up his weapons from under the floor in his basement and decides to take on those who stopped him from grieving for his wife.

Of course, Iosef is not just any asshole, he is the son of Viggo, the 'Mr Big' of Mafiasos (the late Michael Nyqvist). Panic descends when

Viggo hears Wick is coming for his son. At first, he hopes he can pull it back and reason with Wick, so calls him on the phone. When it's clear Wick does not want to negotiate, Viggo has a horrible sense of inevitability... The man himself is coming for them all. Yikes!

Gangsters like Viggo are often portrayed as wise and astute, but not here; instead he is a snivelling coward. Viggo even sells his own son out to save his own miserable skin... But of course he can't face up to this. Instead he will blame fellow hitman Marcus (Willem Dafoe) for 'not doing his job properly' and kill him instead.

Again, John doesn't have to change anything fundamental about himself; he just has to return to what he was before the story even began. John's reputation precedes him. Amongst the Russians, Wick is known as 'Baba Yaga'. These mythic terms and the fact he lurks in the shadows gives John Wick a bogeyman-like presence in the 2014 movie and throughout the franchise. Every bad guy has their own story about Wick: *'I once saw him kill three men in a bar with a pencil ... a fucking pencil.'*

My favourite of the franchise so far is probably *John Wick 3 – Parabellum* (2019), where John is labelled 'excommunicado' for the unauthorised killing of a High Table crime lord on the grounds of the New York Continental Hotel, supposedly neutral ground in the 'assassin wars'.

Starting moments after *John Wick: Chapter 2* (2017) left off, Wick now has a $14 million bounty on his head for breaking the rules. He must evade and kill the assassins dispatched after him, plus this time he must appeal to allies he has helped before, like Sofia (Halle Berry) who trains her dogs to kill. Played to perfection by Berry, what's particularly refreshing about her character is she doesn't want to help Wick but her prior agreement with him is unbreakable as per the assassins' code. This doesn't stop her making her resentment known, such as spitting in his water when they're in the desert!

Secondary characters like Sofia may have to decide to 'fall in' with the protagonist and see the mission his/her way... They must help the protagonist, or they are the enemy. You could say the Voyager's motto is *'join me or die'*. This is why the Voyager turns up so often in genre movies where it's 'life or death', like thrillers. This is particularly obvious in the *John Wick* franchise, but we can see it at work in many others too.

GIRLS ON FILM

In recent years, there's been a significant shift in how the industry views female leads. When I first started out and when I wrote the first edition of this book, female protagonists were often met with suspicion by producers and money moguls. There was a belief 'female leads don't sell' and it was very difficult to get projects with them greenlit.

Fast-forward ten years and it's a very different story. Whilst male leads still outnumber female in produced movies and television across the board, female characters are more in demand in the 2020s than they ever have been in my 20-year career. This has led to a surge in demand for female leads.

Historically female leads have often figured prominently in thrillers (particularly within the supernatural and psychological thriller sub-genres). Even allowing for this change however, it is immediately apparent that female characterisation is much less varied than male characterisation as a general rule; as a result, the notion of the 'usual' character is much more obvious. Frequently, scribes will 'overthink' female characterisation, forgetting that, though gender is (usually) an important part of a person, it is not the *whole* person. This means we end up with a barely warm rehash of the following 'typical' female characters:

- **Kickass Hottie**. Probably the favourite of all supposed 'strong women' in both produced movies and spec screenplays alike, the kickass hottie is a fun fantasy character that most of us love, but she IS overrepresented in both produced content and the spec pile. She is more often than not just a male character with her gender changed. The kickass hottie can do anything physical a man can and look gorgeous doing it... And no produced movie or spec screenplay would be complete without the obligatory shots of her in the shower or in her underwear. Alice in the *Resident*

Evil franchise is the epitome of 'kickass hottie': as the series progresses, Alice's characterisation is drawn with broader and broader strokes, so that, by the fourth instalment, *Afterlife* (2010), she not only 'feels' a clone of other characters in this vein, she literally IS a clone, with many, many copies of her attacking the base! We can't even be sure the one who stows away on the spaceship is the *original* Alice (and really, who cares anyway? She looks hot and kicks ass). Of course kickass hotties CAN be great characters with nuance and layers: one of my recent favourites has to be Lorraine in *Atomic Blonde* (Charlize Theron, 2017), who is basically James Bond with a bad attitude, wearing gorgeous outfits and kicking her way through set piece after set piece. But that's not where her characterisation ends: a bisexual woman, Lorraine is drawn into the conspiracy by a murdered (male) lover, then must try and protect her female lover. Sadly she doesn't succeed (bringing forth the hated 'dead lesbian' trope), but bar that it was a brilliant action film that went against type.

- **Femme Fatale.** The kickass hottie must never be confused with the 'femme fatale' (though she frequently is); the femme fatale is a fantastic character most often seen in the age of the film noir thriller in the 1940/50s. The femme fatale was a mysterious and seductive woman, as well as an arch manipulator and well-drawn character on an equal with her male counterparts. An obvious example here would be Catherine Tramell (Sharon Stone) in *Basic Instinct* (1992). In the past ten years we've seen a resurgence in the femme fatale whose sexiness is surpassed by her cunning: the industry calls this 'The Gone Girl Effect' courtesy of Amy Dunne (Rosamund Pike in *Gone Girl*, 2014). Discovering her husband Nick (Ben Affleck) has been having an extramarital affair, Amy frames him for her own 'murder' while she is still very much alive. Very often when spec screenwriters attempt this character, she is simply sexy and male characters can't help themselves. Yawn. Sometimes the screenwriter attempts to do away with the sexy part and makes the character an ice maiden – but the problem still remains because she is just as boring and two-dimensional.

- **[Negative Adjective] Female.** The 'negative adjective' female is a character most often seen in spec screenplays, particularly in the protagonist's role. Sometimes she will be a 'little girl lost' type and be grieving (most often) for her father, who may have been killed in front of her, or promised her he'd return from a long trip (but didn't). The negative adjective female will be billed most often as 'guilt ridden' (especially in thrillers), but also as 'vain' or 'embittered' (though the latter two more often in the comedy genre). The guilt-ridden female will just as often be responsible for the death of someone close to her: a husband, friend, child, work colleague or, most often, a sister. Frequently the reason will be a car crash or similar accident (thus not 'really' her fault). The guilt-ridden female will often be depressed and a self-harmer, with a tendency towards addiction to alcohol, cigarettes or sex; sometimes all three. It's easy to see what spec screenwriters are trying to do: they're attempting to bring a tragic backstory to their protagonist in much the same way many produced screenwriters do with their male protagonists, frequently via the 'dead wife/girlfriend' trope. But, like that produced thriller content, this sea of negativity, particularly regret, already feels stale and old and is best avoided. A good example of such a female character done well and whose backstory includes grief would be *The Shallows* (2016) starring Blake Lively as Nancy, a young woman whose mother has recently died from cancer. It's played in a low-key, non-melodramatic way, with Nancy portrayed as a capable young woman who is no longer certain of what she wants now such a terrible thing has happened to her family. Unsure whether she wants to continue medical school anymore and wanting to connect with her lost mother, Nancy travels to a secret beach her surfer mom went to when she was pregnant with her. There, Nancy connects with her warrior mother in ways she could not have imagined by having to survive a shark attack.

- **Woman In A Man's World.** It's quite common to find not a single woman included in a produced thriller scenario with a mainly male cast: *The Grey* (2012) kills off its female flight attendant on impact when the plane goes down (though we get a nice view of her dead body eaten by wolves!). Yes, Ottway's wife and Talget's little girl are both 'present' in the narrative, but both are plot devices, rather than characters in their own right. The supposedly non-English-speaking Anna is sidelined in a similar way in *Predator* (1987), for she appears to be there solely to offer exposition to the soldiers: *'When the big man was killed, you must have wounded it.'/'We find our men without their skin... Only when it is hottest, this happens.'* When roughneck character groups include women prominently, they are likely to just be men with their gender changed, such as Vasquez in *Aliens* (1986). Other times, they may be confused representations such as Isabelle in *Predators* (2010), who might be capable of taking on ominous-sounding Black Op missions, but her downfall is her... compassion (sorry, what??). For a short period we were treated to women being at the end of the phone crying while their men were in war zones (*American Sniper*, 2014) or climbed mountains (*Everest*, 2015). The Lindseys from *The Abyss* (1989) or Lindas from *The Perfect Storm* (2000) are few and far between, it seems (and Mary Elizabeth Mastrantonio is nabbing both roles, too!). Like the aforementioned *The Grey*, *American Sniper*, or *Everest* however, spec thriller screenplays like this never seem to remember to include female characters.

- **Mom Warrior.** This role was probably made most famous in produced thriller movies by Ripley's rescue and subsequent protection of Newt in *Aliens* (1986). This is a generally positive representation of women and motherhood that many of the female (and male) members of the audience feel they can relate to, but it nevertheless feels somewhat overdone in the 'women in peril' subgenre. 'Mom warrior' in another subgenre of thriller, however – like sci-fi – still works and I've seen some great representations of her in spec screenplays, plus Sara (Emily Blunt) in *Looper* (2012) is a great representation of a woman conflicted by her past treatment of her son and how it may affect him in the future, signified by her (otherwise unexplained) chopping of the tree trunk root in front of the family home.
- **Crazy Bitch.** Perhaps most evocative of Alex (Glenn Close) in *Fatal Attraction* (1987), the crazy bitch is frequently the antagonist in the

spec thriller screenplays I see. Unlike their produced counterparts, however, the spec crazy bitch is very frequently simply *just* crazy, often for indiscernible reasons, or she crosses over into vengeful female territory, seeking revenge for rapes or other crimes that were 'all in her mind'.

- **Virgin/Slut.** 'Good girls survive and bad girls die' is a dichotomy most typically associated with the horror genre, but it can rear its ugly head in produced thrillers, too, particularly with reference to secondary female characters. Virgins are often 'innocent' types and frequently need rescuing, often quite literally, meaning this character strays into 'damsels in distress' territory. The 'sluts' tag, too, can be hideously literal, like poor Amanda who dies in a single plot beat in *Taken* (2008), as if her 'experience' means she is of lesser worth. Other times, a slut character simply means a vampy female character who can look after herself. She is usually placed in the secondary role function occupied by a male henchman to the antagonist. She will frequently be the main bad guy's girlfriend, but he will usually kill her without a second's thought, as Qualen (John Lithgow) kills Kristel in *Cliffhanger* (1993), though antagonist Thomas Gabriel (Timothy Olyphant) is uncharacteristically enraged by girlfriend Mai's death at John McClane's hands in *Live Free or Die Hard* (2007). Virgin/slut characters hardly ever figure in the spec thrillers I read, however.
- **Damsel In Distress.** Damsels in distress are frequently 'women who need rescuing' and thus are there solely for the service of the plot. Early thrillers like *King Kong* (1933), plus its various remakes, are best known for this character. *The Midnight Meat Train* (2008), *Taken* (2008) and *Lockout* (2012) are all modern thrillers featuring damsels in distress, with only the latter giving the character a little 'something' about her. Damsels in distress don't have to be wholly 'bad' characters, however, especially when they act as the weakest link of a group. It's notable that men sometimes occupy this secondary role function in produced creature thrillers, like Paris (Lewis Fitz-Gerald) in *Pitch Black* (2000), to good effect – especially considering no one rescues him! We're left instead with that impressive last shot with the whiskey fire-breathing, showing

us the ominous sight of the creatures all gathered around Paris before plunging back into darkness, where they tear him apart. In recent years, male care-giver characters such as Steve Harrington (Joe Keery) in Netflix's *Stranger Things* may need rescuing like the princess in the tower, frequently by women or the younger teens.

- **Crone/Psychic Girl**. The female equivalent of the 'mysterious stranger', the crone appears most in supernatural thriller spec screenplays, usually to give away some important exposition and/or lead the main character in a particular direction. She is frequently a horrible, on-the-nose-cliché and best avoided. Sometimes the crone is replaced with 'psychic girl', who will offer strange predictions or observations the hero must work out over the course of the narrative for a very specific and real reason. Anderton (Tom Cruise) in *Minority Report* (2002) kidnaps psychic girl, Agatha (Samantha Morton), in order to escape the authorities and their accusations of 'pre-crime'. In doing so, Anderton *then* attempts to prove Agatha's predictions wrong (which in turn throws up its own problems). The psychic girl is frequently used in spec thriller screenplays but, unlike *Minority Report*, the writer often places finding the 'psychic answer' at the heart of the narrative. As a result, I'm frequently left with the thought: *'Why doesn't she just tell him (the information) if she already knows it?'*
- **Dead Wife/Girlfriend**. Flashbacks of 'better times' involving this female character have formed almost the entire back catalogue of Christopher Nolan's films: even Batman (Christian Bale), it seems, can't save the woman in his life! Though a dead wife or girlfriend *can* work, it has become a lazy shortcut to feed the, usually male, protagonist's motivation, usually revenge. Occasionally a scribe will 'tick all the boxes' in a produced OR spec thriller screenplay with all the clichés: an engagement ring; laughing together while cooking; and even running through a cornfield together. Yargh.

As you can see, just ten seasoned female archetypes is pretty dire; plus many have their 'female-ness' subsequently over-accentuated or, conversely, removed. The end result is the same: we end up with a 'movie woman', rather than an authentic, feeling character (who just happens to be female).

THE GIRL CHARACTER

Whilst cinema-going still skews young in the 2020s, the Marvel Cinematic Universe (MCU) also demonstrates the power of a young female audience, too. When I wrote my first edition of this book, we were in a weird transition period where 'The Girl Character' was bafflingly common.

The most obvious Marvel example back then probably would have been Black Widow (Scarlett Johannson) in 2012's *The Avengers.* As was common at the time, a group of well-differentiated male characters would be joined by a single female character whose vampy 'female-ness' would be her primary attribute.

Writer-Director Joss Whedon was more or less able to get away with this in the first movie; as mentioned, it was largely the way of things at the time. In the space of just three years, there were big changes in terms of audience preferences.

The second *Avengers* movie *Age of Ultron* came out in 2015: this time, Black Widow's depiction was criticised as sexist, leading Whedon to leave Twitter and delete his account.

Many at the time decried the 'trolls' of Twitter, citing Whedon's advocacy for equality and feminism in such quotes as: *''Why do you write strong female characters?' Because you're still asking me that question.'* Fast-forward less than a decade and it appears Whedon is now 'persona non grata' in Hollywood due to a number of allegations from former co-workers, actors on his sets and his ex-wife.

But enough about him. Rather I want to illustrate the massive difference between a character like Black Widow in Phase 1 of the MCU and how things have changed in the subsequent phases as we launch into Phase 4.

It's very clear how female characters have been developed in much more depth to actively attract female audiences in the past ten years. We can see this is in the evolution of Black Widow herself: from taking Steve Rogers' side in 2016's *Civil War;* through to her selfless and heroic sacrifice to gain the Soul stone in 2019's *Endgame;* to seeing her origins and family in her 2021 movie simply titled *Black Widow*, it's clear there's much more to Natasha than Whedon's first two movies portrayed.

In the last decade the MCU has moved forward with a variety of female characters in different role functions too: protagonist, antagonist, secondary and peripheral. The curse of the single, vampy 'Girl Character' in the group seems to have been lifted.

The pragmatic Gamora (Zoe Saldana) from *Guardians of the Galaxy* (2014) is contrasted against her vengeful sister Nebula (Karen Gillan); Suri, Nakia and Okoye (Letitia Wright, Lupita Nyong'o, Danai Gurira) steal every scene in *Black Panther* (2018); plus of course 2019's *Captain Marvel* places Carol Danvers (Brie Larson) in the lead, Marvel's very first female protagonist.

It's also no accident the 'women of Marvel' all come together in the finale battle of *Endgame* (2019) to help Captain Marvel keep the Infinity Gauntlet away from Thanos. (Whilst some fans accused Marvel of 'wokist pandering' for this scene, I was privileged to see the movie at a matinee packed with little girls aged approximately six to fifteen years old. All of them cheered with joy. It was beautiful).

THE SCARLET WITCH EFFECT

Another Marvel fan favourite female character to spring forth from *Age of Ultron (2015)* is Scarlet Witch aka Wanda Maximoff (Elizabeth Olsen). Wanda is a great example of a female character who does terrible things yet we can see WHY she does them, even if we don't condone her behaviour.

Initially introduced as an antagonist with twin brother Pietro (aka Quicksilver, played by Aaron Taylor-Johnson), both siblings hold a grudge against Tony Stark after his weapons decimated their home country Sokovia and killed their parents. After undergoing Hydra experiments that awaken their powers, the twins join forces with Ultron to take down the Avengers.

Of course, Ultron is defeated. Vision (Paul Bettany) is created, a synthezoid made of vibranium and programmed by Tony Stark and

Bruce Banner, awakened by Thor's hammer, his skull home to the mind stone. Alone after the death of her twin in *The Age of Ultron*, Wanda and Vision become star-crossed lovers on a tragic trajectory: Wanda will be forced to 'kill' Vision in *Avengers: Infinity War* (2018) in order to stop the mind stone falling into Thanos' grasp.

Even worse, this heartbreak will be pointless because Thanos simply uses the time stone to undo her and Vision's sacrifice and take the mind stone anyway. This act has far-reaching consequences. When Scarlet Witch confronts Thanos (Josh Brolin) in the final battle of *Avengers Endgame* (2019) she is even denied recognition:

- SCARLET WITCH: *You took everything from me.*
- THANOS: *I don't even know who you are.*

Scarlet Witch is unable to subdue Thanos alone during the battle, plus her meaningless sacrifice will have far-reaching consequences beyond *Endgame*. Unlike both Tony Stark and Black Widow whose own deaths are immortalised and celebrated in monuments like those seen at events like HeroCon in Disney+'s *Ms. Marvel* (2022), Vision's is largely sidelined.

The unfairness of this drives Wanda's grief into a frenzy. She bewitches the town of Westview in Disney+'s *WandaVision* (2021) TV series, creating a family-friendly sitcom-world in which Vision lives and they have two children, Billy and Tommy. She eventually is forced to give it up and lose both Vision and the kids, but her tragic arc does not end there either.

Cast again as the antagonist in 2022's *Doctor Strange in the Multiverse of Madness*, Wanda longs to be reunited with her imaginary children. Discovering new character America Chavez (Xochitl Gomez) has the ability to hop between the multiverses, Wanda opens the 'Darkhold', a book of spells that corrupts everyone it touches. In doing so, Wanda attempts to take America's power for herself so she might take over a version of herself in 'Earth-838' where she still has Billy and Tommy.

Despite Doctor Strange's and Sorcerer Supreme Wong's best efforts (Benedict Cumberbatch and Benedict Wong), Wanda almost succeeds in stripping America of her power (which feels like a metaphor for the stripping of rights away from women and minorities in the USA, but that's a debate for another time).

Knowing she can't beat Wanda, America gives Scarlet Witch what she truly wants: her beloved sons. Yet confronted with their 'mother' from another realm, Tommy and Billy are afraid of the Scarlet Witch and reject her.

Wanda-838 tells her to take solace in the fact the children will be loved, which Scarlet Witch concedes. Reeling from all this, Scarlet Witch realises what she has done and redeems herself, destroying the Darkhold in every multiverse so it can't tempt others ever again.

Why there are ANY multiverses where Wanda has children when they were imaginary in 'our' reality via *WandaVision* is unclear. Some fan explanations point to the fact Vision is not in Earth-838 and that version of Wanda appears to be a single mother. This means she may have given birth to her boys herself the 'old-fashioned way' in 838 or even created them with magic peacefully (ie. without taking a whole town hostage).

Whatever the case, it's super-refreshing to see a layered and nuanced antiheroine like the Scarlet Witch appear in multiple versions in various movies and series. It was such a short time ago that female characters had to be 'perfect' and idealised wives and girlfriends – if they were featured at all.

It was also not long ago feminist commentators said female lead characters needed to stand alone because male partners or children 'weakened' them! Yet for many women in the audience it's the exact opposite: love for their families strengthens their resolve, it doesn't take it away. Scarlet Witch is relatable to an historically under-served demographic, not only in action/fantasy movies but TV series.

IT'S RAINING MEN

So, as we know, it's a white heterosexual man's world when it comes to produced movies in general, so it shouldn't surprise us that it's often the same in thriller, especially if Will Smith or Denzel Washington aren't available. Yet it's not just the protagonists and antagonists who reflect this worldview; sometimes a lot of the secondary characters do as well. Check some of these out for size:

MAIN ROLES

- **Detective.** The detective may literally be a detective or member of the police force, or may act like one, following a trail for clues *for some reason*. The detective is perhaps one of the most versatile characters of the thriller genre, straddling any number of sub-genres and types, given thriller's capacity for suspense and mystery. Memorable detectives of produced movies include Jeff Jefferies in *Rear Window* (1954); JJ Gittes in *Chinatown* (1974); Mills and Somerset in *Se7en* (1997); Leonard Shelby in *Memento* (2000); and Teddy Daniels in *Shutter Island* (2010). As mentioned previously, in the spec thriller screenplays I've read, detective characters are frequently Suspect Number One in the case of a missing wife or girlfriend, so must clear their names (and/or rescue said wife or girlfriend if she is still alive).
- **Maverick Cop.** Cops aren't to be confused with detectives: these guys aren't trailing a succession of clues so much as blowing shit up and talking cool while doing it. *Bad Boys* (1995) is typical of this section of the thriller genre, as is John McClane in the *Die Hard* franchise. This trope was so popular for so long it felt like every cop was a Maverick for a VERY long time. As mentioned in Chapter One however, police procedurals in particular have changed substantially in recent years, especially in the post-BLM protests era.
- **The Vengeful Hero**. A (usually) male antihero bent on revenge, the antagonist in his sights for a very personal reason. The call to action is usually a dead wife, girlfriend and/or children, as demonstrated in the *Death Wish* franchise, *The Crow* (1993), *A Man Apart* (2003), *Death Sentence* (2007) and *Law Abiding Citizen* (2009). A comic-book hero, such as Batman or Spider-Man, will essentially be a vigilante, working against the forces of evil in order to deal with the emotional fallout of dead parents or another family member. Occasionally, a bodyguard might swear vengeance,

such as Creasy (Denzel Washington in *Man on Fire* (2004), and sometimes kidnapping stories feature vengeful antiheros, such as Bryan (Liam Neeson) in *Taken* (2008), who will stop at nothing, even torture and murder, to get his daughter back. I see lots of vengeful heroes in the spec pile, in blood-soaked narratives that ironically sap the jeopardy, possibly because our hero takes too long to despatch the bad guys. Often a vengeful hero will be a detective and/or a gangster as well, working through a number of leads to find that 'Mr Big'.

- **Lone Wolf.** Westerns were once the place to see the lone wolf hero and it was a role undertaken almost exclusively by Clint Eastwood in his youth. The lone wolf is capable of extreme violence and his integrity is rarely in question, especially when it comes to protecting women and children. We tend to know little about the lone wolf, other than what we see of him in the moment: he has no past and, sometimes, no future either, as he will frequently die protecting those more vulnerable, or he will travel off into the horizon. Antagonists are more likely to be lone wolf types in thrillers of recent years, such as Chigurh (Javier Bardem) in *No Country for Old Men* (2007), though recently *Drive* (2011) utilised the lone wolf hero in the form of Driver (Ryan Gosling).
- **Gangster.** British gangster movies are often derided by movie purists, but are arguably the backbone of the British film industry output and have a rich and varied history. Protagonists may be 'rude boys' (complete with quirky quips) like the fellas in *Lock, Stock and Two Smoking Barrels* (1998) or 'businessmen' like XXXX (Daniel Craig) in *Layer Cake* (2004). Though the spec pile appears to be full of gritty, realist-style gangster thrillers, produced gangster movies have shown us that the sub genre may incorporate singing, as in *Hard Men* (1997); dream sequence, as in *Sexy Beast* (2000); or be set in other time periods, like *The Bank Job* (2008). Generally speaking, gangster movies often have rapid-fire dialogue, larger-than-life characters and glamorous portrayals of guns and drugs. Female characters are typically sidelined, usually there for decoration. Spec gangster thrillers frequently follow the 'Mr Big' scenario mentioned earlier, but in recent years have also taken

to placing a young male hero from a working-class background at the helm. He will be forced to look after younger siblings because their mother is a drug addict, alcoholic and/or not interested in her children. He will be an underachiever at school and recruited by a local 'father figure' type gangster, whom he will then have to turn on *for some reason*.

- **Prisoner.** Nearly all muscle-bound action-hero types have done prison movies, with Stallone and Schwarzenegger launching the successful *Escape Plan* (2013–2019) franchise. Prisoners are frequently framed for things they didn't do, especially in the revenge subgenre. If our prisoner protagonist is guilty, however, the audience can be sure whoever was on the receiving end of our hero's crime *totally* deserved it, such as the redneck guy who perves on Poe's wife in the prologue of *Con Air* (1997). Prisoner thrillers very rarely turn up in the spec pile, which always surprises me, since setting a thriller in a prison is the epitome of 'contained thriller' and could be achieved on a low budget relatively easily.
- **Roughneck.** A roughneck is typically educated at 'the school of life' and frequently an outdoors kind of character, whose usual job is something highly specialised, like mountain rescue or climbing, such as Gabe Walker (Sylvester Stallone) in *Cliffhanger* (1993) and Peter Garrett (Chris O'Donnell) in *Vertical Limit* (2000). Roughnecks will often be oil-rig workers (*The Abyss*, 1989; *The Grey*, 2012) or in the military (*Aliens*, 1986; *Predator*, 1987). Nature will often go against them in stories that incorporate action/adventure and being cut off/isolated from others so that survival is quite literally a race against time. Shows of physical strength are often placed as being of paramount importance in this section of the thriller genre, though the more interesting give us an insight into the psychological effects of isolation as well, as in the aforementioned *The Grey*. Spec thrillers are not often set in the great outdoors but, when they are, they are invariably done well, taking advantage of a hostile landscape. I've read great thrillers set in deserts, outer space, the Australian Outback, the Arctic, the plains of Africa, under the sea and hundreds of miles underground, to name but a few.

- **Everyman.** The most celebrated everyman character is obviously David Mann (Dennis Weaver) in *Duel* (1971), though it's worth remembering Hitchcock frequently put the everyman at the heart of his films, most notably in *North by Northwest* (1959). After dropping out of favour for many years, the Everyman is making a minor comeback, especially in television with protagonists like John Nolan in *The Rookie*. That said, if spec writers want to include the Everyman trope in their work they will have to accept it would be a calculated risk since, inevitably, ill-informed script readers may consider the characterisation 'sketchy'.
- **The Outsider.** Subtly different to the everyman, this character often finds himself in the wrong place at the wrong time, such as Robert Clayton Dean (Will Smith) in *Enemy of the State* (1998). Other times the character makes himself the outsider by lashing out at people and things he sees as the problem, such as Foster (Michael Douglas) in *Falling Down* (1993). Other times it's his expertise that places him on the outside, because others do not believe him, such as Brody (Roy Scheider) in *Jaws* (1975), or others do not act quickly enough based on his scientific predictions, such as Dalton (Pierce Brosnan) in *Dante's Peak* (1997). I most often see the outsider character in spec science-fiction thrillers: usually a scientist of some kind, he will prophesy the end of the world because of *something* the government is doing and/or ignoring and will be proved right (of course). Interestingly, very often there is very little this scientist can do in these spec sci-fi thrillers, and mankind is ultimately doomed.

SECONDARY CHARACTERS

Secondary characters are frequently misunderstood and/or under-sold in spec thriller screenplays by writers. Stripped down to the barest minimum, secondary characters usually have one of two role functions:

- Help the protagonist or antagonist to achieve his/her goal.
- Hinder the protagonist or antagonist from achieving his/her goal.

How and why they perform one of the above role functions is what motivates the character, so we need to know who they are to really appreciate this. Going back to Joss Whedon, his notion of 'everyone has a reason to live' is key in understanding the purpose of secondary characters:

> *'Everybody has a perspective. Everybody in your scene, including the thug flanking your bad guy, has a reason. They have their own voice, their own identity, their own history... If you don't know who everybody is and why they're there, why they're feeling what they're feeling and why they're doing what they're doing, then you're in trouble.'*

Whedon is spot on. Everyone in the story should think the story is about them. No character should get up in the morning thinking, *'My role is to help or hinder Character X.'* That way you end up with cardboard-cut-out characters who are merely plot devices. Every character should feel authentic and rounded, there for their own particular reasons, with their own way of looking at the world.

Crucially, it is also worth remembering these secondary characters should *not* take over from the protagonist's and antagonist's respective missions. Again, it is about balance. Here are some popular and recognisable secondary character roles in produced thrillers, plus some comments about how they often fare in spec thriller screenplays:

- **Best Friend/Henchman.** The best friend is inevitably a member of the protagonist's team and the henchman the same, but on the antagonist's side. Both characters turn up the most in thrillers combined with action/adventure, science fiction and/or fantasy. Generally speaking, both will die, the best friend often just before the resolution, to spur the protagonist into the last battle with the antagonists, though sometimes this happens much earlier, such as Captain Jimmy Wilder's (Harry Connick Jr) death in *Independence Day* (1996) or Goose's (Anthony Edwards) in *Top Gun* (1986). These two character role functions are frequently well drawn in spec thrillers, possibly because they are the most recognisable.

- **Coach/Mentor**. If our protagonist must learn a particular skill in order to tackle the issue at hand, then a coach or mentor will step into the breach, like Morpheus (Laurence Fishburne) in the *Matrix* franchise. Their greater knowledge and teaching of the protagonist helps feed the audience the necessary exposition to understand science fiction and fantasy worlds, as well as thrillers with paranormal elements where priests and 'experts' (male or female) may deliver this important role function, such as Kalina Oretzia (Embeth Davidtz) in *Thir13en Ghosts* (2001). Frequently scribes will concentrate more on the exposition than the character in spec thriller screenplays, in a 'Here comes the science part!' type of way. This is a shame, since the mentor character can be combined with all kinds of other elements, my favourite being the 'stealth mentor'. This is when a mentor character poses as the antagonist (or even IS the antagonist), yet dispenses much good advice and truth bombs throughout. An obvious example would be Erik Killmonger (Michael B. Jordan) in *Black Panther* (2018): whilst his methods are terrible, he is absolutely right when he says Wakanda has failed in its duty of care, both to him and their black brothers and sisters in America and across the world. This is what prompts T'Challa (Chadwick Boseman) to change how things are done in Wakanda.

- **Crazy Dude**. The crazy dude can be of varying importance in the narrative. Mac (Bill Duke) in *Predator* (1987) is possibly the best example of this character role function played straight, since he becomes more and more unhinged throughout the narrative until he gets himself killed by the creature. Sometimes the crazy dude is the antagonist, such as Lt Hiram Coffey (Michael Biehn) in *The Abyss* (1989), or an important secondary/comic relief device, such as Ruby Rhod (Chris Tucker) in *The Fifth Element* (1997). Occasionally mental illness is played to good effect with authentic looks at trauma and psychosis: *You Were Never Really Here* (2017) is one of the few movies that get it right. Otherwise generally-speaking television is where it's at for authentic portrayals of mental illness and trauma, with both *Russian Doll* (2019–2022) and *Stranger Things* (2022, s4) hitting the bullseye. In contrast, antagonists are frequently crazy in spec thriller screenplays and their plans literally insane, with no real logic or purpose behind them. Crazy dudes in secondary role functions in spec thrillers often fare little better.

- **Comic Relief.** The thriller genre doesn't have to have a comic relief character and typically doesn't in the supernatural subgenre. They are frequently present, however, in thrillers with action/adventure, fantasy or science-fiction elements, especially those with an enigmatic hero at the helm, such as James Bond, or any with Will Smith in the cast so he can utilise his famous line, *'Oh hell, no!'* Spec thrillers in comparison are most often staid and sombre affairs, with little room for comedy, never mind an actual comic relief character.
- **LGBTQ Characters.** LGBTQ characters are frequently sidelined by mainstream movies in general, with only 'coming out' stories and romantic comedies tending to feature them prominently. Produced thriller movies are no different, largely ignoring LGBTQ characters, though when they do appear they will frequently be villains, with their sexuality or gender identity coded as an automatic threat. Television tends to have better LGBTQ characters generally, plus they often turn up in properties where diversity is celebrated as part of the natural story world. One such example would be post-apocalyptic thriller series such as *The 100* (2014–2020) and *See* on AppleTV (2019–2022). Spec thriller screenplays will sometimes attempt to include LGBTQ characters, though nearly always lesbian couples are favoured over relationships featuring two men. (Even worse, one of those women will often die as a result of a toxic trope known as 'Bury your gays' or 'dead lesbian', a trap even *The 100* sadly fell into).
- **Geek.** Geeks often figure in prominent positions in thriller narratives in this technological day and age, such as Rat (DJ Qualls) in *The Core* (2003) and Matt Farrell (Justin Long) in *Live Free Or Die Hard* (2007). Even before the Internet was in every home, however, thrillers still put geeks at the centrepiece of narratives, including *Sneakers* (1992) and *Hackers* (1995). Spec

thrillers usually include hackers as a *deus ex machina*, often leading me to wonder in notes why they didn't just hack into the 'mainframe' (or *whatever*) in the first place? Yes, yes, that way there's no movie – in which case, why draw attention to this plot hole via technology in the first place? Sometimes a writer's lack of understanding about what computers are capable of lampoons a futuristic narrative: the adaptation of Veronica Roth's *Divergent* (2014) had to deviate substantially from the book on this basis. In the book, the antagonist starts a plan for societal domination and only leaves ONE minion watching over the computer, which stretched credulity when the goodies have to fight their way to the control room to turn it off. Even worse, apparently there isn't Dropbox or WeTransfer in the future either, cos the goodies steal the hard drive and there are no back-ups! In contrast, there is a much more dramatically satisfying showdown in the movie.

- **Blind Prophet/Mysterious Stranger.** Blind prophets pop up in thrillers, often as a warning to the protagonist, and can literally be blind (as in *Minority Report*, 2002). The mysterious stranger will also give warnings, usually based on their experience, such as Montgomery Wick (Scott Glenn) in *Vertical Limit* (2000). This character will often be insufferably smug in spec thrillers, or even know what is going to happen next – albeit failing to tell the rest of the group, for no apparent reason. It's no accident the stories mentioned are all extremely old; the blind prophet is a stale trope that's largely fallen out of fashion in recent years. However, we can see it at work in the AppleTV dystopian thriller *See* (2019–2022), a story world in which in nearly ALL characters are blind. In this story, certain characters such as Paris (Alfre Woodard) are 'PreSages' – people who have a strong emotional connection to other humans and the spirit world. Crucially however they are not psychic, nor can they tell anyone what will happen next in the plot, which would suck the jeopardy and intrigue out of the story, just like in those spec thrillers.
- **Corporate Lackey/Jobsworth.** These guys will be part of the team against the protagonist, if not the antagonist themselves. Burke (Paul Rieser) in *Aliens* is a particularly good example of this.

Jobsworths in spec thrillers will be two-dimensional and largely unsympathetic characters and, more often than not, a comment on capitalism and/or the Conservative or Republican parties. Politics is rarely about black-and-white issues, so characters with these backgrounds need more shades of grey.

- **Foreign Weirdo.** Foreigners are to be viewed with suspicion – according to conspiracy or spy thrillers, at any rate. Similarly, sometimes a character's 'foreignness' is part of their supposed 'quirks', like Lev (Peter Stormare) in *Armageddon* (1998). Unfortunately, many spec thrillers I have read have followed suit, making foreign characters 'weird', rather than celebrating diversity.
- **Red Herring/False Lead.** Typical in detective and spy thrillers, the red herring or false lead will frequently die, thus seemingly cutting off the detective's trail. Sometimes the lead *is* real but dies very early on, like Peter in *Taken* (2008), forcing Bryan to pursue another avenue. This character is frequently missing altogether from spec thrillers, even mysteries. As a result, the protagonist will 'tread water' during the course of his investigation, often looking things up on the Internet for pages and pages, which is undramatic.
- **The Expendable Hero/False Leader.** An expendable hero may be used to illustrate the sheer strength of nature in natural disaster thrillers, such as the excruciating moment in *Dante's Peak* (1997) when one man throws another survivor from the train carriage, only to land in the lava himself. Other times, secondaries may sacrifice themselves to save the rest of the crew, such as Braz's and Searle's agonising exposure to extreme heat in *The Core* (2003) and *Sunshine* (2007) respectively (played by Delroy Lindo and Cliff Curtis). Other times, a character may be set up as a leader of a group, only to die minutes later, such as Apone (Al Matthews) in *Aliens* (1986). In recent years, the MCU has delighted in bringing forth the Expendable Hero trope over and over again: Professor X (Patrick Stewart) has died in multiple movies now, most recently *Doctor Strange in the Multiverse of Madness* (2022). Marvel also appears to like casting alternative versions of characters or

storylines on this basis too, swiftly killing them off or 'snapping' them out of existence – figuratively or literally. Despite this rich history in produced thriller content, expendable heroes hardly ever appear in the spec thriller screenplays I've read. This seems a real missed opportunity in terms of characterisation and 'good' writing, particularly when I can recall those few expendable heroes and false leaders I've read even YEARS later.

Now, from adults in thrillers, let's move on to representations of children.

THE KIDS ARE ALRIGHT?

I personally believe the last 20-30 years has been somewhat of a golden age when it comes to family films. In this era of Pixar and Dreamworks gold, like *Encanto* (2021), *Turning Red* (2022) or the *How To Train Your Dragon* franchise (2010–2019), plus other strong contenders like Disney's *The Bridge to Terabithia* (2007), *Wreck-It Ralph* (2012) and *Zootopia* (2016), it's easy to forget that child characters are often not as well drawn in other genres, especially when their representations are not meant for children. It's a struggle to understand why children are represented so badly both in the spec pile and in produced thrillers. As all parents know, no one child is the same as another and kids frequently have takes on the world that could educate and inspire adults, especially in survival situations. Yet, typically (and, again, shockingly), it would seem we see children in one of just THREE major archetypes in spec thriller screenplays and produced content:

- **Spooky Kid.** A staple of the supernatural thriller and perhaps inspired by the classic *Don't Look Now* (1973). Of all 'spooky kids', Cole 'I see dead people' Sear in *The Sixth Sense* (1999) must be the most emulated child character of the thriller genre, with children frequently being psychic in some way. Some writers attempt to turn this on its head and make 'spooky kids' actual ghosts, as in *The Others* (2001) or *The Awakening* (2011). Very often, the spooky kid is a cardboard cut-out in the spec thriller screenplay: he or she will not feel real, but will utter strange 'sayings' or suffer nightmares that will come true in some way.

- **Helpless Child.** Frequently part of the 'woman in peril' subgenre of thriller, typically girl children such as Gracie (Tessa Allen, *Enough*, 2002) or Sarah *(Twilight's* Kristen Stewart, *Panic Room*, 2002) must rely on their 'warrior moms' to get them out of the predicament, often creating further complications themselves in doing so, such as Sarah's diabetes and resulting near-coma in the latter. The key with the 'helpless child' is not to make the child *the problem*, but to appreciate that having a child with your heroine makes them especially vulnerable. A child may accidentally expose the heroine's hiding place or make bad decisions based on fear or inexperience; they may have specific medical needs like Sarah's diabetes or learning difficulties. None of these things is the child's fault and your heroine must protect them at all costs, without judgement, just like a parent, regardless of whether s/he is biologically related.
- **Inquisitive Brat.** Possibly the most interesting of the three representations, because they are the nearest to 'real' kids. Whether protagonists or secondaries, brats are often highly reactive in the thriller genre, having to deal with things even adults would struggle with, such as demolition of their homes, as in *The Goonies* (1985); alien invasion, like Rachel and Robbie in *War of the Worlds* (2005); or time-travelling strangers, such as Cid in *Looper* (2012). Often, thriller narratives involving brats will couple with action/adventure and allegory, as in *The Lion, the Witch and the Wardrobe* (2005). In spec thriller screenplays, however, brats are nearly always either too young for their years or conversely too old, with very few getting the balance 'just right'. Kids are smart and resourceful, but even a very bright child is *still a child*, with a kid's (frequently left of the middle) logic and ways of looking at the world. Kids are not stupid, but nor are they mini adults.

TEENAGE CHARACTERS

Many spec screenwriters have cottoned on to the fact that child characters make their spec screenplays expensive to produce, once things like fees, tutors and chaperones are factored in. This means child characters were disappearing for a long time from spec screenplays in general, and spec thrillers are no different. In the previous edition of this book I said it was a great shame because a well-placed, well-conceived child character can potentially make all the difference to the group dynamic of your characters and the situation they find themselves in. Consider all your favourite thrillers, particularly if they are supernatural in some way (including creatures) or psychological: I bet there is at least one child in the cast, no? Yes, child characters are expensive, but if you can really nail him/her and make the character seem authentic and real, there's a strong chance your writing will gain the attention you seek, simply because those authentic and real-feeling child characters are so rare.

However, there is a way you can have your cake and eat it on this issue and that's by including a teenage character in your cast of characters instead. It's worth remembering teenage characters – especially those in the 'mid range' of 15 or 16 – are frequently played by actors over the age of 18. This means they are not subject to the same laws governing pay and hours of work, nor do they need chaperones or tutors, as they count as adults. And, like all other child characters, teenage characters are generally badly drawn by the spec screenwriter.

In the past ten years, child and teenage characters have finally started to make a comeback in the thriller. It's not difficult to figure out why: the MCU has shown the way, placing many teen characters as secondary characters, or even front and centre, such as in its TV series on Disney+ such as *Ms. Marvel* (2022). In addition, TV series like *Stranger Things* (2016–2023) have proved people will watch thriller shows with a (mainly) young cast as long as they are dealing with peril. Though the main cast were all under eighteen at the beginning, the audience has watched them grow up without issue; in addition, the original 'teenage' characters have always been in their twenties. So, if you can turn expectations on their head and offer a fresh and relevant representation of a teen in your script, it's a sure solution: do it!

UNUSUAL CHARACTERS

> *'What's 'the word of mouth' factor for your script? What's in it that everyone is going to talk about ... whether that's a great hook, the twist, an unusual character, a fucked up situation, but still feels contemporary and relevant to us now? (Even if it's historical)?'*
>
> **– Samantha Horley, screenwriter, producer and ex-sales agent**
> (@SamanthaHorley)

It's important to note that, bar a couple, none of the archetypes and tropes on the lists are inherently 'bad', but they *are* nearly all overused and/or overly simplistic. There's plenty we can do as screenwriters to define our characters and make them differentiated from 'the usual'. By considering our characters' role functions and motivations, we can add extra elements we may not have seen before; we can combine or take elements from one tired trope and contrast them against a new background, creating a new way of looking at a character. In addition, reflecting on unusual characters in produced content, and considering what makes them different, helps us achieve the same in our own drafts. Here are three unusual protagonists that have caught my eye:

RAY IN *WAR OF THE WORLDS* (2005)

War of the Worlds was a gigantic, epic adaptation of one of the most famous stories ever, by one of the most prominent teams ever: directed by Steven Spielberg; written by Josh Friedman and David Koepp; and starring screen hero-for-hire Tom Cruise. This makes it even more surprising, then, that, at its heart, the film has arguably one of the most interesting and unusual characters in American blockbuster history: Ray.

Ray is by no means a hero. Instead, he's an ordinary guy with no special skills whatsoever; a real average Joe (as opposed to those characters who may be presented as such, but are, in reality, exceptional in some way). Like many male protagonists in this genre, Ray is estranged from his wife, but, unlike those other protagonists, there is no brooding about the past, and the ex-wife doesn't say stuff like, *'I still love you, Ray, I wish it could have been different, oh boo hoo, it's all so tragic.'* Instead, she is now pregnant and happily married to Another Guy. Like many male protagonists, Ray is a bad father: even Ray's own kids, Robbie and Rachel (Justin Chatwin and Dakota Fanning), think he's a loser and don't want to be left for the weekend with him. But what's different here again is that Ray is not a bad father because he's too obsessed with work and being 'exceptional'; he's a bad father because he's lost touch with his kids and their needs. He doesn't know who they are: he hasn't been around and they've been doing this pesky thing called Growing Up. In other words, Ray is like many, many absent parents who have taken their eye off the ball and, in turn, Robbie and Rachel are representative of many, many kids from a broken home. It's not that they don't love him, but they've moved on and their father seems kind of irrelevant to them now. This means going to see him is a duty and therefore a monumental drag.

We sympathise with both Ray AND the kids in this set-up: on the one hand, we can see the kids' POV; they can't rely on him, so act out and behave brattishly, thus making us empathise with Ray's plight, too. He can't do anything right as far as the kids are concerned, not even something as small as playing baseball in the backyard. All of them are in a shit situation and, despite Ray's protestations that they should try and get along and make the best of it, we know they won't, because it's *always* been this way. What's particularly inspired about this characterisation is actually two things:

- **It hits the bullseye audience-wise.** With divorce and broken homes at an all-time high all over the world, kids and adults everywhere can relate to this situation and thus the characters, which is perfect for a family-orientated film (remember, *WotW* was just a 12A in the UK, a PG13 in the USA, meaning accompanied children could watch this movie with adults at cinemas, even considering its bloodthirsty and frequently threatening content).

- **We don't think Ray will be able to cope.** Can you imagine this story from Rachel and Robbie's mom's point of view? You wave goodbye to your kids; you don't want to leave them with your feckless ex but *you have to*. Then Armageddon strikes whilst they're with him! The horror! If I was Ray's ex, I'd have been writing the children off as done-for. But, of course, from this inauspicious start, Ray comes into his own: he WILL get the children to Boston, come hell or high water… *And he does*.

What's great about this film is the believability of Ray's struggle to get the children to safety. Whilst the backdrop of alien invasion is huge and fantastic (and essentially a disaster movie), parents in particular can relate to Ray. Every decision he makes feels authentic and plausible; we can imagine ourselves in his place, whether it's having to leave Robbie to go to Rachel, who is so much younger, or killing Harlan (aka the crazy guy in the basement, played to perfection by Tim Robbins) to stop him drawing attention to their hiding place. As a result, whatever happens in the plot, it feels so much more ominous and threatening because we're rooting for the characters and *we're just not sure they're going to make it*. Wikipedia credits Koepp, rather than Friedman, with taking the writing of Ray in this direction. If true, for all his brilliant collaborations with Spielberg, I believe *War of the Worlds* may be the pinnacle of Koepp's career, as he gives us a hero who is not only fresh and relevant, but feels completely believable. How many big action blockbusters can say that?

DRIVER IN *DRIVE* (2011)

As mentioned in the previous section on character archetypes, Driver (Ryan Gosling) is very much the 'lone wolf' type. We know relatively little about him, other than what we actually see, such as his stunt driving, working at the garage or walking up the hall of his apartment building. As with other classic 'lone wolf' narratives, Driver is a protector – and, as with his predecessors, we see him literally drive off into the sunset at the end. In an age where screenwriters are told we should know EVERYTHING about our characters, Driver is an enigma.

For the first half of the movie, *Drive* is essentially a love story; Driver finds his humanity in Irene and Benicio (Carey Mulligan and Kaden Leos). So, when Irene drops the bombshell that her husband, Standard (Oscar Isaac), is returning from jail, it would have been easy to imagine Driver becoming some kind of antihero by killing him in order to take his family. From there, he would then have had to pay for his actions, presumably by Benicio's hand later, a story so typical it dates back thousands of years: in Sophocles' play about the nature of consequence, *Electra*, Orestes and his eponymous sister avenge the murder of their father, Agamemnon, by killing their mother, Clytemnestra, only to recognise their siblings will most likely avenge *her* by killing *them* (thus taking us into revenge thriller territory). Yet *Drive* avoids this well-mined story with panache and, instead, Driver is thrown into a turmoil of double crosses when he attempts to help Standard pay his debt, only for Standard to end up murdered by the pawn-shop owner; subsequently, a hit is put out on Driver by mafiosos Nino and Bernie (Ron Perlman and Albert Brooks). Unusually, Irene and Benicio are not killed outright, with Driver avenging their deaths. Instead, he protects them, even at huge cost to himself: financially (he could take the pawn-shop money on a number of occasions and does not); physically, because he walks into Bernie's trap willingly, 'allowing' himself to be stabbed; and also emotionally, because, in showing his savage side, he isolates Irene (she can never feel the same way about him as she did by the river once she has witnessed what he does to the man in the lift).

But Driver is only a great character because he is contrasted against a cast of complex and unusual secondaries. Irene, though a little oblivious and heavily idealised – we essentially view her through Driver's eyes – is not your average heroine: in this kind of movie, we would expect far more histrionics from her. It would have been easy to make Standard a villain, but he is a loving father and husband who has made many mistakes and now wants to put them right; he is not what we expect. Shannon (Bryan Cranston) is shady, but a good guy; we want him to get away, as Driver insists he must (even though we know he inevitably won't). And, most importantly, though they are both antagonistic forces to be reckoned with, both Nino and Bernie have softer, more human sides, too; neither believes they are a 'bad' guy and both have grown weary of killing and the various problems a life of crime creates. In the pizzeria, fearing retaliation, Nino and Bernie discuss tying up the loose ends – or, rather, Shannon and Driver, as well as Cook (James Biberi), blithely eating in front of them. Bernie's subsequent exasperation at having to murder Cook, saying to Nino: 'Now you clean up after me' is brilliantly done. Similarly, Nino's lament that he is not taken seriously by his peers (*'I'm 59, Bernie! They still pinch my cheeks!'*) or Bernie's sorrow at killing Shannon when he'd rather have raced the car with him, is palpable; Bernie almost seems kind when he actually kills Shannon, telling him *'that's it... no pain'*.

So it's important to remember that *Drive* is the sum of all its parts. With its 1980s-style soundtrack, highly stylised shots/feel and graphic violence, *Drive* is a cult hit for a niche (adult) audience, rather than a big studio tent-pole movie like *War of the Worlds*. Driver is an instantly recognisable character, but one who seems out of his time, which draws us in. Surrounding Driver with such a variety of unusual secondary characters is a master stroke, because immediately we can grasp that Driver is meant to be an enigma, rather than an empty void.

JILL IN *GONE* (2012)

Now to consider a much smaller, indie film: *Gone*. A detective character, Jill (Amanda Seyfried), vows to track down the man she believes kidnapped her a year earlier and whom she thinks has her sister captive in the film itself. No one believes her story, even the police, thinking she has mental health issues (which she does, evoking the old adage, 'Just because you're paranoid, don't mean they're not after you').

I read a lot of spec thriller scripts involving sisters. The sisters may be literal, like Jill and Molly (Emily Wickersham) in *Gone*; 'as good as' sisters, in that they have been friends for years, usually since school or through a traumatic period in their lives; or they may be involved in a sexual relationship (though this is frequently underplayed by the writer, with one usually an older-sister type character to the other, hence my inclusion in the 'sisters' terminology). What unites these characters is the fact that these sisters, literal or otherwise, are usually all the other has: dead parents or isolation from their peer group for whatever reason will mean that *when* – and it's nearly always when, not *if* – one disappears, the other is left alone, the only hope and saviour of the one who has gone missing, with no one else willing to help.

As a result, then, *Gone* feels a little familiar plot-wise. Similarly, as plans go, Jill's to retrieve Molly (and, indeed, the serial killer's, in luring Jill towards his trap) doesn't really stand up to scrutiny, since it seems unnecessarily convoluted. But that doesn't really matter, because Jill is such an intriguing character. Jill is beautiful and blonde, played by teen favourite Amanda Seyfried (despite being in her late twenties), but what's perhaps most interesting is the fact that Jill is also a *compulsive liar*. We witness this element of her character develop throughout her investigation as she tells enormous whoppers to get what she wants from the various people she comes across. As a result, the viewer is unsure if Jill's account is entirely reliable, placing us in uncomfortable limbo between Jill and the police as Jill becomes more and more reckless (and, seemingly, less and less reliable). This then gives an impressive resolution even more impact, without relying on the tired trope of 'it was all in her mind'. Best of all, the resolution wrong-foots us *again*, for Jill, having had her revenge, tells the police she was imagining it all.

So, though *Gone* is not a perfect movie, Jill is a fascinating character in her own right, especially as, typically, lying is not a trait we might associate with a young woman of her background – or, indeed, supposedly likeable protagonists in general. But, really, why not? *Gone* shows us very convincingly a character can do *anything*, even something that usually has negative connotations, like lying, if it fits the narrative, tone and scope of the story.

UNUSUAL SECONDARIES

As mentioned in the secondary characters archetypes list, the best secondaries help or hinder the protagonist or antagonist in his/her mission, but mustn't 'take over' from that mission. The best produced thrillers appreciate secondary characters are not cardboard cut-outs, but rounded and believable, with strong motivations and histories all their own, just like those in *Drive*. Here are some others that spring to my mind:

- **Burt and Heather in *Tremors* (1989).** Taking up residence in the isolated valley of Perfection, Burt and Heather (played by Michael Gross and Reba McEntire) have prepared for every eventuality of apocalypse... but *not* 'underground goddamn monsters' as Burt laments on the bulldozer towards the resolution of the movie. It would have been easy to write Burt and Heather as gun-toting nut jobs with every right-wing viewpoint imaginable (and assign them an antagonist's role in the group while doing so), but the writers of *Tremors* admirably avoid walking into this predictable character cliché. Burt and Heather's viewpoint is cast against Val and Earl's from the start, but never once do we feel Burt and Heather *are* the problem. In fact, when Val and Burt argue at one point, peacemaker Heather steps in, dragging Burt away: *'I know... [Val] thinks he knows everything.'* This is masterful because we are reminded that Val is no expert in this situation; none of them is. Burt and Heather feel three-dimensional and real because they are devoted to each other and to life itself: they want to live, but they will take no prisoners. This means that, when one of the monsters breaks into their underground basement, we assume they will die – probably by blowing themselves and the monster up. So when they succeed in killing the creature without the need for suicide, we are as elated as the rest of the cast back on Chang's roof in town. It is also worth remembering Burt has some of the best lines in the film, the pinnacle probably from that scene: *'Broke into the wrong goddamn rec room didn't you, you bastard?!'*

- **The entire cast of *Con Air* (1997).** Talking of dialogue (see what I did there?), providing killer lines for your entire cast and not just your protagonist or antagonist is a sure-fire way of getting your script noticed, not only by agents and filmmakers, but actors too. Consider a film like *Con Air*, in which most of the characters get fantastic dialogue, providing us with an insight into their motivations from the offset, whether they're a liberal thinker like

Vince Larkin (John Cusack), who provides the fabulous running commentary as our villains get on the plane; the never-ending sass of Pinball (Dave Chappelle), who provides the catalyst for the coup on board; or Garland Greene (Steve Buscemi), a serial killer who regales Poe (Nicolas Cage) with his various murderous exploits like a mild-mannered neighbour at the garden fence. Even a very small part like Guard Falzon (Steve Eastin) gets his own distinct flavour and motivation: this guy loves his job! Falzon really enjoys lording it over prisoners, from his 'None of this impresses me' speech on boarding the plane, to a rare moment when main antagonist Cyrus the Virus (John Malkovich) is bested after he asks sarcastically, *'Oh stewardess, what's the in-flight movie today?'* and Falzon replies, *'I think you'll like it, Cyrus. It's called "I'll Never Make Love to a Woman on the Beach Again" and it's preceded by the award-winning short, "No More Steak for Me, Ever".'*

Intriguingly, revisiting *Con Air* in the 2020s is quite revealing: what was considered risqué or bizarre is now commonplace. The phrase 'white privilege' was not in the mainstream in the 90s, yet Diamond Dog (Ving Rhames), points out he too hates Cyrus 'The Virus' (John Malkovich) but recognises the white guy has the literal way out of jail, a powerful metaphor for said privilege. Garland's talk of psychopaths and how mothers can unwittingly help create them was considered woo-woo in the 1990s but 30 years later is now accepted as correct in psychiatric circles. Similarly, there is, unusually for a 'roughneck' cast, one LGBTQ character on board the plane. Named 'Sally Can't Dance' (Renoly Santiago), s/he is a cross- drug dealer (who may or may not be transgender). Though a caricature, some believe Sally to be good representation (if not entirely progressive). Talking to trans friends, many report loving Sally for three reasons: LGBTQ characters were not part of the action genre generally in 1997 (and still aren't!); she is not hassled by the other prisoners or seen as bad for being trans or cross-dressing, just for being a villain wanting to escape prison; plus, even when Poe strikes her in the resolution, he 'affirms her gender' by slapping her, rather than punching her like he does the other convicts.

Now obviously no one has to like any of these things or re-evaluate how they feel about *Con Air* which is, at foundation level, an extremely crass and cheesy popcorn flick that is otherwise very much a product of its time. As a movie, *Con Air* is 100 per cent nuts and, like Marmite, definitely an acquired taste: you either love it or you hate it. As screenwriting a large cast of secondary characters goes, however, it's a masterclass.

- **Lynne in *The Sixth Sense* (1999).** And from the ridiculous to the sublime: Lynn (Toni Collette) is a working single mom to Cole (Haley Joel Osment) in this supernatural thriller and a real breath of fresh air. I read mother characters a lot in this genre who are uncaring and/or emotionally detached from their children (or, conversely, dead, so literally not there), yet Lynn is neither of these things. She is the type of mother we all would want: she fights for Cole whenever she gets the chance, whether that's warning off bullies or insisting to doctors Cole needs help. She is deeply troubled by Cole's behaviour regarding the 'supposed' ghost activity in their apartment, begging him to tell her what's wrong when he runs to her, mute and shaking. But, understandably, Lynn does not want to reward what she sees as attention seeking. She does not know what to do for the best. This is why she sends him away from the dinner table when he won't admit to taking the bumblebee pendant, which joins up neatly in the striking denouement in the car near the resolution, when the dead cyclist appears at the window. Throughout the movie, we can sense Lynn's sorrow and frustration growing, so this brilliant moment when she realises for the first time Cole is telling the truth is both memorable and moving as mother and son bond over what had previously caused them nothing but conflict.

- **Marie in *The Bourne Identity* (2002).** It's kind of sad really that Marie (Franka Potente) is destined to become the over-used dead wife/girlfriend archetype in the next instalment of the Bourne franchise, *The Bourne Supremacy*, because she's a really great character in the first movie. Her collusion with Bourne (Matt Damon) is both insightful and believable: she's cast from the offset in the embassy as a freethinker, hence Bourne targeting her. He knows she won't blindly turn him in, but equally he knows she's not a paranoid leftie, either, so he must earn her trust. It would have been really easy to characterise Marie in a very one-dimensional way: she's attractive and so is Bourne, so it stands to reason they may get it on, but we're not asked to suspend our disbelief over this. Marie is no 'kickass hottie', pulling combat skills out of nowhere; though she finds herself in over her head, her reaction to various (incredible) events is completely plausible, such as shock when the assassin goes through the window: *'Why would he do that??'* Her loyalty to Bourne is not called into question, either, which is a refreshing change; too often the female companions of 'exceptional' heroes like Bourne are turncoats, even if it's against their will by blackmail. We're also not asked to believe she would blindly go on the run with him 'no matter what': he sends her away for her own safety and reunites with her at the end.

- **Pest in *Attack the Block* (2011)**. As a creature thriller, *Attack the Block* borrows heavily style-wise from its obvious Hollywood influences and it does so extremely well. Like *Con Air*, secondary characters are full of comedy quips from start to finish, plus many of them feel rounded and believable, like Burt and Heather from *Tremors*. Yet *Attack the Block* is not afraid to go against audience expectation, killing off its teenage characters at various junctures, such as Dennis (Franz Drameh) in the girls' apartment or Jerome (Leeon Jones) in the smoke-filled halls. In addition, unusually, Pest (Alex Esmail), the dedicated comic relief character, is surprisingly philosophical throughout, underlining the notion of 'many a true word said in jest'. When Sam, the older female character (played by Doctor Who's Jodie Whittaker), boasts about how her boyfriend is working away in Ghana 'to help the children of Africa', Pest pipes up, *'What about the children of Britain?'* This single moment impressively strips away the frequently middle-class notion of charity being needed 'far away', the subtext being 'charity should begin at home'. No mean feat for a film about a bunch of kids fighting extraterrestrials in tower blocks with fireworks.

So, when you're thinking about secondary characters for your spec thriller screenplay, think first about their motivation: help or hinder. Then about how they are going to do it and, most of all, why. On top of that, you can add whatever you like, including fantastic dialogue, troubled group dynamics and opposing viewpoints, paradoxical behaviour or even heavyweight philosophy.

AVOIDING CHARACTER CLICHÉS

But now we reach the biggest conundrum: what screenwriter sets out to write a stereotypical or 'usual' character? Answer: none. I often find myself being agreed with at seminars and workshops, only to find those same writers have created the very characters they want to avoid in their specs. So why is this? During my work with screenwriters and reading thousands of thriller screenplays, both movies and TV, I usually find it's one of the following:

- **They've gone OTT on backstory**. I have long ventured that good characterisation is not about creating endless character profiles so you know what your protagonist or antagonist had for breakfast and what his or her ambition was when s/he was five years old. I've seen countless screenwriters tie themselves in knots over backstory, when all that really is, is distraction. We're dealing with character in the here and now – we need to know what makes characters tick, sure, but at the same time as they deal with the problem or issue presented to them in the narrative. Consider all your favourite characters and what you know about their back-story, and how: chances are, those backstories help POWER the situation the characters finds themselves in. They will dig deep to get over the situation in the *here and now* as opposed to think back to endless flashbacks from 'before'. When flashbacks are used, it's usually because it has a direct bearing on what is going on in the main story: consider *The Handmaid's Tale* and how Offred (Elisabeth Moss) remembers her time as June, which in turn helps her to stand up to her oppressors in Gilead. As veteran TV screenwriter, show runner and playwright Sally Abbott

(@SallyAbbott3) says: 'Backstory has to play out on the page, otherwise it's extraneous.'

TIP: ***A single moment alluding to what happened 'before' is worth much more than extensive flashbacks, prologues or over-analysis via dialogue. When you do use flashback, make sure it doesn't 'take over'.***

- **They're writing for what they imagine the marketplace wants.** And now, of course, for the other end of the scale! When faced with criticism of their characters as being two-dimensional, some writers rebuff it with the notion characters don't 'need' depth, because there are so many produced movies with poor characterisation. This seems to happen most, I've found, with writers attempting female protagonists. Whilst it's certainly true lots of produced movies have terrible characterisation, that does NOT mean we need to exacerbate it as screenwriters; we can be part of the problem or part of the solution, as the saying goes. On a less philanthropic note, creating well-drawn, three-dimensional characters is one of the most likely elements that will get your script noticed, so those writers are intentionally sabotaging their scripts' chances in the marketplace.

TIP: ***Avoid cardboard-cut-out characters: don't make them *all* about the role function and forget about the rest. Audiences don't always remember plots, but they do remember characters… and the same goes for script readers, producers and execs. As CEO of Women in Film and Television (@WFTV_UK) Kate Kinninmont (@WomenInFilmKate) wisely points out:*** **'Most screenwriters are men, but, increasingly, the gatekeepers at the studios and broadcasters are female. If you want to get past them, give some thought to your female characters. We're all tired of clichés and stereotypes. Give us some wit and irony; give us some originality; give us some life!'**

SUMMING UP...

- Do your research. Work out the role functions of various characters in produced thrillers, what their motivations and histories are and why various characters keep your interest (or not).
- At base level, secondaries need to help or hinder your protagonist or antagonist. Everything else is piled on top.
- Balance your backstory – not too much or too little. Make sure it plays out on the page.
- Remember the character archetypes we've seen before – and think about how they can be changed or combined to create new ones.
- Remember screenwriters are not casting agents – but know there are pointers to giving us a flavour of who characters are. Don't rely on the 'usual', remembering that women, homosexuals and characters belonging to other ethnic groups are not 'issues', but people.
- Consider, 'Why this character?' Think about whether the character in your mind has something about them and if they are best for your story. Don't go blindly with the first one that comes to your mind.

Having thought 'Why this story?' and 'Why this character?', you're ready now to consider how you will write – or indeed rewrite – your spec thriller screenplay.

PART TWO

WRITING **YOUR** THRILLER SCREENPLAY

'A writer is a person for whom writing is more difficult than for other people.'

– Attributed to Thomas Mann

PITCHING & PREPARATION, PART 1: **PREMISE, LOGLINE & DRAMATIC QUESTION**

'Hook them with a good logline... If it's cliché, their eyes will go blank. If it's a flawed concept, they will frown. But if it's a good idea, they won't mind chatting about it; it won't feel like work.'

– Micho Rutare, writer/director, development exec
(@MichoRutare)

MARKETABLE SCREENPLAYS

Over the years, I have seen many writers succeed at jumping through the various hoops to production and beyond. Some have credited their success to luck and/or being in the 'right place at the right time'; others to various formulas, courses, books and ways of writing. And good for them. Myself, I believe the harder you work, the luckier you get. Similarly, I do not believe in formulas or 'ways' of writing. There's hard work involved getting your vision on the page, but the skill is realising it doesn't stop there: you must ensure your vision doesn't get watered down and bent out of shape during the development process, then again when it goes through finance and production, and again via distribution. Filmmaking is, in short, an almost superhuman effort!

So you may have seen produced screenwriters insisting on the likes of Twitter that the key to getting where they are is 'just' writing a great screenplay. You may have been confused at this, because, as far as you're concerned, your spec screenplay is great. Maybe you've had good feedback from a couple of industry professionals; perhaps it's placed in a couple of contests; maybe you've pitched it at various festivals or online. But nothing's come of it. So those produced screenwriters going on about 'great screenplays' being the key must be full of hot air, right? Here's the bad news: they're not. That annoying produced screenwriter on social media saying it's 'just'(!) a question of writing a great screenplay is completely, 100 per cent RIGHT. But what is a great screenplay? Don't confuse a great screenplay necessarily with great writing. Instead, think 'great screenplay' = MARKETABLE screenplay. Agents and filmmakers don't care what a great writer you are; they care whether your screenplay is an *easy sale*. But a marketable screenplay needn't mean selling out. It doesn't have to be 'either/or' and crossing your fingers; I have known many spec screenwriters write screenplays they were 100 per cent passionate about, yet still sell them. So what makes your passion project marketable?

WANTED: A GREAT STORY WITH GREAT CHARACTERS

It all comes down to this... There are two things everyone in the industry wants from a screenplay, regardless of genre: a great story, with great characters. We all know this, really. It's what we want as audience members, so it stands to reason the people setting productions in motion would want it, too. But how to achieve it? After all, no spec screenwriter starts by saying: *'You know what? I'm going to write the MOST MEDIOCRE story ever, with the DULLEST characters imaginable.'*

Yet I see mediocre stories, complete with dull characters, all the time in the spec screenplay pile. And, yes, some of these mediocre stories have been written really, really well with great dialogue; a well-drawn arena; interesting visuals or something else. Some of the characters in those screenplays might be funny, or interesting, or unusual on their own merits (though, without a story goal, can they truly be 'great'? The million dollar question). But guess what? None of this lights my fire. I don't RECOMMEND them… and *not* because I don't think the writer has talent. It's because I know people are looking for a great story, with great characters. It is not optional. It is as simple as this:

- Great writing + mediocre story = NO SALE
- Mediocre writing + great story = SALE

Every time I blog or tweet about this issue, I am met with the outraged cries of spec screenwriters, over 90 per cent of them new writers. 'Surely this can't be true?' they wail. 'It's the execution that counts!!' No. A hundred times, no. It is NOT the execution that counts. Think on this – if it *was* the execution that counts:

- Only the most talented writers would ever be produced.
- With no eye for the market, those talented writers would be writing some of the crappiest ideas imaginable.
- It wouldn't matter how 'good' the writing was – even those uber-talented writers would STILL not be able to make them float!

The reality? If this were true, we would have a hell of a lot more crap on the market than we do now. So it's GOOD the industry puts story and central concept at the forefront whilst sidelining that tricky notion of 'it's the execution that counts'. I have seen mediocre writing with a great story sell over great writing with a mediocre story literally hundreds of times. And I, for one, am glad this happens as it means we have far more chance of hitting the bull's eye in terms of that elusive great story with great characters. But how do we find that 'great' story? By investing in your premise and central concept.

PREMISE

Your premise is the first building block of your screenplay. Obvious stuff, perhaps, yet this is frequently the part most often neglected or glossed over by screenwriters when writing spec screenplays. Too often, a writer will get an idea and blindly forge forward with it, not putting it under the microscope first to see if it really stands up to scrutiny. As a result, whether at first draft stage or further down the line, the story will go awry, simply because those first building blocks were not put in place properly. A lack of care over premise can affect your screenplay, even multiple rewrites down the road. Why take the risk? It is also worth noting premise is what SELLS your thriller screenplay – or not, as the case may be. If your premise doesn't have a clear central concept and/or a strong hook, then it will be like the hundreds of thousands of others in the spec pile. Nail it, however, and you could find your thriller screenplay in demand.

CENTRAL CONCEPT AND HOOK

> *'The business is so full of material, it's essential that your idea can be pitched in a couple of sentences. Can people quickly see the dramatic hook? When you tell people about the idea, do you see their eyes brighten with interest?'*
>
> **– Kurti & Doyle, scriptwriters**

The central concept is how your audience 'understands' your story: consider how you pick a movie or TV series on a streaming service. If it's by picking up or scrolling through titles that *look* interesting from the main image and then saying to your friend or partner, 'Oh, this one's got (that male/female STAR) in we both like'; 'This one's directed by (NAME)'; or 'This one's from the same team that produced that (PREVIOUS MOVIE) we liked', then congratulations: this is probably how 90 per cent of people do it. From there, your friend or partner might ask, 'What's it about?' To which you reply with a short précis of the story, without even thinking. For example: *a lawyer has to go on the run from the government when he accidentally comes across classified secrets* (*Enemy of the State*, 1998).

The hook, then, is paramount to thriller in potentially engaging the audience and may be presented one of two ways:

- **The Commercial Hook.** Most commonly associated with big-budget blockbusters, a commercial hook is that *thing* that grabs a potential audience by the short and curlies and makes it want to see that movie, no matter who is in it, who's made it or, really, even how it plays out. In short it signs up first and foremost for the spectacle, rather than the storytelling – and this works, because who can't recognise these commercial hooks, even without the titles attached:

  Cloned dinosaurs run amok on an island. (JURASSIC PARK)
  Monster creatures from two separate franchises seen together for the first time, slugging it out underground. (ALIEN VS PREDATOR)
  Alien giant robots try and take over Earth, but only other giant robots can stop them. (TRANSFORMERS)
  The origins of a well-loved cultural superhero. (This one could be any of them!)
  As a screenwriter, it's really important not to be snobby about commercial hooks. Whilst you may not like these kinds of movies, knowing what makes a film hook 'commercial' really could mean the difference between potentially selling your screenplay – and wasting your time. We can learn a lot from Hollywood in this regard, whose mantra is frequently:
  'Write me a low-budget picture that creates a $200m sequel!'
  A low-budget thriller screenplay needn't have a commercial hook; but everyone wants one. Think of the *Saw* franchise… and how little money the original was made for, plus what came next. Or *Moon* – and how it meant director Duncan Jones was able to make *Source Code* next.

- **The Dramatic Hook.** But, even if your hook is not immediately commercial, you can appeal to filmmakers, agents and execs via that old classic: the 'great story'. You can do this via your dramatic hook, which frequently grabs the audience and asks them to imagine themselves in the protagonist's place; I find it easiest to do this in the form of a question. As with the previous section, blockbusters may also contain dramatic hooks, just as low-budget pictures may have commercial hooks. So if we consider *Enemy of the State* again, Robert Clayton Dean is an ordinary family guy who is in the wrong place at the wrong time and is pulled into a nightmare, facing adversaries much bigger than himself. The hook, then, might well be – as is often the case with thrillers – *'How will he escape?'*

The short version when considering the hook:

- Commercial Hook = appeals to a cultural DESIRE in the audience. Dinosaurs, robots, monsters, zombies, vampires, serial killers, superheroes etc have this kind of appeal. People are aware of the concept and sign up for 'larger than life' shenanigans.
- Dramatic Hook = appeals to a cultural FEAR such as your children being kidnapped and being held hostage; home invasion/ destruction (the house, country or planet); having to go on the run; stalking etc. Asks the audience member to put themselves in the protagonist's place: 'What would YOU do?'

Can hooks be both commercial AND dramatic? Absolutely. In fact, many of the best thrillers appeal to both cultural desires and fear. See if you can spot and break down which ones do this.

WINNING AND LOSING

So we need an idea of your premise, concept and hook in your logline. But frequently the loglines you see posted online or hear at pitchfests neglect at least one of these elements. If you can nail all three with a killer logline, you have your best chance of a read request from that elusive agent or producer. But how to do this?

We already know it's usually the antagonist, rather than the protagonist, who is in the driving seat of the thriller, whatever sub-genre or element we're using. So obviously the premise is from the antagonist's point of view, right? Nope! It should still be the protagonist's POV, because it's *their* journey we're watching, not the antagonist's (this is where it gets potentially confusing and why many writers get into script meltdown further down the rewrite line). Basically, you need to come up with a premise from the protagonist's viewpoint that includes the problem the antagonist is presenting him or her with; it's what audiences sign up for – to see if the protagonist wins or loses against the antagonist. For example, consider *Safe House* (2012) and its logline, taken directly from IMDB:

> *A young CIA agent is tasked with looking after a fugitive in a safe house. But when the safe house is attacked, he finds himself on the run with his charge.*

Immediately, it's apparent whose film this is: the young CIA agent's; our protagonist, Matt Weston (Ryan Reynolds). The fact he's 'young' is important as it connotes he is inexperienced and/or ill-equipped to deal with the situation (the safe house coming under attack); this creates even bigger problems for him in the story and asks the audience to empathise with his plight or imagine itself in his shoes. But the biggest problem is not the attack – it's the fact that Weston is not only on the run; he's also still in charge of that fugitive the logline mentions: our antagonist, Tobin Frost (Denzel Washington). Frost is, of course, not only a dangerous man, but hugely more experienced than Weston, making the battle for power between them all the greater. Who wins and who loses may be inevitable (nine times out of ten the protagonist wins) but, in the best thrillers, we still want to know *how* it will play out.

IT COULD HAPPEN TO YOU

When it comes to thriller, the second key element is the notion that 'it could happen to you'. Whilst many thriller premises are indeed fantastic and even set in different times and places, there's a very human element of expectation involved. Remember Ray in *War of the Worlds*? Though aliens were invading, we're watching his very human struggle of trying to protect his children and get them to safety; this is something we can all relate to, as who wouldn't do the same? Even in story worlds where the protagonist has specialist training, like Weston in *Safe House*, we can still believe what Weston does – go on the run with Frost – because we can imagine ourselves doing the same thing in his place (why wait in the back room, as the safe house comes under attack, when you can escape? Anyone with half a brain would take the opportunity to flee and worry about the consequences of that decision later). We can even apply 'It could happen to you' to subgenres and cross-genres of thriller:

Creature Thriller. You're no longer the hunter, but the hunted.
Conspiracy Thriller. A Higher Power could set out to get you.
Crime Thriller. You could find yourself on the wrong side of the law.
Women In Peril. The man/people in your life could turn on you.
Supernatural Thriller. Forces 'beyond' could try and attack you.

As you will see from my examples, all of the antagonists above are 'stronger' – if not literally, then metaphorically – than 'you', the potential protagonist. Thriller seeks to put the viewer in the protagonist's place in a way that horror does not, which is much more voyeuristic in its process: *look at the people dying/being possessed/being eaten, etc.*

WHAT ARE YOU WRITING?

Before we go any further, let's consider WHAT you're writing. In the first part of this book, I took you through a number of craft elements such as concept, characters and structure, as well as thriller genre conventions. I also broke down how spec screenplays differ as features (aka movies or films) and how spec television pilots have gained added currency in the 2020s thanks to the streaming revolution.

Lots of my 'Bang2writers' come to me unsure whether they are writing a movie or TV series. They confess they are unable to tell what the difference is, and/or whether they have 'enough story'.

So, first things first. As you may have noticed from watching movies at the cinema or on your device, the average movie is somewhere between ninety minutes and two hours. Generally speaking, the more famous a filmmaker is, the longer they can get away with; this means if you're a new writer, you want to go more towards the shorter side: 80 to 90 minutes (so 80-90 pages) is frequently the length of scripts I see coming across my desk from private investors in particular.

As mentioned in part one, most produced thriller movies have very obvious plotting. This means the journey your character goes on will be very clear, going from A to B to C in an obvious way. It will likely be very light on subplot; it may not have one at all, with the writers focusing on other narrative techniques to bring out complicated thematics instead.

We can see this 'pathway' for the characters in psychological thriller *The Gift* (2015), which was written, directed and starred Joel Edgerton and produced by Blumhouse. At first, Joel's character Gordo presents as the antagonist, bringing married couple Simon (Jason Bateman) and Robyn (Rebecca Hall) unwanted gifts. He says he knew Simon at school, which Simon denies. Over the course of the movie, Gordo's antagonistic and creepy presence starts to change and we begin to relate to him instead of Simon. By the end, we realise Simon is a liar and the antagonist and Gordo is the protagonist who has delivered a very important lesson that 'things are not always what they seem', both to Simon and Robyn, but also us, the audience.

It's true that a movie like *The Gift* has 'enough story' to be a TV series as well. In fact there are many thriller movies that have been adapted as TV series for Netflix and Amazon Prime, as well as terrestrial television: *Bates Motel* (2013–2017), *Limitless* (2015), *Cobra Kai* (2018–2022), *Hanna* (2019–2022) and *Resident Evil* (2022) are all either direct adaptations and/or spin-offs of the original movie concepts they are based on.

Disney+ have also shown the studios are willing to exploit ALL possible elements of a single property in the 2020s: at the time of writing this book, there were at least eight *Star Wars*-related TV series, including fan favourite *The Mandalorian* (2019–2020) and *Obi Wan Kenobi* (2022). The MCU is even bigger in the TV space, with a whopping sixteen TV series: at the time 2022's ground-breaking *Ms Marvel* was hailed as the 'best' and highest-ranking Marvel property, TV show OR movie.

But how does this help us decide what we're writing? Well, if we were to adapt *The Gift* as a TV show, there would need to be some significant changes. Whilst there's 'enough story' for a movie that's one hour and forty-eight minutes, that's only roughly three episodes of a TV show which are typically forty-five to fifty minutes. A good start, but not enough.

If you look on your TV platforms, you'll discover the average run-time for a TV limited series is approximately eight to ten episodes. (While you may see fewer or more episodes, they tend to be outliers unless they are mini-series of four episodes, which are enjoying a small comeback though whether they stay remains to be seen).

I always recommend aiming for approximately eight episodes. I also recommend planning for at least three 'story strands' PER EPISODE. Yes, you read that right: THREE. Lots of writers – especially British writers – think television episodes are typically two strands: a main plot and a subplot. Whilst that was true in the UK for a long time, if we study television history we can see this begin to change around the 1990s. It first became popularised by the success of behemoth properties like the sitcom *Friends* (1994–2004), though by the end of the century it had made its way into crime thrillers on TV like the iconic *CSI* franchise (2000–2015).

So while many UK thriller TV series doggedly continued with the two-strand structure for a long time, since the streaming revolution many have been forced to adopt the three strands. This is not because of 'homogenisation' or 'Americanisation' as some commentators insist, but because audiences are more media literate than ever. As mentioned in this book already, audiences can decode character motivations, plotting and tropes in an instant. This means MORE story is needed to keep them occupied, not less.

THE PITCH DECK

In the 2020s, it's very common for writers to be asked for their 'pitch deck' for a spec limited series on TV, or for a feature film. You may have heard them called 'series bibles', treatments, 'sizzlers' or packages too.

I go into the exact requirements for a pitch deck or package in the second half of this book. You will find a list of everything you need to include in yours on p289, but as you may guess the average pitch deck involves such things as a one-page pitch, detailed plot beats and character bios. It also includes more business-type stuff, such as casting and finance.

Many writers lament the rise of the pitch deck, saying the script should 'stand for itself'. This is a version of 'it should be the execution that counts' argument. As mentioned already – rightly or wrongly – it's not the execution that counts. It is what it is.

Instead of looking at the pitch deck as an imposition on your time and/or creativity, look at it as an added OPPORTUNITY.

A pitch deck – like its name suggests – gives you an added chance to sell your story 'off the page'. It can help make the script reader and their bosses (such as agents, producers or development execs) excited about reading your spec TV pilot or feature. Pitch decks have many advantages, such as:

- A good pitch deck knows that it's concept that gets 'bums on seats' at the cinema, or people queuing up movies and TV series on their watchlists. If a writer is unable to sell their OWN story 'off the page' in the pitch deck then, there's a strong chance the script won't either.
- It's a sad fact of life, but many producers and investors hate reading scripts. This means they need an additional document that can help them judge whether reading the script is worth their time. A good pitch deck cuts to the chase and helps them make this decision.
- Most writers are not good at pitch decks. This means that if you are, you may get noticed by industry pros quicker because you have demonstrated you know how the industry works.
- Many spec scripts are not well written. However, your pitch deck may illustrate the concept has solid potential, meaning industry pros may buy the script anyway and develop it with you or another writer.
- Whilst your pitch deck or script may not get bought, if yours is good, you may get work writing them for other people or companies.

But what SHOULD you write in the 2020s – TV or film? More on this, next.

WHICH IS PREFERRED IN THE INDUSTRY – SPEC TV PILOTS OR FILM?

This is one of those frustrating 'how long is a piece of string' questions. Whilst it used to be spec features were preferred, it's more hazy in the 2020s. 'We're more agnostic about format now,' says Julian Friedmann, agent and founder of The Blake Friedmann Literary Agency in London, 'sometimes we even send out two different pitches for the same story: one as a limited TV series, the other as a film.'

So if you really can't decide which you want to do, there's a precedent there: create pitch material for both! Do be aware however that you need to know the difference between film and TV. Here's a breakdown of what your film requires:

- A typical movie is 90-120 minutes maximum (and you probably want to err towards the shorter side if it's an indie film)
- Your main plot will take up approximately 80-100% of the story 'space'
- Your movie may have a subplot, but it will typically be much 'lighter' than we'd see in a TV subplot… or it may have no subplot at all (many thriller movies don't, especially when they stay with the protagonist in most or even EVERY scene)
- Your movie may make use of an overt plotting archetype of some kind, ie. The Hero's Journey or similar
- Your thriller probably won't be an ensemble of characters (though it can be)

In contrast, when we're writing a TV series, we need to consider the following:

- 8-10 episodes = 8-10 hours. That's a LOT more story!
- Each episode needs 3 'story strands' for modern audiences.

- This works out as 1 x 'A' story (major storyline); 1 x 'B' story (minor story); 1 x 'C' story (human/serial element that takes us to the next episode.
- The 'A' story probably takes up approximately 50-60% of the story space; the 'B' story probably takes up 30-40%; leaving approximately 10% to the 'C' story.

I've heard some producers and actors often say they prefer serials/ limited series in the 2020s because 'there's more room for character'. This might suggest to some TV thrillers are not as plot-led as movies, which is not true. The difference is we can see MORE characters and see more details of their lives, especially in ensembles, but also secondaries too. In movies, a secondary character just doesn't have the time to go off and do their own thing *related to the A story* in ninety minutes; when there's ten hours, they can in the B story or C story. It really is as simple as that at grassroots level, (though there are other considerations such as 'the dramatic question' or 'story engine' of your show too). First however, let's consider your thriller logline.

CRAFTING YOUR OWN THRILLER LOGLINE

Like premises, writers often neglect their loglines, too, meaning they screw up their chances when pitching their projects, especially online. A good logline should give the reader (or listener, if a verbal pitch) a clear idea of its premise. This is why I always recommend writers get feedback on their loglines and rewrite them if necessary, as well as their one-page pitches and scripts. What's more, being able to deliver your loglines conversationally really gives you the edge when you're asked, 'What are you working on?'

I like to use what I call 'logline hacks' in order to avoid describing 'around' the story (a huge problem for most spec screenplays of ALL genres). My personal favourite is:

When [Inciting Incident Occurs] a [specific protagonist] must [objective] or [stakes].

When a logline describes 'around' the story, it usually means the writer has fallen back on cliché language use such as '[character] must face his/her demons'. I have seen this phrase in so many thriller loglines and it hides what's going on because it could literally mean anything! As a result I have no idea what the premise could be which is an automatic PASS (aka rejection).

However, using the logline hack (not to mention the B2W Logline Cheat Sheet, which you can download for free at www.bang2write.com/resources), can help you make sure you have dealt with the following for your thriller logline:

- **The 3 Cs:** clarity, conflict, characters. A good logline is clear, outlining what is at stake, who is in it and why this is a story. Too often, loglines are clumsy and don't reveal these three things. If you can't identify the '3 Cs' in your own logline, no one else will either… and your concept will misfire. Always double-check with these three things in mind.
- **The central concept/the hook.** Being able to pinpoint the seed of the story and imagine yourself in the protagonist's place are key elements of a marketable thriller screenplay. Frequently, spec thriller loglines read or sound like dramas, giving little indication of what's at stake, so execs', agents' and filmmakers' interests are not piqued.
- **The notion of 'winning/losing' and 'it could happen to you'**. The lone protagonist, isolated from his/her peers *for some reason*, is a key element of thriller and frequently s/he is up against an antagonist or antagonistic force much bigger than themselves. Thrillers are essentially David and Goliath-type stories, which is universal and very much part of our culture, so easily understood by audiences. Taking advantage of the two universal notions of 'winning/losing' and 'it could happen to you' is a great shortcut in coming up with your premise and crafting your logline so as to sell your idea off the page and get that all-important read request for your screenplay.
- **The shorter, the better.** Writers are frequently asked to pitch in 25–60 words maximum. Nailing those three all-important elements of

premise, central concept and hook is a tall order – which is why you should never rush your logline and always get others' opinions on it.

- **High concept can be low budget.** A lot of writers confuse the notion of 'high-concept' thriller with being high budget. Whilst most high-budget thrillers are indeed high concept, it's perfectly possible for a low-budget thriller to be high concept, too. High concept refers to the clarity of the concept within the film – the easier it is to 'see' the hook and/or the central concept, the more high concept it is.
- **Loglines are not taglines.** Frequently writers make the mistake of confusing taglines with loglines. Whilst a logline is that all-important story précis, taglines refer to those you find on movie posters. The most famous tagline ever has to be 'In space no one can hear you scream' (guess where from?). It's not compulsory to avoid writing taglines, as long as it's in addition to, rather than instead of, a logline. However, as with everything, if including a tagline, make sure yours is crafted well and not the first thing that comes into your head. Nine times out of ten a writer will write 'What would YOU do?' on a pitch document. One to avoid, definitely!

SPEC TV PILOT LOGLINES

But wait: you're not writing a feature-length screenplay, but a TV pilot. As mentioned in the first section of this book, spec TV pilots are more in demand than ever thanks to the streaming era. But writers can't 'phone it in' like Tony Jordan says; because of this fundamental shift in the industry in the last decade, competition is huge, so getting noticed is difficult.

This means your logline for your spec thriller TV pilot must ROCK. But are there any major differences between TV pilot thriller loglines and ones for movies?

As with so much of writing, it can depend. There are some best practices in selling your TV thriller 'off the page', however:

1) Use everything listed in the previous chapter for movies for your TV pilot – the hook, winning/losing, the 3 Cs etc.

2) Make sure you have TWO loglines – one for the series as a whole, one for the pilot you will be sending out.

3) Put them BOTH on your one-page pitch or treatment.

That's it – no big secret. As with all prep and selling documents, there's no special way or industry standard for this, but the above can really help in submissions.

RETURNING DRAMA SERIES VERSUS SERIAL (AKA 'LIMITED SERIES': WHAT THEY'RE NOT)

'What you must compress is why anyone should read the damn thing in the first place. Get your head around the "why" not the "what" – to sell your script. You are trying to kidnap 90 mins of someone's else life, remember? That's not about selling your pages, it's about selling you. Have faith in yourself. The conviction required to read what you have written will follow.'

– Gub Neal, producer (@GubNeal)

As mentioned in the previous sections of this book, TV thriller serials are big business in the 2020s. Audiences love them because they are 'bingeworthy' and they can involve themselves in long character arcs and mysterious, intriguing plot work.

So, are you writing a returning drama series or a serial? Do you know the difference? How is your spec screenplay thriller TV pilot structured? If the answer is 'I'm not sure' to any of these questions, then you need to find the answers pronto because producers WILL ask you in meetings!

Annoyingly, like anything in screenwriting different people have different ideas of what 'returning drama series' and 'serial' mean... and there's no agreed, definitive definition! However, for the sake of ensuring there is no confusion as I continue to describe various TV series in this book, I am going to look at the terms as the industry *tends* to use them, based on my experience in the UK script reading trenches.

Returning drama series tend to have two to three story 'strands' per episode. The American model of three story strands seems to be most popular in the last 25 to 30 years, though before this in the 1960s to early 1990s you will probably discover two is the standard.

What's more, sometimes how many 'strands' is dictated by what the story is… A returning drama series that usually has three *may* default to two, especially in plot-led episodes with high stakes, especially in the case of season finales.

Frustratingly, a serial also tends to have the same number of story 'strands' as a returning drama series – two to three average, with three being modern audiences' demand. So it can't be that, either!

So let's look to television history. Before the streaming era, American returning drama series tended to have VERY long series runs – often somewhere between 20 and 24 episodes. In contrast British returning drama series did not tend to have such long runs, typically running for somewhere between six and ten episodes (with smaller runs of two to four episodes usually referred to as 'mini-series').

We can't look to series longevity for answers on what sets the returning drama series and serial apart either. In the past, American returning drama series usually continued as long as audiences tuned in: it was not unusual to run for ten to twelve series or beyond. Some sitcoms did the same.

Whilst some series commissioned before the streaming era are still going (at the time of writing, *Grey's Anatomy* was on its nineteenth season, with *The Simpsons* on its thirty-third season, though arguably neither of them are thrillers at heart), it's unlikely they would run as long as this if commissioned in 2023. This is because in the Netflix era, American series typically run for three to four seasons maximum (occasionally five). Nowadays, British series don't tend to have seemingly never-ending series runs either: it's very unusual for British series to go beyond four or five seasons too.

Before I go into what's different between returning drama series and serial in detail then, let's consider what 'makes' a returning drama series using a case study of an iconic American TV crime franchise.

Crime Scene Investigation (*Las Vegas*)

There is a difference between returning drama series and serials (aka 'limited series'). In returning drama series there will be a main story that forms that 'A' story which I will call 'story of the week' – to illustrate, let's consider *Crime Scene Investigation (CSI).*

Whilst the series has inevitably dated considerably since its first episode in the year 2000 (with the original *CSI: Las Vegas* only ending in 2015, some spin-offs still going and a reboot of the original beginning in 2021!), it remains one of the most influential crime series to grace television.

Whilst some of the original *CSI*'s storylines and depictions now feel sensational and exploitative to modern sensibilities, its subversion of gender and racial tropes helped set the current conversation on diversity in motion.

Whilst its LGBTQ representation was lacking, it still employed a diverse ensemble cast at a time many series were all-white, neurotypical and able-bodied, plus it placed characters who are STILL unusual at the forefront.

Pathologist Doc Robbins was a double amputee (played by Robert David Hall who also had both legs amputated after a car accident in real life). Fans also believe series protagonist Gil Grissom (William Petersen) and Sarah Sidle (Jorja Fox) were coded as neurodivergent at a time when autistic representation was more or less nil.

These were not the only commentary on disability: for Grissom's storyline on his impending deafness, renowned actor and star of *Children of A Lesser God* (1986) and 2021's Oscar-winning *CODA* Marlee Matlin guest-starred. There was also an episode which centered a case involving little people (s3, ep4, 'A Little Murder') where series regular and lab technician Nick must confront his own prejudices against so-called 'dwarves'.

In terms of gender representation, there was an eclectic mix of female characters who were depicted as being both highly skilled at their jobs alongside their own complex personal lives. Across the entire franchise female characters were depicted as cops, supervisors, lab technicians and pathologists. Though most of them were very beautiful and looked like models (as is the case with TV series generally) they were not all Moms, wives or white, either.

Even better, *CSI* didn't care whether viewers found female characters 'likeable' either, despite the climate at that time that largely demanded it. The aforementioned Sarah Sidle from *CSI: LV* was a 'Marmite' character with fans either loving or hating her. Though her manner could sometimes be brittle and demanding, she was depicted as an ultra-observant near-genius who would stop at nothing to get the job done… Characteristics most often associated with male characters, even in the 2020s!

My personal favourite however was *CSI: LV*'s night shift supervisor Catherine Willows (played by Marg Helgenberger). Catherine's past was as a Las Vegas showgirl, performing in the casinos to fund her way through college after her abusive gambling addict husband left her and her daughter in the lurch. She never acted ashamed of her roots, nor was she punished for them: in fact, her hard-won social mobility was frequently praised by colleagues, plus her experience of handling boastful and unpleasant high-rollers often helped the team. She was not above using her feminine wiles to break a case, either: she once promised a prisoner for every question he answered truthfully, she would unbutton a button on her blouse!

However I would wager CSI's most influential and lasting legacy is the 'version'. Like many stories of its time, CSI was non-linear in scope as the team examined cases. In contrast to many other police procedurals before and since, CSI did not tend to use flashbacks.

Instead a team member would speculate what *could* have happened based on what they knew so far. Viewers would then *see it enacted as if it had*. Often these 'versions' were found to be incorrect as the team worked the case. As new evidence came to light, those suspects would be disregarded and the final version would reveal the 'true' murderer.

Crime Scene Investigation – Returning Drama Series Format

So, each episode of *CSI* had two of those main story 'strands' but crucially, one would be 'smaller' in scope than the other... Let's call them the A strand and the B strand. The third story strand is what I call the 'serial element' that takes us from episode to episode.

It becomes obvious how it plays out when we consider how the format of a memorable franchise like *CSI* works:

- **Teaser.** We may see the victim alive (and how they die), but we ALWAYS see the victim dead. The CSI crew gather around the body, various details are shared to set up the episode to come. CUE CREDITS and the famous theme tune, courtesy of The Who.
- **STRAND A – Story of the week (Murder Investigation # 1).** Story Strand A will take up the most story 'space' here – approximately 50-60% of the script. The team investigate a murder which often has a ticking clock element, which is a staple of the thriller genre – ie. they need to get results before the killer strikes again; before the court case is over; or before a suspect leaves the country. This 'story of the week' will resolve by the end of the episode, like a mini feature-length story of approximately 45 to 60 pages.
- **STRAND B – Story of the week (Murder Investigation # 2).** Story Strand B in contrast will usually take up 30-40% of the story 'space' (dependent on how much space Story A takes). In the case of the *CSI* franchise, this may be an entirely separate investigation into a different murder. Alternatively, it may be a secondary team working on the same murder as in Story Strand A but they're looking into another element of the case, ie. the 'B Team' looking at ballistics and other lab-based stuff, while the 'A Team' are out in the field. Again, this 'story of the week' will resolve by the end of the episode.
- **STRAND C – Serial Element.** The serial element of returning drama series usually operates within the 10% of the story 'space' left by the A and B strands. The serial element in returning drama series is often character-led, examining their relationships, problems

and worldviews and *Crime Scene Investigation* was no different. This serial element will NOT resolve, but typically take us from episode to episode of that season. An obvious serial element of the original *CSI* was team leader Gil Grissom's aforementioned increasing deafness due to a hereditary condition passed down by his mother.

Sometimes however, the serial element 'seeds' other issues that become the focus of finales in the series. In *Living Doll* (s7, ep24, 2007), Sarah Sidle is captured by the Miniature Killer (named so for the intricate miniature scenes the killer constructs and sends to the CSI team).

In the season finale, Sarah's ordeal formed the 'A' strand as the rest of the CSI team strive to find and rescue her. Yet before this finale, the Miniature Killer had 'popped up' before in series 7 as part of other investigations in the 'B' and 'C' strands. The finale did not come out of nowhere but provided a very satisfying serial arc, with *Living Doll* retaining a very respectable 8.9/10 star rating on IMDb a whopping sixteen years later at the time of writing this book.

Now let's consider how a classic returning drama series thriller like *CSI:LV* compares to a modern streaming hit serial/limited series like *Stranger Things* (2016–2023).

Stranger Things (2016–2023)

Stranger Things is a mixed genre project, mixing both horror and thriller tropes with relatable human drama. Here's a short plot summary of the pilot episode:

It's November 6th, 1983 in the provincial town of Hawkins, Indiana. Before we meet any of the main characters, we join the action at the Hawkins Research Laboratory where something terrible occurs. Crucially we don't know exactly what it is, we only know people are dying horribly for some reason.

After that, Will disappears within the first few minutes of the pilot, plus we know something supernatural is at work before we have even set eyes on a demigorgon or know where Will (Noah Schnapp) could have gone. The Dramatic Question – *'Where is Will?'* – has been cemented for us from the very beginning of the pilot and for season one.

By the end of the episode, we've been introduced to all Will's friends – Mike (Finn Wolfhard), Dustin (Gaten Matarazzo) and Lucas (Caleb McLaughlin) – as well as Jonathan, Will's older brother (Charlie Heaton). We also meet Will's mother Joyce (Winona Ryder). From the offset we understand Joyce will do literally ANYTHING to get her boy back. She goes to local sheriff Jim Hopper (David Harbour), who is a hard-drinking smoker; he is not unduly concerned about Will, despite Joyce's worry. It's also important to note that whilst all this is going on, we also meet Nancy and Steve, two older teen characters (Natalia Dyer and Joe Keery).

Meanwhile, a young girl in a hospital gown walks through the woods: this of course is Eleven (Millie Bobby Brown), who has escaped from the research laboratory. Back at the lab it's clear something very severe has occurred but Eleven's 'father' Doctor Martin Brenner (Matthew Modine) believes she can't have gone far.

Eleven breaks into a local café and steals food, causing the owner to call the cops. Later a woman claiming to be from social services shoots and kills the café owner but Eleven escapes back into the woods.

To appease Joyce, Hopper is trying to organise search parties for Will but it is not going well. Joyce is angry at him and she and Jonathan decide to make missing posters. As the search continues, Hopper mentions he has a daughter who lives with her mother; a bystander mentions Hopper's daughter actually died.

Will's friends take it onto their own shoulders to find him and go searching in the woods at night on their own. This is when they find Eleven and this forms the ending of the pilot.

The Serial Format of *Stranger Things* (s1)

In the space of approximately forty-five minutes of screen-time, the *Stranger Things* pilot deftly creates those three story 'strands' relating to the problem of 'Where is Will?':

- **Story Strand A: The deadly event at the research lab, followed by Will's disappearance (Horror element).** This is the 'A' story and involves our main players: Will's friends and brother, plus his mother and local law enforcement, headed up by Hopper. This is NOT resolved by the end of the pilot episode. This part of the pilot and ensuing series is filled with Horror tropes where monsters exist and the supernatural can kill you. The scientists' deaths and Will's abduction are the stuff of nightmares, plus we will see other Horror elements later in the series, such as the infamous moments the walls come alive with monsters. Lots of critics and commentators talk about the influence of Stephen King on the show and it's most obvious here.

- **Story Strand B: Eleven's escape into the woods (Thriller element).** Other characters such as her doctor 'father' are introduced here, as well as various peripheral characters despatched to recapture her. We don't know who Eleven is, how she's connected to Will's disappearance or why she might have been in the lab in the first place. We do sense she is 'dangerous' – but at this point we think this is because shady government officials are willing to kill to keep her existence a secret. Again, this is NOT resolved by the end of the episode. This part of the pilot takes advantage of thriller tropes, especially those to do with government conspiracies, cover-ups and tests on innocent subjects. (Though few critics or commentators seem to talk about the fact *Stranger Things* is a mixed genre piece, I am reminded here of the thriller novels of Dean Koontz in the 1990s, especially *Sole Survivor* (1997), in which a widower called Joe has to rescue and protect a young girl 'grown' in a government laboratory who also has supernatural powers. The girl is numbered CCY 21-21 and names herself Nina after Joe's daughter who also died in the plane crash that killed his wife).

- **Story Strand C: Teen love triangle (human element).** Nancy and Steve are teenage characters not in the 'inner circle' of what's happening with Will, but crucially Jonathan – Will's older brother – is. He has the hots for Nancy and during this series we will witness a 'will they/won't they' with Steve cast as an obstacle that gets in their way. This is the 'human' element of the story that's NOT supernatural in a Horror OR thriller way. Instead we relate to the characters because most of us over eighteen will have been in some kind of love triangle or seen one in friends' lives.

The problem is very obvious here: 'The Disappearance of Will Byers' is posed in the pilot's title and Will vanishes in the first few minutes of the episode. Story 'strand' A forms the basis of the whole of season one of *Stranger Things*, with Eleven's arc in story 'strand' B running parallel with it and intertwining with Will's in places. As the season continues Eleven becomes Hopper's surrogate daughter and by being shown real love and acceptance for the first time, Eleven finds her place in the world.

This all makes sense because by understanding where Eleven has come from, the boys, Joyce and Hopper are able to get Will back. Meanwhile the 'will they/won't they' thread of Nancy and Jonathan continues across the season, with Nancy ditching Steve for Jonathan.

THE DRAMATIC QUESTION

As mentioned, the serial and returning drama series have 'crossover' in terms of how they're structured. They both tend to have three story 'strands' per episode, leading some screenwriters to conclude serials and returning drama series are more or less the same thing.

In contrast, other writers and producers may disagree that returning drama series and serials are NOT the same but may struggle to vocalise *exactly* what's different about them.

Let me have a go. Through my work as a freelance script editor, I've been fortunate enough to work with a cross-section of professional writers, directors and producers from both Britain and America, as well as a number from European countries too. These writers have worked in television as well as features, plus I've also interviewed many for the site at www.bang2write.com and at events like London Screenwriters' Festival, both live on stage and on Zoom.

This experience has afforded me a unique insight into how a cross-section of writers' rooms and various projects work. One thing that has cropped up in many of these conversations with professional writers and producers has been the notion of serials and what they call the 'Dramatic Question' of a show.

The Dramatic Question is a compelling question that writers establish by the end of the pilot that the audience has to watch the series to answer.

'Dramatic questions are not pretentious or thematic,' explains Shruti Saran (@shrutesnladders), who writes for Netflix, 'They're always really simple.'

Here are some examples that Shruti generously shared on Twitter (reproduced with permission):

- *Succession* – Who will succeed Logan Roy?
- *Stranger Things* – Where is Will?
- *Mad Men* – Who is Don Draper?

'I love the Mad Men one especially, because that show is not about a larger mystery or competition but it still has a strong Dramatic Question from the jump,' Shruti says.

The Dramatic Question is integral. It is posed by the end of the show's pilot episode and – this is the crucial part – *the viewers must watch the whole season to see it answered*. Indeed the Dramatic Question is the element that ties a TV serial together.

Thinking about Shruti's examples then, here are some Dramatic Questions I have identified in recent British and American TV thrillers:

- *Ozark* – Will the Byrdes get out clean?
- *The Handmaid's Tale* – Will Offred/June survive Gilead?
- *Sons of Anarchy* – Will Jax manage to balance fatherhood and the motorcycle club?
- *Peaky Blinders* – Will Tommy abandon his roots to get to the top?
- *Vigil* – Will DCI Silva uncover the murderer on the submarine and live to tell the tale?
- *Killing Eve* – will Villanelle and Eve ever be together?

As you can see, none of these Dramatic Questions are clever or fancy in any way.

'A lot of pilots either don't establish strong Dramatic Questions or they just ask, '*WTF is happening?*' says Shruti, 'That is not an actual Dramatic Question, it just means your story is confusing. Also, too many Dramatic Questions dilute the story. You want ONE good one.'

CAN THE DRAMATIC QUESTION OF A SHOW CHANGE SEASON TO SEASON?

Absolutely, yes. Whilst some serials have the same Dramatic Question for EVERY season – *Stranger Things* does not. Will returns from the Upside Down at the end of season one, plus it would be rather boring if each season just exiled a character to the same place! (We'd also imagine the characters rather stupid for being unable to plan ahead for this potential problem).

Modern audiences are exceptionally media-literate and require escalation wherever possible. The more specific the Dramatic Question, the more likely writers have to reinvent it, season to season. Here's my version of the differing Dramatic Questions in every season of *Stranger Things* 1-4:

- Season 1: *Where is Will?*
- Season 2: *WTF is the Mind Flayer?*
- Season 3: *What the hell is beneath the mall?*
- Season 4: *Who is Vecna and what does he want?*

Of course, you may be looking at these Dramatic Questions and thinking I am waaaay off. A friend of mine insists S2 is actually, '*Can we trust Will?*' because of his connection to the Mind Flayer. I like this but feel it doesn't cover the whole season. ALL the characters in s1 were connected in the search for Will ('*Where is Will?*'), whereas '*Can we trust Will?*' only really covers his friends. In contrast, '*WTF is the Mind Flayer?*' in my mind covers all the characters – in discovering what it is, why it has come back and how to fight it.

The point of this exercise is not to demonstrate I am right and she is wrong, however. There's no 'right' way for *audiences* to interpret a story. They will bring their own thoughts, lived experiences and worldviews to everything they watch on TV or in the cinema.

Looking at the Dramatic Question of each season of *Stranger Things* is also illuminating from a genre perspective. According to the Rotten Tomatoes site, s3 is considered the 'weakest' of all of the seasons by both critics and audiences alike, with s4 considered a 'return to form' by most viewers. Though many are recognising this intuitively and are unable to explain exactly why (especially as s3 is still excellent and certified 'fresh'!), I thought I would have a go.

As mentioned already in this case study, the show has always been a mixed genre piece, balancing Horror and thriller tropes concurrently. Season 1 presents as a Horror in the first instance: a place where monsters exist and even adult professionals like scientists are not safe (the subtext being children will be in even more danger). From there, '*Where is Will?*' and '*WTF is the Mind Flayer?*' 'cement' Horror as the frontrunner over thriller.

Though I haven't counted the number of scenes, I feel comfortable venturing it's 60-40 in Horror's favour in both s1 and s2. In contrast, I would say s3 is the opposite in it favours thriller over Horror. For every scene where troubled antagonist Billy is surrounded by exploding rats and melting townspeople, it feels like there's many more where Hopper and Joyce and Steve and Robin – the power 'couples' for this season – are taking on Russian spies or trying to avoid torture. Eleven, whose arc usually uses thriller tropes, does not differ in this season either, though she takes on the 'human element' with her budding relationship with Mike, not to mention her friendship with Max.

So it should not be surprising that s4 of *Stranger Things* is being heralded as a 'return to form' – it literally is, with the season returning to a focus on Horror over thriller!

The Vecna thread is true Horror: it's creepy and weird, working as an impressive metaphor for trauma and depression as his victims are literally broken by their experiences. Steve, Nancy, Robin, and new character Eddie must face the Upside Down in order to get the truth about Vecna, with only Dustin, Max, Lucas and Erica to guide them out again.

Hopper, Murray and Joyce's threads continue in the thriller vein as they get kidnapped by Russia and taken behind The Iron Curtain, but it's much smaller this time. The boys in California – Mike, Will, Jonathan and new character Argyle – are also on a thriller arc, trying to escape the US government who wants them dead because of their connection with Eleven.

Eleven continues in her thriller arc, attempting to recover her powers with Brenner after losing them closing the gate under StarCourt at the end of s3. Her thread also converges with One, who is murderous and vengeful, her antithesis; this in turn connects with both Nancy's trauma at seeing Barb's death in s1 and Max's watching Billy die in s3. This ties Eleven's arc into both thriller and Horror, which makes sense: she is the lynchpin of the whole series.

The Handmaid's Tale s1-4: *Will Offred/June survive Gilead?*

In contrast, the more 'open' the Dramatic Question at the start of a series, the less likely they will have to change it, season to season. Let's breakdown how this works, using *The Handmaid's Tale* as an example.

The Handmaid's Tale is a very different show to *Stranger Things*. Launched in a politically charged time against a backdrop of Donald Trump's presidency and women's marches, the dystopian series remains ominously prescient.

It's also significantly different in tone and direction: it's one part human drama as individuals are forced to take on the personal horrors of a totalitarian regime, to two parts political and spy thriller as clocks count down, ultimatums are issued and women plot against their masters.

What's more, the series is a very definitely NOT a 'four-quadrant' thriller. Its target audience is predominantly female adults, though the Hulu series also targets men who may share socio-political interests such as reproductive rights. This led to the series' first launch in 2017 not only being advertised in women's magazines such as *Vogue* and *Vanity Fair*, but also an advert during that year's Superbowl.

Another difference to *Stranger Things* is *The Handmaid's Tale* has the same Dramatic Question every season. The reason we can invest in this same question – *'Will Offred/June survive Gilead?'* – is because what it means for Offred/June (Elisabeth Moss) to 'survive' the totalitarian regime can depend on the events in that season.

In season one of *The Handmaid's Tale,* most of the events centred around Offred's Commander's Home – the Waterfords (Joseph Fiennes and Yvonne Strahovski). We discovered necessary exposition about how Gilead had come to be, plus what the rules of this unholy new regime are.

These events are contrasted against when Offred was June: how she'd been a professional woman, a mother to Hannah and wife to Luke (O-T Fagbenle), instead of the silent submissive she is now as Offred (which she must act like for her own safety). We wonder if she will survive these horrendous new conditions she is forced to live with, especially if she is unable to conceive a child in time.

In season two, Offred has to contend with a different kind of survival. She is pregnant with a baby – but it's not the Commander's. His wife Serena Joy 'arranged' the pregnancy by forcing her driver Nick (Max Minghella) to 'provide', so is in on the secret; but she may or may not reveal it if it suits her. Again Offred's life is on the line, especially as she refuses to stop searching for her other child Hannah who is still living in Gilead. She ends up sending baby Nicole to safety in Canada and her husband Luke takes responsibility for the child while campaigning to get June out.

In season three, Offred's survival is in question again. In disgrace for kidnapping baby Nicole, she is sent away from Serena's Joy home to a new posting; the only reason she is not hanged is because she is one of the few fertile women left in Gilead. Her new commander (Bradley Whitford) is one of the architects of Gilead but has grown disillusioned with the regime. With his secret help, she manages to arrange the 'Angel's Flight' – 80 children and servant women flown out of Gilead to safety in Canada. She is unable to locate Hannah for the flight, however.

In season four, June manages to escape Gilead but the story is not over. She is reunited with husband Luke and daughter Nicole but is unable to settle in Canada due to a combination of post-traumatic stress and the fact she has had to leave Hannah behind in Gilead. At the end of the series, it's clear June has made up her mind: she is going back. She will get Hannah back... or die trying.

As we can see illustrated here, the Dramatic Question of *The Handmaid's Tale* is very stable here because it is so open: 'Will Offred/June survive Gilead?' is an integral part of the show, season to season. In contrast, *Stranger Things*' is much more specific in season one, so they have had to change their Dramatic Question every season.

WHICH IS BETTER: AN 'OPEN' OR 'SPECIFIC' DRAMATIC QUESTION?

This is a bit of a 'piece of string' question, especially if we are writing spec thriller TV pilot screenplays! After all, the average spec screenwriter will write only the pilot episode of a speculative television series, plus a pitch deck of the resulting episodes for that season.

It's unlikely that writer will need to plot out subsequent seasons in that pitch deck; when they do it can feel like overkill. This is because producers like to put their own 'stamp' on stories they option. What's more, if that TV series is produced and gets a second season, audience response to the first may help inform what happens next too.

So B2W's advice here is don't worry about whether your Dramatic Question is 'open' or 'specific' in that first season of your series. Put your energy into crafting a compelling Dramatic Question of ANY kind.

It's the Dramatic Question which will hook industry pros' interest... just make sure you avoid the question '*WTF is happening?*' I see this in the spec pile all the time and like Shruti says, that just means your story is confusing.

THE STORY ENGINE VERSUS THE BIG IDEA

But perhaps you don't like the notion of the Dramatic Question, or perhaps you have heard other professional writers and producers talk about these things using other terms. I know I have, because as mentioned there's rarely a time everyone calls scriptwriting terms the same thing in this business!

One such phrase you will have likely heard or read is 'The Story Engine'. The Story Engine powers our TV series consistently, which in turns propels the story forwards. It's particularly useful in TV series writing (particularly serial storytelling) and is probably closest to Shruti's notion of the Dramatic Question.

Louisa Minghella (@MinghellaLouisa), a literary agent with The Soho Agency, says, 'The Story Engine asks what is happening that needs resolving by the end of the series. It could be a broken relationship, a mystery unravelling, an illness, something that needs finding. In the finale you may introduce a second Story Engine to get us to watch season two!'

I like to visualise 'The Story Engine' as one of those plastic wind-up toy trains parents give to toddlers. It becomes obvious that whatever is going on in the series must take us from episode to episode. Each episode escalates from the pilot towards a huge event in the finale in all genres, which is why I call Act Three 'The Showdown'.

This is most obvious in TV thrillers like it is in movies. The season finale will frequently be the most shocking, most explosive, most memorable part of the story. This is why season finales in TV thrillers often contain literal explosions, battles, revelations and the deaths or redemptions of favourite characters.

'The Story Engine is interconnected with what I call "The Big Idea",' Louisa explains, 'The Big Idea is more integral to your story's construction; basically a core theme. Everything about your story is there because of the Big Idea. What are you SAYING with this story? Why is this story meaningful beyond the Story Engine? What compels us to watch it?'

THE BIG IDEA = THEME

If we consider Louisa's notion of The Big Idea in relation to *Stranger Things* again, we can see this core theme in action.

Stranger Things was initially considered an adult property: it's literally a '15' rating on Netflix in the UK and a 'TV-14' in the USA, meaning it's not recommended for children who are not teenagers. This has not stopped the show's tween fanbase of approximately eight to twelve years old loving the series! (I would have had nightmares for weeks at the same age from watching the show, yet my ten-year-old has two posters of Eleven on her wall, as well as a plushie demigorgon!).

Combining this surprise audience as well as its intended audiences of teens and older Millenials and younger Gen Xers means *Stranger Things* became a surprise hit with 'the four-quadrant audience': male, female, young and old. Young tweens in particular love it so much it was awarded Best Family show in the 2021 Kids' Choice Awards.

With hindsight, it's perhaps not so surprising. *Stranger Things* is a powerful story about friendship, redemption and the victory of good against evil. These are all appealing things for audience members of ANY age. As the history of successful stories show, we like to invest in such themes.

'The Big Idea is so important because it gives you a reason to have every single character that is in your show, it is integral to what order the scenes come in, what each episode explores, and how the Story Engine comes into being,' says Louisa.

This is very clear in *Stranger Things*. Its Big Idea can probably be summed up as:

'What WOULDN'T you do for your friends and loved ones?'

Every single character in *Stranger Things* orbits this Big Idea – whether it's Joyce smashing up her home with a bat to find Will; the boys taking in Eleven and hiding her; or Hopper facing down government agents.

Even antagonists orbit that same Big Idea... they're just the antithesis of what the 'good guys' are doing, because they want to cover up what's going on and don't care who they have to hurt or silence in the process.

Similarly, the core theme aka Big Idea is very clear in *The Handmaid's Tale* as well. As a comment on misogyny and reproductive freedom, the show feels scarily prescient, especially when we consider the repeal of the historic Roe Versus Wade ruling in 2022.

The reason the show feels so prescient is because Margaret Atwood wrote the original source novel about things that were really happening, even back in the 1980s and before that. Indigenous, poor and disabled women have had their reproductive rights controlled, curtailed and taken away for decades in various countries across the planet. Sadly it was only when Atwood spotlighted these injustices with a white protagonist that this concern became mainstream and the iconic red handmaid's gowns and white 'wings' (bonnets) became the motif of the movement.

'Having the Big Idea and the Story Engine in place in your mind is not only going to make your idea and execution tons better, they'll solve at least 80 per cent of your writer's block. What should come next, you say. What are the Story Engine and Big Idea? How can they be uncovered/moved forward/explored?' explains Louisa.

But should writers include such things as 'The Dramatic Question' or Big Idea and Story Engine in our pitching documents such as treatments as pitch decks?

The answer from Louisa is a resounding YES: 'Don't be afraid to stick them in your treatments! If they're good, it will help us as readers visualise the series beyond your pilot script and will make everything more compelling.'

The Legacy of *Lost* (2004–2010)

From modern serial storytelling, let's consider where it all began. Love it or loathe it, *Lost* is one of the most influential TV series in modern screenwriting. At a time returning drama series was the standard, *Lost* favoured serialised storytelling when most people knew Netflix as a postal DVD service. (Yes really! By 2007, Netflix had delivered its billionth DVD in the mail... and apparently two million customers were still subscribed to this service in 2022).

Lost was the brainchild of JJ Abrams (*Star Trek, Fringe*) and Damon Lindelof (*Watchmen, The Leftovers*). The logline on IMDB reads: 'The survivors of a plane crash are forced to work together in order to survive on a seemingly deserted tropical island.'

Fans became obsessed with the show long before social media and watch parties were a thing.

Blending a mixture of thriller and adventure elements with relatable human drama, *Lost*'s appeal was irresistible to audiences. It became an international hit very quickly, with questions (note: not THE Dramatic Question!) on everyone's lips such as (but not limited to):

- What's behind The Hatch?
- Who are 'The Others' and what do they want?
- What's The Smoke Monster?
- Why haven't the survivors been rescued?
- Are they all dead (with the infamous fan theory: 'is this Purgatory')?

It's important to note however that none of these questions I listed form the overall Dramatic Question of the show which I would venture is simple and enduring.

The Dramatic Question At The Heart of *Lost*

As mentioned already, the Dramatic Question is always clear and simple and *Lost* is no different. I would venture it is:

'What is The Island?'

Literally everything in the show revolves around this Dramatic Question, whether it's trying to leave the Island, discovering who 'The Others' are, or why people seem to fall under its spell.

Whether *Lost* answered this Dramatic Question in its polarising finale depends on whom you ask. I've heard Bang2writers wax lyrical about how beautiful that final episode is; others claim it is the most frustrating piece of writing they've ever seen.

I don't mind admitting I didn't really 'get' *Lost* first time around. Back then I wasn't much of a television fan and mostly watched movies. I'm a plotting junkie and though I was yet to come across the concept, I don't care for JJ Abrams' notion of what he calls 'The Mystery Box' where a writer drops their audience 'in the middle of a mystery-in-progress that leaves them wanting to know the answers in both directions' (JJ Abrams in his 2008 TED Talk, *The Mystery Box,* available on YouTube).

Forced to wait a week between episodes then my interest waned, especially as I was a new mother with limited attention due to babies and toddlers screaming over the episode (no live rewind back then if you missed something!). As a result I quite literally lost the thread somewhere around episode fifteen of season one and didn't go back.

Revisiting *Lost* in the 2020s

Disney+ launched in 2020 just as lockdown one of the Covid pandemic happened. Like so many people with kids in the house, we subscribed for the sake of our sanity. There's nothing like a musical to keep fractious children amused in international emergencies!

Disney did not miss a trick with their adult subscribers, however. Having acquired Twenty First Century Fox in 2019, it wasn't long before Disney put the entire back catalogue on Disney+. They also put other adult content from their other subsidiary companies on too. This meant adult subscribers suddenly had access to countless movies and TV series that were very definitely not for children… and one such series was *Lost.*

I decided to revisit the whole of *Lost* and find out what the Bang2writers were going on about, once and for all. I ended up bingeing all six seasons in the space of about two weeks. I discovered the following:

- In contrast to 2004, in 2021 bingeing the series one episode after another really added something and made a HUGE difference to my enjoyment this time around. I was able to invest in the characters much more and overlook the sometimes languid plotting that annoyed me first time around.

- I was also surprised by the diversity of the characters, not to mention how their representations were so nuanced and layered. The character tropes had aged very little, even in contrast to many much newer series. The diversity of the cast means there are multiple shots and strands where there are few or even NO white characters for many minutes at a time, unusual even in the 2020s.
- What's more, the characters often go against audience expectations, even in modern times. Jack (Matthew Fox) might be a doctor, hero and leader (as we expect from a white male lead) BUT he is also irascible, petulant and awkward. His need to save everyone is presented as a BAD thing, an actual flaw!
- In contrast, Kate (Evangeline Lilley) is an antiheroine which is more in keeping with modern sensibilities of female leads. She is also on a redemption arc: she is not a good person deep down at the beginning, but self-serving, looking out for number one. We see this mirrored in Juliet (Elizabeth Mitchell) too.
- Locke (Terry O'Quinn) is an interesting character because back then older characters are rarely as stoic, agile and commanding as him. The Island gives him a 'miracle' in granting his wish to walk again so he can try and lead the group. Though I wasn't thrilled by yet another wheelchair-using character presented in this light, it's a character trope 'of its time' and makes sense within the context of the story and his character. Locke's sorrow at leaving the Island and subsequent suicide off-island (with his form being overtaken by The Man In Black on the Island) was an intriguing twist, too.
- Hugo 'Hurley' Reyes (Jorge Garcia) is a larger-bodied character (aka fat, though I must point out my use of this word implies no judgement. When writing this book I contacted body-positive activists online for advice on appropriate terms to use, many of whom told me to 'just say fat!'). He is an unlikely hero not only because larger male characters are usually comic foils but also the fact media in the 1990s to early 2000s were besieged with rampant fatphobia. His storylines did not revolve around his eating then, but his mental illness: he believes his lottery win is a curse to those around him.

- Charlie (Dominic Monaghan) is a rock star and addict. When we first meet him, he conforms to our expectations of 'junkies' lying and cheating to get a fix. Many shows would have chosen to make Charlie 'the weakest link' or made him an antagonist because of this, but Charlie's arc is so much more. Over the course of his arc he becomes a protector and saviour, supporting the pregnant Claire (Emilie de Ravin) and even sacrificing himself for the other survivors.

- Sayid (Naveen Andrews) is an Iraqi, yet he is presented as dashing, heroic, desirable, frequently with his shirt off (this was even more surprising given the events of the time, such as 9/11 and the Second Gulf War). Our 'typical' white cowboy Sawyer (Josh Holloway) is also presented as desirable like this but in contrast to Sayid has much darker motivations and doesn't seem to want to redeem himself. Both are also antagonistic but vulnerable, depending on the situation.

- Sun and Jin (Yunjin Kim and Daniel Dae Kim) are East Asian, but unusually are holistic characters. They have problems in their marriage but these stem from other people and outside pressure. Their love story is tragic but more in keeping with white 'star-crossed lover' tropes like *Romeo and Juliet*, leading some fans of the show to declare their arc the best TV romance of all time.

- Various antagonists are presented and redeemed, or those who were 'good' may cross over to the other side. This is most obvious in Michael (Harold Perrineau) who begins as a crash survivor, forced to turn against the rest of them when his son Walter is kidnapped by The Others.

Other elements I discovered included the fact 22-episode runs feels WAY too long for such an involved serial. Some episodes felt bloated and unwieldy, filled with 'moments' for the sake of it.

At six seasons, some fans feel *Lost* went on 'too long' too. This instinct is good: in 2020 Damon Lindelof revealed the show was only ever supposed to have three seasons.

That said, JJ Abrams wanted to rival 90s phenomenon *ER* in terms of diversity, plus his interest in 'longitudinal narratives' and his controversial 'mystery box' theory really shook things up in terms of storytelling. I went to university to study screenwriting in the year 2000 and everyone was talking about 'fragmenting the narrative' back then. I'd venture Abrams and Lindelof were closest in managing that.

What About THAT Ending?

Did I like the ending this time around? I actually loved it. Whilst the religious allegory with The Man In Black (Titus Welliver) and his brother Jacob (Mark Ross Pellegrino) was a little heavy-handed for my tastes, Jack's sacrifice to ensure the others get off the Island and subsequent deliverance into the 'Flash Sideways' really worked for me.

According to the Lostpedia online, The Flash Sideways world is a metaphysical realm; 'the main characters created a metaphysical realm to find each other after their deaths... Though they all died at different times, the characters appeared in the realm together, letting them meet and remember the "most important part of their lives" which of course is their time together on the Island. From there, they can finally "move on".'

So what was the Island? For me it was a magical place where people can process and confront their place in the world. For some, like Hurley and Jack, the Island became their home and final resting place. For others, like Kate she had to learn how to do something selfless – which in her case was rescue Claire from the Island, the real mother of Kate's adopted son Aaron.

The Longitudinal Narrative

Whilst I am not a fan of 'The Mystery Box' (largely because it becomes 'WTF is happening?' too easily), another *Lost* alumnus can shed some light on what makes television serials so bingeable.

Javier Grillo-Marxuach is a screenwriter and producer who worked on *Lost* with Abrams and Lindelof. He's gone on to write on other HUGE thriller TV serials such as *The Witcher, Dark Crystal: Age of Resistance* and *The 100*.

What Javier calls 'The Longitudinal Narrative' is when writers start with 'the big picture' of the show. This informs the season, so we can step back and see how it all fits together... which in turn means writers can find out **where and how** their pilot kicks the story off.

'You start with the big picture, by putting up the ten poles of the season up on a whiteboard,' says Javier. 'Then you start narrowing it down... As in "Okay, we know this is going to happen halfway through the season." Put the entire season into the major events. Then start working down from those in terms of plot, character, and so forth.'

I love this approach because 'drawing the story' on whiteboards or a big sheet of paper really helps me focus. It's what I do with Bang2writers who are writing television pilots too. We look at the season as a whole, often starting with the big finale and plotting backwards. This allows us to 'find' where the season begins, avoiding the temptation to start 'too early'. It also means we can ensure characters are DOING things and it's EVENTS – *not* just talking about stuff! – that's pushing the story forwards.

So if Dramatic Questions, Story Engines and Big Ideas don't work for you, perhaps The Longitudinal Narrative will.

The B2W plotting worksheet (overleaf) was created to help writers look at their stories as a whole feature-length screenplay or pilot, but it can also be used to plot an entire season arc.

When it comes to story 'strands' for individual episodes, I like to use different colours. Alternatively, you can add extra arrows if you prefer. There's lots of case study breakdowns to demonstrate on the B2W main site.

Of course, you can 'draw the story' like this even if you're not writing a TV pilot. It's possible to use the worksheet for feature-length thriller movies, or even novels if you want (I do). Visual reprsentations of plot can really help us figure out set up/ pay off, what we're missing, or in keeping events 'tangible' in leading towards an epic showdown.

My personal favourite? I like to plot BACKWARDS. I find the 'biggest' event and make it that showdown and then travel back down the arrow to 'find' the beginning. I find it stops me starting the story 'too early'. But the more you practice like this, the better you will become at doing this foundation work 'your' way.

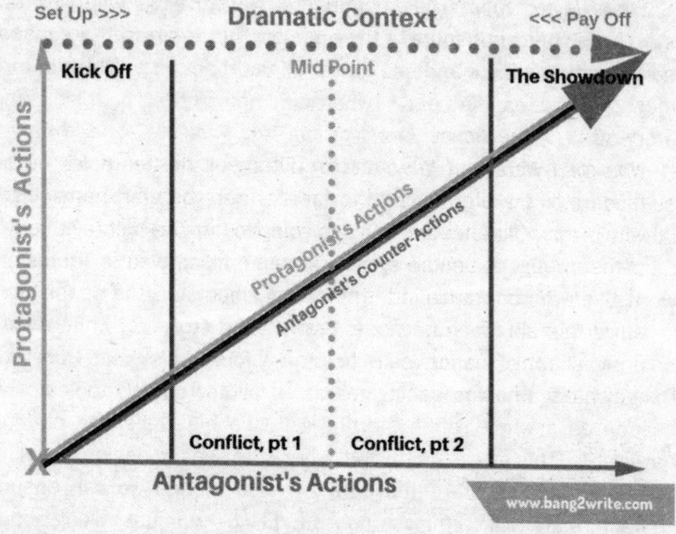

You can download your free copy of the B2W plotting worksheet at www.bang2write.com/resources.

TITLE

By the way, if you don't have one already, now is the time to get yourself a good title. Many writers sabotage their chances again here, picking titles that sound wrong for a thriller in general or the sub- or cross-genre they're attempting. When thinking about your thriller's title, ideally it should give the audience a clue about:

- The tone
- The story
- And/or the characters or elements within them

In particular, try to avoid song titles (they're everywhere in the spec pile); titles that have been used lots of times before (check out IMDB and Google first); or weird-sounding titles (i.e. this is a technique more associated with the comedy genre: *Eternal Sunshine of the*

Spotless Mind; *To Wong Foo, Thanks for Everything, Julie Newmar*, etc). Let's check out some of the titles of various movies I've already mentioned:

- ***CSI*** aka ***Crime Scene Investigation, The Rookie, Castle, Brooklyn Nine-Nine, Person of Interest, Lost***. Exactly what it says on the tin: these projects are named after situations, jobs or the characters within them. No need to reinvent the wheel. *The Mentalist* is the same, though it arguably doesn't travel well: whilst a 'mentalist' in the USA is a magician who can manipulate others with their amazing brain powers, in the UK a mentalist is 'an eccentric or mad person'. That said, Patrick Jane is not the most sane of people and it didn't seem to matter to the success of the series over here.
- ***Stranger Things.*** Did you know? The original title was *Montauk*, an alleged military conspiracy about experiments on children that apparently went on at Camp Hero after World War II. However this title requires prior knowledge of that; if you have none, the title makes no sense. However every English-speaking person has heard the phrase 'stranger things have happened' so this title WORKS as it intrigues as to what these stranger things could be.
- ***The Handmaid's Tale***. This sounds literary and is meant to: the original source material riffs off classics such as Chaucer's The Knight's Tale, The Miller's Tale, etc. Whilst that may put off people who don't like literary stuff, this series is for people who DO.
- ***Die Hard*** – does exactly what it says on the tin again. It screams 'Kickass Hero dispatching lots of Bad Guys'. Sign me up.
- ***Predator*** – this is going to be violent and probably involve a monster, no?
- ***Tremors*** – could be about earthquakes, sure, but then, given that the story relies in part on geology student Rhonda's seismographs (which predict the monsters' approach underground), this is a clever subversion of audience expectation.
- ***Con Air*** – lots of convicts. On a plane. Well, durr. And *obviously* there will be mayhem of some kind.

- ***The Sixth Sense*** – we associate this with psychic/supernatural powers, which is essentially exactly what we get. Boom, done.
- ***Safe House*** – this is another clever subversion of expectation: we associate safe houses with spies, etc, and figure they're 'safe' (hence the name). But, obviously, this safe house is *not* safe, else there wouldn't be a movie about it. Immediately we want to know why.
- ***Attack the Block*** – again, another title that does exactly what it says on the tin in terms of action, like *Die Hard*, though it also holds some information back, like *Tremors*, i.e. 'Something is attacking the estate or "block"; come and see what it is.'

However you choose to tackle your thriller's title, remember what has gone before. Don't choose something that's used too frequently, is too vanilla or too wacky, either. And try and keep your title punchy and to the point: just like your thriller screenplay.

So, now you have your great title and your killer logline. What next... the actual script, right? Not quite. At the risk of seeming completely boring, next up is the outline and various steps to stop you straying off track.

SUMMING UP

- Write two loglines for your spec TV thriller pilot: one for your drama series as a whole AND your pilot episode.
- Know what you're writing: a feature or a TV show, plus how they differ.
- Know what you're writing: a returning drama series or a serial and how they differ.
- Understand your Dramatic Question at the heart of your thriller (aka Big Idea, Story Engine, Theme).
- Know what came before and inspired your own TV thriller and how yours is different, don't just rehash what we've seen before.

- Understand characters need deep work to feel nuanced and layered.
- Use the 'Longitudinal Narrative' to figure out your series plot-wise as well as your characters' individual arcs leading to the series finale.
- Pick a title that doesn't hide what your story is really about.

PITCHING & PREPARATION, PART 2: **THE OUTLINE**

RECIPE FOR SUCCESS?

Now you have your premise and killer logline (plus your Dramatic Question etc if you're writing a TV series), it's time to write an outline. By 'outline' I mean a set of notes or prose version of the screenplay designed to help you, the writer, negotiate your way through the plot. These outlines are not to show the outside world (though you may want to show to feedback-givers, via peer review or paid reader). I've seen outlines run to anything between five and thirty pages and, yes, admittedly, they can be quite dull documents both to write *and* read. But they really are worth an attempt and I'll explain why shortly.

An outline is the scriptwriting equivalent of a kitchen recipe. Outlines are not selling documents, but extended 'notes to self', if you like. Many spec screenwriters shy away from writing an outline in the first instance. They will say they'll only go off track, anyway; that outlines kill spontaneity; that they'll miss opportunities in the plot regardless, so might as well get started on the draft.

Whilst I am sympathetic to these viewpoints, if you want to progress FAST in your screenwriting career, you need to write outlines. As screenwriter Simon Uttley (@siuttley) points out, *'It's not about strait-jacketing later creativity, it's about guiding you through to that first FADE OUT.'* So, the *more* work you do at foundation level, the *fewer* drafts your spec thriller screenplay will need. And guess what: the fewer drafts you need of one project, the more new projects you can write in the long term... And the more projects you can write, the more likely it is you can break through by getting one of them noticed.

THE RIGHT PRESCRIPTION

It goes without saying that there's no right way to write an outline, especially if you're essentially writing a note to yourself about *how* you are going to tackle the story of your spec thriller screenplay. That said, having read lots of screenwriters' personal outlines over the years, I would venture the ones who are the most *prescriptive* about what they want to achieve with reference to structure and character in the story are the ones who go off track the least and have the most success with their drafts. But what do I mean by prescriptive? As we know from previous chapters, thrillers need to:

- Be thrilling, first and foremost.
- Set the tone and story world from the offset and must not be too 'backwards looking'; we're concerned with the 'here and now'.
- Be highly structured, to increase tension and jeopardy more and more as the narrative progresses, with the biggest thrills (for whatever reason) in the resolution.
- Provide a shift in dramatic context from flight (non-engagement) to fight (engagement).
- Have an antagonist who drives the action and a reactive protagonist.
- Have secondary characters who help/hinder them in their respective missions.

In considering the above, I think it helps to break an outline down to the following questions before tackling what happens in the actual plot, and with whom:

- **Where does the story start?** Whether you start right in the middle of the action and 'rewind', or try a much more 'slow burn' technique in introducing us to your characters and story, you need to think about *why* we start at that particular point and not somewhere else in the story. Don't just start at where it 'feels' right; make it work. This is a plot *construction*, not a plot *happening*.

- **Where does the story end?** Many writers paint themselves into a corner by the end of their spec thriller screenplay, meaning characters' actions often feel rushed and nonsensical. The greatest produced thrillers have resolutions that are not predictable but which are *inevitable*: a subtle difference. This in turn makes their resolutions 'obvious': OF COURSE John Book will have to face the bent cops in the Amish barn without a weapon to hand in *Witness* (1985); OF COURSE he will have to outwit them first with brute force via the corn silo, then with the support of the usually pacifist Amish people... And OF COURSE Book will leave the settlement *without* Rachel. Neither can sacrifice that much, even if they do love each other. Anything else would be just plain ridiculous and undermine everything that went before it.

- **How does it get worse before it gets better?** Act Two is called the Conflict for a reason – you need shedloads of it! Yet many spec thriller screenplays will run 'on the spot' for most of this act, which is simply no good. Your protagonist must progress forward plot-wise every step of the way in the thriller, and most of his/her steps will take place in the conflict. The antagonist will place obstacles in front of the protagonist, but s/he must keep dealing with them. My children like to play video games like Super Mario: the little characters are in their cars attempting to go from A to B, avoiding giant wrecking balls and mushrooms and weird freaks. They also have to collect rings and other stuff in order to 'power up'. Your spec thriller screenplay's protagonist is much the same: they're in their little car, trying to get from A to B and collect the good stuff as they go, whilst the antagonist is throwing all kinds of shit at them, trying to stop them before it's GAME OVER. Underestimate the importance of that journey in your thriller screenplay and you will find your protagonist's car breaks down and you're gonna have to phone the scriptwriting equivalent of the AA.

- **What do my characters do and feel about all this?** Of course, it's not all about plot, construction or not. The best plots have great characters that feel rounded, relevant and believable and are ultimately memorable. So we're back to this notion of *who* your characters are and *what* motivates them to do what they do in that plot. Someone – I forget who, unfortunately – tweeted me once with the excellent observation: *'It's not 50/50 character and plot; it's 100/100 character and plot.'* Though maths was clearly not the tweeter's strong point, it stuck in my head because, screwy or not, it's 100 per cent true.

Writers who strive to provide answers for these four questions in their outlines are much more likely to write a well-conceived, genuine spec thriller screenplay, as opposed to a drama in which the characters run around a lot.

BLUEPRINTS

In writing an outline, it can pay dividends to think of plot being a *construction*, rather than a *happening*. If you build brick by brick from its foundations, you are far more likely to create a screenplay of substance, with characters of worth. But, like my building analogy, you're much more likely to do that if you have a proper, coherent blueprint you can follow. As TV showrunner Emilia di Girolamo posits, *'It's far easier to fix plot flaws in a short outline than a whole screenplay... if a story won't work on a page, it really won't work on ninety of them!'*

So let's break down that *basic* plot structure of the thriller genre and consider how it can work for our own screenplays when we write our outlines. Note this can be the entire plot construction of a single thriller movie, or it can be the baseline for a TV thriller series arc, whatever you want to call it:

- **Step One: ACT ONE – SET UP. Keywords: Catalyst. 'Here and Now.' Start as you mean to go on.** *Protagonist presented with problem by the antagonist; the protagonist *needs* to solve it (s/he can't just walk away).* So, what is the killer logline? Whatever it is, we need it to inform our Set Up. We need to hit the ground running and we need to make sure the tone and story world is set up alongside our characters (not one, *then* the other). We need to get a flavour of our characters and their motivations here (especially with reference to any catalysts that kick off any action/reasons) but, crucially, we don't need to 'shoot our load' on this. We should discover things like characters' motivations and backstory and whatnot *as* we go along. We don't want it all upfront and we certainly don't want a stack of flashbacks, etc, detracting from the 'here and now'.
- **Step Two: ACT TWO – CONFLICT. Keywords: Non-engagement/ Resistance. Attempt to escape (literal or metaphorical).** *Protagonist is presented with variety of obstacles by the antagonist...* In our outline, this is where we may end up writing what is essentially a list of behaviours and events, with our protagonist doing all s/he can to avoid this crap and/or escape (if appropriate): 'And then... and then... and then...' Don't worry about this. Don't forget this document is primarily for YOU, that all-important blueprint to keep you on track in the story. Don't gloss over events; instead make sure each one is more problematic than the last. Remember Super Mario: dodge those mushrooms. Whatever you do, don't have your hero/ine 'running on the spot'.
- **Step Three: MIDPOINT. Keywords: Moment of clarity.** *Things get worse/eye of the storm (as appropriate).* This is frequently the moment where your protagonist makes that big change from non-engagement to engagement with the antagonist, or they at least start thinking about it. Give them a great reason to change their thinking and engage for the first time directly with their nemesis. It can be anything you want. You're the writer!
- **Step Four: ACT TWO – CONFLICT. Key words: Engagement. Fight to the death (literal and/or metaphorical).** *Those obstacles keep*

coming and the protagonist must keep overcoming them, even though each obstacle is more difficult than the last. Despite engaging for the first time, very often your protagonist will be propelled into something far worse than before and this loss of hope will make them figure they have nothing to lose, so they might as well go out fighting. Their struggle becomes bigger: in big-budget blockbusters, this will frequently mean the monsters or aliens will take over the rest of the world, so the hero/ine will decide to take on what is essentially a suicide mission to stop this from occurring (though we know it usually won't come to that). In smaller thrillers, it may be a sense of personal honour: the protagonist decides the antagonist cannot be allowed to win and do this to someone else.

- **Step Five: ACT THREE – RESOLUTION. Key words: Loss of hope. No way out? Last minute saviour/destroyer. Payoff.** *Looks like all is lost for the protagonist... It looks like the antagonist is going to win... And then the protagonist turns it around *in some way* and solves the problem (or not, as the case may be).* Typically, your protagonist will be cornered in the last section of your thriller outline. There will seemingly be nowhere left for him/her to go. And this is typically where something you seeded earlier in the screenplay will come into play as a big Payoff. It can be anything and it can be anywhere: Set Up, Midpoint, Conflict... As long as it's not mentioned for the first time in the resolution, otherwise it will become a *deus ex machina*, conveniently delivering your hero/ine from evil. Its function can save your protagonist and destroy your antagonist, or vice versa... but we must believe the *opposite* of whatever you want to play out until the very last second to really make your thriller thrill.

So, as you can hopefully see, your outline needn't be a 'tick the boxes' or 'paint by the numbers' job. Remember the B2W plotting worksheet here, as well as all the various plotting archetypes such as The Hero's Journey, Voyage and Return, Rebirth, etc. Plot construction is not formula, but a framework: you can use it to create any narrative you want in the thriller genre and its many sub- and cross-genres. It is bendy and can incorporate any number or types of characters and their motivations. Remember, all we need in any spec screenplay is a beginning, middle and end – and not necessarily in that order. You have the foundation and then you build stuff on top of that. So don't get ants in your pants about outlines; they're not out to get you. They are just blueprints; a plan of how you will tackle your story. Boom. Done.

THE FINISH LINE

> *'The non-negotiable for getting a script written in the 2020s is the same as it would be in any other decade. Time management. You have to devote hours of your week to the writing. And that can be a monumental task if you are juggling another career plus social and family life. But it's the only way you get to FADE OUT. Carving out a part of your day or a day of your weeks where you are devoted to the work on the script is non-negotiable. You have to build your church and attend each week.'*
>
> ***– Eric Heisserer, screenwriter and show runner***

Most spec screenwriters write one or two projects at a time per year, but, in my experience, very few sign off on drafts, preferring instead to tinker with them for months and months and, sometimes, even years. Whilst no screenplay is ever truly 'finished', it does not make sense to keep returning to them indefinitely. Yet many writers will do this and then ask me why they are not advancing. The reason is simple: you have to let go of your previous work in order to move on to the next level and create even better work!

So, to avoid this bizarre kind of 'repetition compulsion' and to make strides in your writing career, consider writing at least one new project and signing off on it every single year. That's right! Every single year. Stop tinkering and redrafting and reworking. Factor this in from the very beginning: give your project a start date and an end date and, if it won't work, or people consistently don't respond to it, don't be afraid to junk it. No writing is ever wasted. You can take those characters or plot threads out of the draft that is not working and put them in another screenplay. *Have the guts to 'finish'.* Only that way will you be able to really capitalise on your strategy for getting your work out there, which I go into in more detail in the next section of this book. But first, the script pages. Yay! Except there's one more thing... Are your first ten pages the best they can be? That's next, plus another look at set up and how it's working in your actual script pages.

SUMMING UP...

- Invest in your premise – make it easy to grasp and you access your potential audience.
- Remember the key ingredients of a great thriller premise: the hook, plus the notions of 'winning and losing' and 'it could happen to you'.
- A great thriller logline should be told from the protagonist's POV.
- Remember the 3 Cs: clarity, conflict, characters. If we don't know what's happening to whom and why, we don't care.
- Avoid making your thriller sound like a drama.
- Never use a tagline instead of a logline.
- Make sure your logline and title really sell the central concept. Get feedback on them and make sure they grab people. Great characters are born out of great plots and vice versa.
- Outlines are blueprints: nothing more, nothing less.
- Well-conceived outlines can mean fewer drafts down the road.
- Being 'prescriptive' with your outline with reference to plot construction can really help ensure you have a great foundation.
- Remember the difference between movies and TV; returning drama and serials (aka limited series).
- Have the guts to 'finish' your screenplay – and factor this in from the beginning! Manage your time well.

THE FIRST TEN PAGES & SET UP

OPEN/CLOSE TEST

'Nothing beats a great first page for getting industry attention. Make sure your first page tells a story and sets the tone.'

– **Pilar Alessandra, script consultant** (@onthepage)

Whilst officially you have ten pages to 'wow' your reader, agent or exec, and hopefully get that all-important full read, the reality is that you actually have just ONE page. That's right! They may not even actually *read* your script, they may literally open and then close it just as quickly, having skimmed the first few sentences only. But how can you avoid this? With three simple steps:

- **Make sure your opening IMAGE grabs the reader.** I'm always surprised by how few writers think about the *first* thing we're supposed to see as the script opens. Typically, a character will be walking somewhere, or we open with black – both of which are really, really boring. Think of all the thrillers you've seen and how they open: what image introduced us to the story? How did they grab your attention, or was it a slow burn? Did that first image set the tone and help us get an idea of what was to come? Or was it something random and seemingly out of place that joins up somewhere else in the story? Whatever you do, pique the reader's interest; don't open on something without a really good story reason.

- **Avoid cliché, notes to reader and overdone storytelling devices.** Readers read all day; that's their job. So if you open with something they see all the time or tell them *how* to read your screenplay or bore them, they will stop reading and close your script. End of. It really is as simple as that. So make sure you *know* what all the tired tropes and conventions are; screenwriting and filmmaking follow fashion, just like everything else. Script readers, agents and producers have never been more approachable: many have blogs, Twitter accounts, Facebook pages and appear at events such as film festivals, where they will detail what they feel is 'good' writing and what bores them. So there really is no excuse!

- **Double check the obvious stuff, like script format.** Critics accuse readers of making scriptwriting into a 'beauty contest' and, in years past, they were correct: most of the scripts chucked out before about five to ten years ago were for relatively minor and obvious offences, such as incorrect formatting and/or font. Scripts now generally look better than they did, but there are still lots of irritating and annoying format errors that can interfere with the flow of the read and stop the reader from engaging with your story. So make sure you're not just copying others' mistakes that you've seen in your peers' scripts or online – double check. There are lots of great resources now, so you need never drop any script format clangers ever again. As a result, readers are harsher than ever on this point, as they figure there is no excuse to submit scripts that are out of whack with industry expectation. I have made a one-page script format PDF reference guide and a 'Format One Stop Shop' detailing all the format issues in detail that I see on a regular basis; you can find them both at www.bang2write.com/resources. Alternatively, Google 'screenplay format' and you will find thousands more.

So, congratulations – you got past the 'open/close' test – and your script stayed open. But you're not out of the woods yet... *Now* you have to make the reader want to read past your first ten pages.

THE PERFECT TEN

Google 'screenplay + the first ten pages' and you'll find a stack of articles dedicated to advice on your first ten pages. It seems everyone is in complete agreement: the first ten are a story's most important. The reason for this is practical: a reader at a literary agency, prodco or finance scheme typically reads the first ten pages of your script in order to decide whether it merits a full read (or not). It's a harsh system, brought in to combat the huge number of submissions companies and initiatives get. It works for the most part, with probably 70 to 80 per cent of scripts falling at this first hurdle (with most of *those* sabotaging their chances within just ONE page, as outlined in the previous section).

So what are scripts failing at within the first ten pages these days? Generally speaking, it is nearly always one (or more) of the following seven deadly scriptwriting/story sins:

- **Cliché rears its head after all.** There are any number of clichéd or familiar elements to stories; but, related specifically to thriller, I would argue that one of the most clichéd elements is the 'dream waking' (starting awake from a nightmare, which we see in the first few frames); this will often be swiftly followed by characters getting ready for the day ahead – in the shower, eating breakfast, etc. Then there's 'voiceover overtelling' (typically recounting A Terrible Thing That Happened *Before*, which may or may not inform the story, and which we'll flashback to, over and over, sapping jeopardy in the 'here and now'. Then there's 'the funeral', where a protagonist will be at a lost relative's graveside and be told Something Significant, which will set off the action. As ever, there's no reason for these to not work, but it is difficult to persuade readers they can when they've seen SO MANY bad versions of these.
- **We don't know who the protagonist is... and who s/he is up against.** Within the first ten pages we need to know WHO we're dealing with. That includes the protagonist and the antagonist and/or antagonistic force regarding the situation at hand. An easy way of doing this is by opening with your protagonist and introducing your

antagonist second. Instead, many spec thrillers try to establish intrigue by starting with someone completely different – or even lots of characters, as if inviting us to 'guess' which ones the protagonist and antagonist are. This rarely works and only ends up confusing the reader, which inevitably leads to your spec thriller screenplay being abandoned at page ten.

- **We're introduced to characters first and THEN the story.** As mentioned previously, this is something that happens in all genres, but particularly in thriller, which means we end up feeling like we're 'waiting' for the story to start and is a big no-no. Character and story need to be introduced hand in hand, especially for today's audiences. Don't make us wait!
- **Stop. Rewind… Yawn.** Undoubtedly inspired by *Memento* (2000), lots of spec thrillers open with an intriguing hook, then stop and rewind to a few days' or a few hours' earlier, as mentioned in Chapter One, under the subheading 'Hitting the Ground Running'. Now, rewinding *can* be an interesting technique and I would hesitate to call it a cliché *per se* – but, frequently, spec thrillers do not utilise this device effectively. I've lost count of the number of times I've read a really great hook on page one and turned eagerly to page two… to discover characters eating breakfast or something equally dull. Talk about a let down! Similarly, we might have a really intriguing hook on page one – and then have absolutely no clue what it relates to, as the writer does not return to it (or even mention it, never mind set it up) until the resolution.
- **Montage-a-rama.** The montage can be a really useful device in the thriller when related to story and dramatic context, as outlined in Chapter One. However, lots of writers choose to *start* with montage or have one very early in the draft. Whilst this can be a good choice, nine times out of ten it isn't, because said writer puts one in for style, not story. Cityscapes and changing seasons are the two I see most in the first ten pages of spec thrillers and it rarely adds anything; instead it reduces potential tension.
- **Writers splurge non-linearity all over the place.** Frequently, spec thrillers start with 'Flashback' and I always wonder what exactly we're

flashing back from, if we haven't seen the present yet? Equally, the writers may jam in a load of flashbacks at the expense of anchoring us in that present – so it's difficult to know what story we're dealing with, or whom. Don't forget that notion of the 'throughline', so you can anchor the reader (and thus your audience).

- **The story doesn't state its intent.** It's actually possible to begin a thriller script any way you like – even with clichéd openers and montages and non-linearity – IF the first ten pages state that story's intent in an interesting, thrilling way. But most don't, leaving the reader dangling. But what does 'stating intent' mean, anyway?

STATING YOUR STORY'S INTENT

There's all kinds of advice out there on how to write a rip-roaring first ten pages, but I always think it's more useful to take the emphasis off one's own POV and consider what OTHERS may want from you, the writer, and the pages you send them. As a script reader, I know I want to know the following when I open someone else's screenplay:

- Who the protagonist is
- Who the antagonist is
- What the goal is/what the counter-goal is, i.e. in the case of thrillers, what does the antagonist want/why does the protagonist want to stop him/her?
- What the genre/tone is, i.e. is this a serial killer/conspiracy/supernatural thriller, etc?
- What the story is, i.e. what is the premise? Either the whole of it or a good portion of it; I don't want everything shrouded in supposed 'mystery' and I don't want to 'wait' for the story to start.

... And I want to know the above within the first ten pages. It really is as simple as that. There's no big secret. The difficult thing is getting it down on paper. And now for the rest!

THE SET UP AND PAY OFF

So, as we know from the beginning of this book and from our own outlines, the first act or set up of your thriller screenplay should be able to be reduced to the following:

> *Your protagonist is presented with a problem by the antagonist; the protagonist *needs* to solve it (s/he can't just walk away).*

Looking to produced thrillers, we can see this is the case over and over again:

- In *Aliens*, Ripley is presented with the uncomfortable knowledge that LV 426 has been colonised by families after the board choose to disbelieve her version of events regarding the creature in the first film. Instead, the board believe Ripley went nuts and blew up a perfectly good starship and freight load after the malfunctioning Ash killed the rest of the *Nostromo*'s crew. As a result, we believe it is a case of not only personal honour but responsibility on Ripley's part when she chooses to accompany the marine corps with Burke to the colony when they lose contact: she quite literally thinks they will need her special knowledge of the creatures (which they do in the pay off).
- In *Con Air*, Poe is on the plane with the ringleaders of the bloody coup: Cyrus The Virus; Diamond Dog; Billy Bedlam. Remember, Poe could get off at the first drop (before the coup is detected by authorities on the ground), but *chooses* not to, for the sake of best friend Baby-O (at risk of diabetic coma, now his insulin has been smashed) and Sally Bishop, the female guard (at risk from serial rapist Johnny 23). This not only serves a plot purpose, but makes us realise in the pay off Poe is an upstanding guy who's served his debt to society and is not the same as the rest of the convicts.
- In *Panic Room*, Meg and daughter Sarah are not faced with a metaphorical decision, but a literal one: afraid for their safety (as anyone in the audience would be too, male or female), they

barricade themselves, first, inside the lift, then the panic room of the title. This serves the plot and the resulting irony in the pay off (what the burglars want is actually *in* the panic room).

In comparison to these examples, very often in spec thriller screenplays the reader is left feeling the protagonist could have just ignored the antagonist's actions and/or the situation at hand – either by literally walking away or by going down the usual channels, such as calling the police and getting them to deal with the problem instead. But imagine if Ripley had not cared whether LV 426 had been colonised by families in her overly long hyper-sleep; or that Poe was not friends with Baby-O or did not care about Sally Bishop's fate; or that Meg and Sarah had run out the front door instead?

So, to get your audience on side absolutely, what the set up of your thriller screenplay needs to present is this situation:

If your character does/does not (do this action) and/or make (this decision), there would be no movie.

Ensure that your protagonist cannot just ignore or walk away from your antagonist's actions, and/or the situation at hand, to create a solid set up and lead us into the Second Act or Conflict of your thriller screenplay where whatever you have set up pays off.

SUMMING UP...

- You have one page to impress in the first instance, so double check everything, even format.
- Your opening image matters more than you think.
- Avoid cliché at all costs.
- Find out what the industry thinks is 'good' writing – this is always changing, but has never been easier to find out, thanks to the likes of social media.
- Make sure your first ten pages state the story's intent.
- Make your set up mean your protagonist cannot just walk away.

THE CONFLICT & THE SHOWDOWN

'Language is pacing. Tailor the look of your pages to convey tension and momentum. White space speeds it up; black slows it down.'

– Ed Hughes, Linda Seifert Management (@LindaSeifert)

TWO MUCH

Act Two is probably the most problematic area of any screenplay and the one capable of causing the most headaches in writers. However, Act Two can be even more fraught with issues in a thriller screenplay than your average spec. The reasons for this are plentiful, but the two issues I see most in thriller specs are:

- **The Wasteland.** Whilst some spec thrillers set up well and 'hit the ground running' (thus earning themselves a full read), readers can still find themselves frustrated as early as the first turning point: many of those spec thriller screenplays will then grind to a halt, forcing their protagonists to 'run on the spot' as a variety of events happen *to* them and we end up marking time before the 'showdown' in the resolution. This then turns the Conflict – arguably the most important element of any story, but especially the thriller – into a wasteland of lost opportunity in terms of plot, as we're waiting for the protagonist to *do* something, so tension (thus interest) is lost.

- **The Plot Thickens.** Many writers over the years have confessed to me they feel daunted by the second act of their feature screenplays. A common complaint is this section of the movie feels 'too big' and they haven't 'enough' story. Those writers will then attempt to pile too much in, chucking in extra characters and subplots all over the place and tying themselves up in knots. This means when I come to read it I can't decide who the important people are and what events I'm supposed to be following and why, as it's a veritable melting pot of plot threads and character motivations.

Though very different issues, the end result is the same: protagonists end up 'treading water' or 'running on the spot'. Remember that notion of your protagonist in their little car like Super Mario, dodging the bad stuff and collecting the good stuff to 'power up' for the resolution? More on *how* to do this, next.

BREAK IT DOWN

So, whether your issue is a protagonist 'running on the spot', or a script overloaded with extraneous characters and subplot (or something else), I recommend breaking the second act down into bitesize chunks, so you can see where you're going in the story and why. In his book *Writing Drama*, Yves Lavandier poses the notion of protagonists *'climbing walls, each bigger than the last'*. I think this is a great image for screenwriting in general, but especially thriller. (This is one of the reasons I started drawing the diagonal arrow in the B2W plotting worksheet from the 'bottom' of Act 1 and leading all the way to the 'top' of Act 3, as shown in part two of this book). Think of the protagonists in your favourite thrillers: what 'walls' do the antagonists make them 'climb' in order to get to the resolution? The best thrillers really put those protagonists through their paces, before that final showdown with the antagonist. In breaking down your conflict, think back to the notion of dramatic context, of the thriller 'flight versus fight' and see how it informs your story:

- **ACT TWO – CONFLICT (Part 1)**: *Protagonist presented with variety of obstacles by the antagonist...*
  You've already set up, so we know *who* the protagonist is and *why* the antagonist is a problem for him/her and *what* the situation at hand represents. At the moment, your protagonist's mind is reeling. All s/he wants to do is get away, either literally or figuratively. Perhaps there's a literal problem – i.e. s/he has been kidnapped by person or beast; there's an alien invasion or natural disaster; or s/he is the victim of home invasion or other crime? Or perhaps it's a metaphorical problem: she must solve a mystery or find something out about the afterlife, perhaps before *something else* happens? Whatever the case, your antagonist is cocky here and thinks s/he has bested your protagonist and the antagonist would be right: all our hero/ine really wants is to get away and curl up into a little ball somewhere: *s/he does not want to deal with this shit!*
- **MIDPOINT**: *Things get worse/eye of the storm (as appropriate).*
  This element of your thriller screenplay will depend on the story and how you want to execute it. Perhaps this marks the spot where your dramatic context changes from 'flight' to 'fight', as it does in *Red Eye* (2005), when Jack confronts Lisa in the airplane toilet and we learn of her history as a rape survivor? Or perhaps it will be a moment of quiet, as in *Cube* (1997), as the group attempt to make it through the cubed maze (only to discover later in the resolution they should have stayed where they were)?
- **ACT TWO – CONFLICT (Part 2)**: *Those obstacles keep coming and the protagonist must keep overcoming them, even though each obstacle is more difficult than the last.*

  Whatever you decide to put at the midpoint – a huge crescendo or a quiet whimper – between that midpoint and the end of the second part of the conflict your protagonist will have made a *realisation*: s/he is the only person who can get them out of this. Their time in 'flight' is over... Now is the time to *fight – and beat the antagonist or die trying* (literally, figuratively or both).

  Act Two performs the most important elements of your thriller screenplay. In addition to charting the change in response of your

> protagonist, Act Two also marks the transition of the antagonist: s/he will be sure s/he has won in the first half, but this will change as the second act progresses. Your characters will essentially swap places: the victor in the first half, the antagonist will generally find him/herself the loser by the end of the resolution. Even in cases where the antagonist *does* win – the most obvious being John Doe in *Se7en* (1995) – we are invited to believe the protagonist, in this case Somerset, will win until *the very last second*. Remember how hard Somerset pleads with Mills not to let Doe 'win' by shooting him, whilst Mills agonises for painful moments? It really does look as if Mills will heed Somerset's warnings, making it all the more shocking when he changes his mind at the last second and succumbs to wrath, his own deadly sin.

Being ninety minutes to two hours, the way this works out in movies should be pretty clear. However don't forget we can also relate the above to the 'story strands' of writing television serials or returning drama series too. But what kind of content can we include in Act 2?

REVEALING CHARACTER & PUSHING THE STORY FORWARD

> *'Thrillers require a huge amount of skill and attention to detail. If there are a few scenes out of kilter or not quite punching their weight in any other genre we can forgive it and move on, but get a scene wrong in a thriller and all that tension that you've lovingly created prior to that dissipates and you've got to start all over again building it up.'*
>
> **– Hayley McKenzie, Script Editor, Script Angel**
> (@Hayley1McKenzie)

Tension is everything in the thriller screenplay. This means interrogation scenes are very much part of the spec pile when it comes to police and crime thrillers (both feature-length screenplays and TV pilots). It's not hard to see why: interrogation scenes are a staple of produced movies and TV too. They can be a fantastic way of upping the stakes and tension, especially in Act 2. Plus being contained, interrogation scenes can be quite cheap to film too which means they're a possibility for filmmakers on a low budget.

Unfortunately, the average spec screenplay's interrogation scene often becomes static and boring – the very opposite of what they're supposed to be. This is usually because the writer believes an interrogation scene is made up of non-stop dialogue back and forth. Whilst these scenes may be dialogue-led, they should not revolve entirely around talk.

Chains and chains of dialogue is NEVER a substitute for visuals and in-depth character work driving the scene. But what does this mean? Let's look at two case studies that use the interrogation scene well.

Line of Duty (2012–2021)

Line of Duty is a British police procedural TV series focusing on AC-12, an anti-police corruption unit, created and written by showrunner Jed Mercurio. Running for six series, its 'Who is H?' storyline kept the nation talking, with nearly 10m viewers for its ultimate finale. Unlike many police procedurals that focus primarily on life in the field, 'chasing perps', *Line of Duty* is unusual because it emphasises systemic failures and injustice in the institution of policing itself. But rather than become a drama putting all this under the microscope, it still places thriller tropes at its heart.

Line of Duty is best known for its iconic interrogation scenes, where accused police officers must justify their decisions and defend their actions. These are known to be highly tense, with many reversals of expectations on both sides. One of the most infamous has to be 'Urgent Exit Required' in the season finale (s3, ep 6) when the corrupt DI Matthew 'Dot' Cottan (Craig Parkinson) escapes interrogation by sending a text message, prompting an armed police officer (and fellow corrupt crony) outside to shoot his partner and spray the room with gunfire. Cottan escapes with the other officer into the street, with our intrepid heroine DC Kate Fleming (Vicky McClure) in pursuit. Cottan is spirited away by his other co-conspirators, but not before Kate shoots at the car from a bridge, sending it off-road.

Many screenplays in the spec pile fail to understand what an interrogation scene is really for: pushing the story forward and revealing character. Instead, interrogation scenes become exposition dumps to 'catch up' the audience on the storyline. Whilst this can work *in conjunction* with other craft elements (such as pushing the story forward and revealing character!), it rarely works on its own.

A lot of screenwriters don't understand what 'push the story forward' and 'reveal character' really means, however. Let's break it down: first things first, search 'Dot's Urgent Exit' on YouTube where you should be able to find the scene in its entirety (dependent on territory).

Even if you have never seen *Line of Duty* before, you will probably be able to understand the purpose of that interrogation scene and its subsequent chase sequence is to:

A) Reveal how Dot is connected to the corruption (push story forward)
B) Illustrate the conspiracy is so serious people will kill to protect it (push story forward)
C) Show that both Dot and Fleming will do whatever it takes to hide/unveil the conspiracy respectively (reveal character)
D) Dot and Fleming had a previous 'thing' with each other (reveal character)

So, get on YouTube and take a look if you can. It's a real masterclass.

Prisoners (2013)

In this thriller written by Aaron Guzikowski and directed by Denis Villeneuve, a father Keller Dover (Hugh Jackman) takes matters into his own hands when his daughter and her friend go missing.

As in many thrillers of the past ten to fifteen years, Dover is an antihero. Jackman plays against type: even Wolverine has nothing on Keller Dover (Wolverine is a superhero after all, however gruff and irascible he may be). Dover leaves no stone unturned and literally stops at nothing to recover the two girls, even kidnapping and torturing Alex Jones (Paul Dano), a mentally ill local man Dover suspects of being a sociopathic kidnapper and murderer.

Dover's actions are meant to horrify the viewer, but also ask us: 'What would YOU do?' if the clock is ticking and your children's lives hang in the balance. Whilst we don't – and obviously should never – condone Dover's vigilantism, we also accept we may behave the same way if we were desperate enough.

As Dover enacts a one-man desperate crusade, police pursue multiple leads and the pressure mounts. Detective Loki (Jake Gyllenhaal) finds himself locked in a powerful interrogation scene with suspect Bob Taylor (David Dastmalchian).

The morally ambiguous theme of the movie is reflected most in Detective Loki, who is a 'good cop' in that he does 'the right thing' ... but Loki feels the 'right thing' is fluid and can depend on what the situation needs. As with Dover, this can be an admirable trait... or it can be horrific as we discover in this masterful interrogation scene with Bob.

Believing Bob to be withholding information, Loki becomes more and more irate as Bob persists in drawing something that looks like a puzzle. The time is ticking away and the little girls who are missing could be dying. As a character we know Loki is mostly honourable but not above doing whatever it takes to get important information. This means we are not surprised when he assaults the suspect, though we do believe his sorrow when Bob grabs Loki's gun and kills himself.

This means the interrogation scene is not mere 'banter' back and forth, but again: it pushes the story forward and reveals character very effectively. In addition, the scene contains a triple whammy of dramatic irony, a very unusual but effective technique that can get writers notice in their own thriller screenplays.

Dramatic irony is a literary technique, originally used in Greek tragedy. Dramatic irony is created when the full significance of a character's words or actions is clear to the audience or reader although unknown to the character. It's obvious to us Bob is suffering from guilt or similar, but unlike Loki we realise this may drive him to extreme actions. If Loki had NOT assaulted Bob:

1) Bob would never have had the opportunity to grab Loki's gun
2) Bob's death means Loki has now lost his only lead
3) The answer of where the girls are is literally in the 'puzzle' drawing! That 'puzzle' that angered Loki so much was literally the 'map' Bob promised but was unable to describe.

It's not difficult to understand why many writers believe interrogation scenes in thrillers to be 'static'; they literally are in spec screenplays! But as we can see from both *Prisoners* and *Line of Duty*, they can be dramatic, engaging and visual. This means they should be anything BUT static. There is plenty going on in these scenes: characters moving in and out of the room; visuals of characters' discomfort or triumph; hidden movements under the table etc. This is why interrogation scenes can be so tense and work so well. Lesson? Never mistake one location as being STATIC; they're CONTAINED. A subtle difference, but crucial.

BLOCKBUSTERS AND SET PIECES

Moving on from tension created by characters, another issue writers have with Act 2 is they're not thinking about what audiences sign up for: thrills! One of the biggest draws thrillers have are life-or-death stakes, especially if they're of the big-budget variety: explosions, monsters, giant robots or other things that provide the commercial hook or cultural desire mentioned already in this book.

One of the reasons blockbusters are popular with the four-quadrant audiences is the set piece. Very often these set pieces will be the 'selling point' of the movie: potential audiences will see them in trailers or clips on TV or the internet via social media. Set pieces can be serious, funny or something in-between but ultimately what they ALL must do is EXCITE the audience via thrills, spills and visuals. Whilst most indie filmmakers don't have the kind of budget needed for such set pieces, there's still plenty to learn here – especially when the average spec thriller screenplay is dialogue-led and barely visual at all!

The *Jurassic Park/World* Franchise (1993–2022)

A franchise that does the set piece exceptionally well is the *Jurassic Park/World* movies. They are such popular movies with people of all ages that if you ask someone which is their favourite and why, they will inevitably mention at least part of a set piece as their answer. This is because set pieces are visual and exciting, which makes them memorable.

Set pieces are meant to be visual feasts, yet too often spec thrillers – even ones meant to be blockbusters and high-budget – become chains and chains of dialogue; low-budget ones even more so. Yet we can learn all about visuals from blockbusters like the *Jurassic* movies. Such iconic visuals in the *Jurassic* franchise include (but are not limited to):

- The T-Rex roaring as the banner reading, '*When Dinosaurs Ruled The Earth'* flutters down in the first movie (1993)
- The deaths of the Brachiosaurs on the island in *Fallen Kingdom* (2018)
- The caravan falling off the cliff in the Lost World whilst Sarah, Ian and Nick hang from a rope (*The Lost World,* 1997)
- The concurrent dinosaur chase through Malta to the plane, with Owen on a motorcycle and Claire and Kayla in a Jeep (*Jurassic World Dominion*, 2022)
- The Spinosaurus taking out the aircraft (*Jurassic Park III*, 2001)
- The Indoraptor on the roof in the 'haunted house' sequence (*Fallen Kingdom)*
- The deaths of the mercs and hunters in the long grass via velociraptors in the second movie
- Owen riding a motorbike with velociraptors through the jungle (*Jurassic World*)
- The computer code reflected on the velociraptor as it figures where the humans have gone (first movie)

- Sarah on the glass with it cracking underneath her fingertips (*The Lost World*)
- The satellite phone and the Spinosaurus (alluding to the crocodile and the ticking clock in *Peter Pan*)
- Ian Malcolm and Claire Dearing running with flares and the T Rex (first movie and *Jurassic World*)
- The satellite phone sliding from one side of the boat to the other as they almost drown thanks to the Spinosaurus again (third movie)
- The T Rex as villain AND hero throughout the franchise, with Blue the velociraptor bringing up the rear in *Jurassic World*
- The demise of Indominus Rex courtesy of the T-Rex, Blue the velociraptor and the Mosasaurus (*Jurassic World*)

Whether you like or despise the *Jurassic* movies, it's indisputable the franchise is visual A.F! Can you think of a way of making YOUR film or TV thriller as visual, just on a lower budget? Bet you can – so let's work out what 'makes' a set piece.

WHAT IS A SET PIECE?

First things first, what IS a set piece? Here's a dictionary definition:

Set Piece, noun: 1) A scene, action, or the like, having a conventional form and functioning as part of the structure of a work of art, literature, etc.
2) In a novel, narrative poem, or the like: a passage more or less extraneous to the sequence of events, introduced to supply background, color, or the like.

Note how the definition does not say that set pieces 'have' to be BIG BUDGET. In fact, even the lowest budget screenplay can benefit from set pieces because as we also know, low-budget scripts can still be high concept.

So when it comes to writing our own thriller screenplay, a set piece is a scene and/or series of scenes that:

1) **Has a beginning, middle and end.** Hence the 'extraneous to the sequence of events' part of the definition. Whilst set pieces need to form a part of the plot somehow, the average set piece must also have its own internal logic. Whilst definitely not my favourite in the *Jurassic* franchise, consider the fantastic dino-jeep-motorbike chase in *Jurassic World Dominion* here: story-wise, the characters 'just' have to get to the plane. That could have been just a single moment, but because the franchise is known for chases the filmmakers make the characters really go through an ordeal to do it. The set piece is all about HOW they do that.

2) **Can stand alone.** You don't need to have watched the entire movie to understand the point of the scene, 'cos of point 1 in this list – which is why we see so many set pieces in movie trailers or pictures of them online – and sure enough, if you Google 'Jurassic World Dominion' you will see a lot of video, images and gifs of Chris Pratt on his motorbike racing dinos in the Malta streets!

3) **Has a specific purpose in pushing the overarching story forward somehow** (ie. taking us from one Act to another; or perhaps altering the dramatic context, such as 'flight to fight', or The Showdown in the resolution). In *Jurassic World Dominion*, the dino chase marks the moment Claire and Owen decide to take matters into their own hands and rescue their adopted daughter Maisie from evil shadowy corporation BioSyn.

4) **Frequently reveals character, especially the protagonist versus the antagonist or other threat.** (ie. 'brave and ingenious goody versus deranged and vicious baddie' is a big favourite in the action genre and again, this is obvious in *Jurassic World Dominion*. The dinosaurs are a pre-established threat, plus Owen is already an action hero. However Claire started the franchise as a corporate bot herself. Here she is not only an activist (as she was in *Fallen Kingdom*), she is now a mother too – a 'warrior mom' if you like. It is no accident we are more worried about her making it

to the plane than Owen; she has had farther to go in terms of arc.

5) **Reflects the tone and genre of the piece** (ie. serious and plausible peril; high octane; fantasy action; comedic elements and so on). We can see all of these at work in the 'chasing dinos' sequence of *Jurassic World Dominion* – the chasing dinos are fantasy corporate weapons, plus the motorbike going up and down stairs in particular has a lot in common with other high-octane franchises like *Fast & Furious* or the Daniel Craig *James Bond* movies. In addition, Owen driving the bike straight into the plane as it prepares for take-off, only for the first dinosaur to make it in AS WELL is nail-biting stuff. Owen jumps off the bike into Claire's arms, which swiftly takes a comedic turn: as the lurching plane leaves the tarmac, gravity sweeps the bike AND the dinosaur out of the plane!

So, set pieces can really elevate your spec big-budget sample screenplay. Just be aware of what has come before and how the most popular franchises do theirs, especially as you don't want to rehash iconic moments. When the competition is high just to get noticed, it is worth doing your research. So stream your favourite action and adventure thrillers and make notes!

WRITING A SET PIECE IN YOUR THRILLER SCREENPLAY

> *'I think thrillers represent a lean, tight writing style… A paucity of words increases the impact of those left on the page. Momentum is key… Even more so than your "average" screenplay, thrillers need to attest to the first page advice of David Koepp's "Panic Room" script: "This film is short. This film is fast."'*
>
> **– Ste Russell, agent at Collective Talent**

Some writers want to write set pieces because blockbuster movies are what got them fired up about films and screenwriting in the first place. Yet these writers will often get themselves tied up in knots. They may overwrite their set pieces, accounting for every moment in minute detail; or they may leave everything to the imagination too much, so theirs is barely 'there' on the page. So here's 5 important questions to ask yourself, next time you're attempting to write a set piece:

1) **WHO is involved?**

Keyword: *IDENTIFY. Knowing which characters are involved and why, plus how this relates to the overall story, will help you construct your set piece.*

Set pieces usually revolve around the protagonist but are frequently instigated by the antagonist. As described in the *Jurassic World Dominion* chasing dinos set piece, Owen and Claire have discovered where Maisie is being held and they need to get to her. That would be a bad enough problem by itself, but then the trained dinosaurs are set on them by the BioSyn bounty hunter. Eek!

2) **WHAT do we need to understand?**

Keyword: *EXPOSITION. Here a set piece may underline how the story world works (especially in dystopian, sci-fi or fantasy futureworlds), but also may introduce a character, or a concept that proves important in the story LATER.*

There needs to be a clear goal in a set piece. Owen and Claire have tracked Maisie to Malta, but just miss her. They need to get to BioSyn, which is back in America. This means they need a plane. We've already been introduced to Kayla, who saw Maisie handed over by the bounty hunters. This is where their paths cross over and Kayla decides to help Owen and Claire get their daughter back.

3) **WHEN will it be?**

Keyword: *TIMING. Is there a ticking clock? Plus space out your set pieces.*

Set pieces should be exciting; they should add to the tension and 'rising action' of the piece. Some kind of ticking clock element usually achieves this... ie. Owen must get to the plane before it takes off without him, otherwise he will get eaten by dinosaurs! It's also possible to have too much of a good thing. You need to space set pieces out evenly or risk your story seeming lumpy and uneven. Equally, don't make us wait too long between them, either. Look at each set piece you want to write in isolation and figure out when it will be in the story, to figure out if you need it (or not). Now I don't think *Jurassic World Dominion* did a great job of any of these things, but *Jurassic World* (2015) is as close to the original as you can get for the number of set pieces and how well they play out; I'd venture *Jurassic Park* (1993) is the gold standard for set pieces. Watch both of them in close succession and see for yourself.

4) **WHERE will it be in relation to the REST?**

Keyword: *STRUCTURE. Each one, bigger than the last.*

Great thrillers contain 'rising action', so each set piece is BIGGER than the last. There's no point having the biggest fight, explosion or monster anywhere but the end. This is why the Jurassic movies always include ALL involved characters in the resolution (who are still alive!): protagonist, antagonist and important remaining secondaries.

5) **WHY am I using it?**

Keywords: *GENRE & TONE. Whatever you choose here, you need to be consistent.*

Writing something that will 'look cool' *may* cut it if you're commissioned, but this rarely works for spec screenplays... because they've NOT been made yet! So think about why you're using your set piece: perhaps it is to signpost something that happens later (as with *Jurassic Park:* the T-Rex is both the villain AND the hero in that first movie, chasing and saving our human characters. This means that when she crashes into the visitors' centre in the resolution and saves Alan, Ellie and the children from the velociraptors it is NOT a *deus ex machina* as some commentators insist).

Or perhaps the set piece will create a reversal or twist (as with *Jurassic World* when the velociraptors turn on the humans in favour of Indominus Rex 'The raptors have got a new Alpha!')? Or maybe it's a fun moment to reveal character as with Ian Malcolm attempting to be a hero by luring the T-Rex away from the children with the flare in the first movie and making such a hash of it he almost gets himself killed; or Claire's 'We need more teeth' and doing similar, only doing a MUCH better job whilst running in heels!

Incidentally, both these fan favourite moments feed into the hero/villain arc for the T-Rex: throughout all six movies she is both a threat and a saviour. This is why we cheer when she takes on bigger dinosaurs such as the Indominus Rex or the Gigantosaurus and worry when it looks as if she might die, defeated… only to cheer again when she wins. This is one of the reasons *Jurassic Park III* is so hated by T-Rex fans: she loses and is killed by the Spinosaurus, considered a huge misstep in the franchise.

LOW-BUDGET SET PIECES

Again, most spec screenwriters who want to make their scripts themselves, or get them optioned for production do not have the kind of budget the big franchises do. That said, it's still possible to write set pieces that won't break the bank and get your writing noticed (especially considering most screenwriters won't write set pieces in their thrillers at all). There's lots of ways to create BIG ideas on a low budget, without an explosion or dinosaur in sight.

Yet we can still look to those big-budget set pieces to help inspire our own smaller or low-budget versions. I watched about 25 action thrillers back-to-back for research purposes for this book and discovered the following scenarios were frequently featured in set pieces:

i) Chase Sequences

This should come as a surprise to no one, especially as I broke down the chasing dinosaurs set piece from *Jurassic World Dominion* in this book too! Now, *Fast & Furious* style drag racing is most likely out of bounds for the low-budget filmmaker; it's also likely *Mad Max: Fury*

Road motorbike stunts and smashing lorries are too. But chases on foot – especially in deserted places like warehouses or woodland – could be a low-budget alternative. (Just be aware even just chasing people up and down stairs is a health and safety consideration, not only for the actors but the camera operator).

ii) Breaking INTO or OUT OF Somewhere

Bank or museum heists or prison escapes come to mind here, plus we have seen lots of these set pieces in action in blockbusters: the *Mission Impossible* (1996–2023) and *Ocean's Eleven* through to *Ocean's 8* (2001–2018) are the most obvious series, as is the *Escape Plan* franchise (2013–2019). Yet you could have your characters break into/break out of absolutely anywhere that is more budget-friendly. What if your protagonist's loved one is locked in an unknown room by an antagonist and your character has to figure where they are before they can rescue them? What if your character is held prisoner by an abusive spouse and has to figure out how to escape their home?

iii) Escape to Safety

Disaster thrillers frequently have characters needing to make a literal leap of faith into mid-air in order to escape certain death behind them. Virtually any Dwayne 'The Rock' Johnson action thriller will have him have to make that leap, just like all the action men that preceded him such as Bruce Willis, Arnie and Stallone. In the *Transformers* franchise (2007–2017), nearly all the characters are in peril from collapsing buildings at some point and must leap to safety. Sometimes characters will need to make that leap in a vehicle, such as the characters trapped in the bus in *Speed* (1994) when part of the intersection is missing but they can't slow down. When characters are not leaping, they're running such as the 'escape from sunlight' set piece Riddick and friends have to make on the burning planet Crematoria in *The Chronicles of Riddick* (2004). Sometimes they will escape to safety by melting into crowds or parades like in *The Fugitive* (1993), though we don't tend to see this as often nowadays as it's considered a cliché, though sometimes we can see subverted versions such as the Skrull's escape on the subway in *Captain Marvel*, 2019). When characters are not leaping, running or camouflaging, they're trying to outrun disasters and alien invasions via plane (*Independence Day*, 1996); or motorbike (*Deep Impact*, 1998). Other times they must crash headlong into the atmosphere and risk burning up to get to safety (every disaster movie set in space ever, but especially *Gravity*, 2013). Sometimes their vehicle to safety becomes a trap, like the gyroscope in *Jurassic World: Fallen Kingdom* when it falls off the cliff into the ocean and starts filling with water. Obviously all of these set pieces mentioned are SUPER expensive (and frequently require set builds or CGI), but low-budget filmmakers can still learn from them and do their own versions on a smaller scale. The key is understanding characters need to get from to A to B – how do they do that while keeping costs down AND making it as tense as possible for the audience?

iv) Hostage Situations, Sieges, Barricades & Attacks

I'm always surprised by how few sieges and hostage situations I see in the spec pile. Classic thrillers like John Carpenter's *Assault on Precinct 13* (1976, remade 2005) as well as modern movies like *The Taking of Pelham 123* (2009) and *Copshop* (2021) show us they can be fertile ground for thrillers. They're also great for the low-budget filmmaker because they have a great excuse for the action being contained! Of course the hostage situation or siege is not the set piece usually, but when those on the outside try and breach the perimeter. These may be the 'good guys' trying to rescue those trapped against their will, or it might be bad guys or monsters trying to get in past blockades meant to protect. In the British creature thriller *Dog Soldiers* (2002), the characters have barricaded themselves in a remote farmhouse because werewolves are trying to kill them. There's a brilliant moment in which Private Spoon (Darren Morfitt) is caught in a hallway between two doorways with werewolves on the other side of each of them: he must ensure one stays closed and slide across the floor to kick that one closed too, otherwise the monsters will get in. What if your character was trying to keep someone – or something! – out like this in YOUR low-budget set piece?

v) Attacks & Battles

Marvel is probably the gold standard for the finale battle: the devastating loss of half the cinematic universe at the end of *Avengers Infinity War* (2018) is followed by the inevitable return of our lost heroes in *Avengers Endgame (2019)* which had even the usually reserved British whooping and cheering in the cinema! Attacks and battles like these are usually the home of fight choreography and explosions, so usually the picture most people have in mind when they hear the phrase 'set piece'. The cheesy favourite has to be the hero walking away in slo-mo, not even flinching as something blows up behind him (this might have been a staple of action movies in the eighties to the mid noughties, but you don't see it so often now). Explosions cost a packet and are rarely used in low-budget movies; plus even short fights can be prohibitively expensive because they usually need to be under the supervision of a stunt co-ordinator and take a VERY long time to film. That said, low-budget martial arts thrillers exist, plus there are ways to make things explode on a low budget. I have provided coverage for produced movies that have done all these things at budgets of a million dollars or less. If you really want to include explosions and battles in your low-budget film, it's a question of understanding what's possible for what money… and whether the reality will live up to the picture in your head. If it can't, you may want to find another big finale.

And now for the showdown in your thriller screenplay, possibly the most undersold element of many spec thrillers, yet the most important in terms of dramatic satisfaction if you want your reader to come away with a positive view of your writing and to recommend you 'up the chain' to a producer, director, initiative, contest or agent.

THE SHOWDOWN

So you've put your protagonist through his or her paces, pitting them against the antagonist every step of the way. You've made him/her change from wanting to simply run away to wanting to directly engage with the antagonist. Now you're ready to write – or rewrite – your resolution, which, in the case of thrillers, I call 'The Showdown'. Why? Because this is where the main pinnacle of the action should be. The showdown is most often played out in hand-to-hand combat or other confrontations (such as those between humans and spirits) or, least often, a moment in which a character must make a devastating decision or choice, as in the previously mentioned *Se7en* or *The Mist* (2007). Let's remind ourselves what the resolution generally signifies in the thriller genre:

> **ACT THREE - RESOLUTION:** *Looks like all is lost for the protagonist... It looks like the antagonist is going to win... And then the protagonist turns it around *in some way* and solves the problem (or not, as the case may be).*

The key element of the resolution in thrillers is that notion of all seemingly being beyond the protagonist's grasp, even though s/he has decided to fight now. It is 'the darkest hour before dawn', the last and highest wall to climb. In comparison, then, spec thriller screenplays frequently undersell the resolution, whooshing through proceedings, so it all feels rushed and even tied up in a neat bow. Other times, spec thrillers will stagger towards the resolution in fits and starts, so the story goes out with a whimper, rather than a bang, which is generally dramatically unsatisfying. Most often, however, the resolution feels 'back ended': in other words, writers will pay off huge chunks of exposition here, much like *Scooby Doo* cartoons: 'You did this... because of this... so this happened.' *All that's missing is, 'And I'd have got away with it if it wasn't for you pesky kids!'*

So rather than dropping any of those clangers in the resolution of your own thriller screenplay, I'd recommend considering the following:

- **Use action if action is expected...** If your thriller screenplay contains action throughout – be it martial arts or other hand-to-hand combat, explosions or gun fights – make sure you write the biggest AND most difficult fight in the resolution, else the reader (as the audience's representative) will feel cheated. Do not have all the big fights up at the beginning; if your story is the type that uses brute force, then don't keep the fights all at the same level either. Remember that notion of walls, 'each bigger than the last': if your protagonist is going to literally fight his/her way through the situation, make each fight bigger and better than the previous one until we reach the showdown, which should be the very pinnacle of the action.
- **...But be truthful and honest.** A lot of female protagonists are let down by their writers in both spec thriller screenplays and produced content in that they use their wits and guile for three quarters of the screenplay, only to turn to brute force in the resolution, as if this is the only way to escalate the story and for a female character to really 'win'. Yet women generally use violence when there is no other option and most frequently for self-defence, preferring shock/ambush tactics to enable escape, rather than prolonged hand-to-hand combat as, generally speaking, men are stronger than women. That said, we have seen great fight scenes involving women in the thriller genre: Mallory (Gina Carano) in *Haywire* (2011) is a great example, though it is important to remember she is a spy with specialist training and kills Paul because she has been burned by Kenneth (Ewan Macgregor). In other words, she only resorts to violence when she has to. But sometimes characters 'suddenly' have an ability for violence we feel a little incredulous over, regardless of gender: for example, in *Death Sentence* (2007), Nick Hume (Kevin Bacon) is billed as a 'mild-mannered executive', yet, upon forcing the court to drop the case over his son's murder and donning a leather jacket, Nick is miraculously able to dish out extraordinary amounts of violence to people who would have been far more used to street justice than he. If we compare Hume to Clyde Shelton (Gerard Butler) in a similar revenge thriller, *Law Abiding Citizen* (2009), Shelton is

presented as capable of horrendous violence from the offset, after seeing his wife and daughter murdered before his eyes ten years' previously. That gap time-wise enables us not only to believe his mindset has gone dangerously awry, but that he has also been training. So think of how your character would use violence. Do not blindly stick a fight in there because it would look cool or seems a logical conclusion. You need to be truthful and honest about your characters' abilities (including how they might grow), instead of magically pulling combat skills seemingly out of nowhere.

- **Resolution means confrontation.** I call it The Showdown for a reason. In a thriller, your resolution quite literally needs a confrontation in order to resolve. How that confrontation is represented depends on the story and subgenre of the thriller, and frequently means a literal fight of some kind, though sometimes a difficult choice (which, more often than not, the protagonist must refuse or 'lose'). The two exceptions are usually the supernatural thriller and psychological thriller. In the supernatural thriller your protagonist may also be offered a choice but, just as often, some kind of realisation, which is frequently represented via the twist ending, *The Sixth Sense* (1999) and *The Others* (2001) being the most famous (and most imitated in the spec supernatural thrillers I read). In psychological thrillers, protagonists must also come to a realisation, most frequently about the identity of the antagonist, as in *Fight Club* (1999) and countless other thrillers about identity and so-called split personalities. Occasionally, a detective character must realise they are on a wild-goose chase, as Leonard Shelby (Guy Pearce) does at the end of *Memento* (2000), thus joining up with the shock hook of Teddy's shooting at the beginning of the movie. Whatever you decide to do, in the absence of an actual fight, there must be something meaty to reward the reader (and thus the audience) for sitting through your whole screenplay!

SUMMING UP...

- During Act Two, your protagonist goes from 'flight' to 'fight'.
- S/he will stop trying to run away (literally or metaphorically) and engages directly with the antagonist for the first time.
- Remember thrillers need to be visual, even when they're contained – like in the interrogation room. Avoid letting your thriller turn into chains of dialogue instead.
- Tension must grow as the plot leads towards that big finale – we need to doubt the protagonist is going to make it.
- Learn from set pieces in blockbusters – can you create some at a low budget? If you can, your screenplay will be in demand.
- This in turn takes us towards the moment where all seems lost for the protagonist before we enter the resolution.
- Ensure your protagonist and antagonist 'swap places' – where once the antagonist was cocky, sure s/he would win, now the protagonist is the victor.
- In cases where the antagonist ultimately wins, make us believe the protagonist will win until the very last second.
- Ensure the biggest and best fights and/or most dramatic choices/ demands on your protagonist are in this section.
- Put simply: *save the best 'til last.*

So congratulations! You've written your spec thriller screenplay. Now it's time to get your script out there for feedback, in readiness for selling it 'off the page' to agents, producers and filmmakers via your pitch material. But, what's more, you need to sell yourself...

PART THREE

SELLING YOUR THRILLER SCREENPLAY

'Dreams do not come true just because you dream them. It's hard work that makes things happen. It's hard work that creates change.'

– Shonda Rhimes

FEEDBACK & THINGS TO CONSIDER

A PEP TALK

Generally speaking, nowadays writers know they need feedback before they send their screenplays to agents, producers and filmmakers. Gone are the days of obvious first drafts in the spec pile as standard. As mentioned previously, screenplays generally look like actual screenplays, too: I have seen a massive decrease in scripts written in the wrong font and laid out in the wrong way. Equally, gone are the days of a writer jealously guarding his/her loglines, sure someone is out to rip them off. The average spec writer knows ideas alone cannot be copyrighted and that this is actually a good thing, else we would soon run out of things we could actually write about!

Interestingly, however, a new problem has surfaced: writers seem to have forgotten they are the authority on their own work, especially when it is speculative. This means many writers feel frozen even by good or encouraging notes, or even by requests from industry professionals to read their work! In other words, the pendulum has swung too far the other way: writers may no longer be egocentric nightmares, accusing script readers and producers and agents of trying to stifle them, but now they are typically nervous wrecks, seeking approval and freaking out about the slightest thing. Again, the end result is the same because they don't advance – and end up tinkering, redrafting and reworking, never finishing their work or signing off on it, as stated in the chapter in section one about outlines.

So before you think about getting feedback on your thriller screenplay, think on these points:

- You are the writer.
- You know what is best for the work.
- You know what you first conceived (hopefully via that great premise and killer logline).
- You know what the intention is: what the story is 'supposed' to do.

Keeping these four elements in mind when approaching notes and feedback is not optional; it is absolutely essential. Not to inflate your ego, but because, at foundation level, you must stay true to your intentions (whatever that means), otherwise you will find yourself pulled in every direction. That is not to say you can't take the screenplay in a new direction if someone gives you some gold feedback that excites you; sometimes two heads ARE better than one. But don't change things for the sake of it and don't fold to someone else's vision of your thriller screenplay. It is a spec script. It is yours. No one else's... But – and there's always a but!! –

...Remember what I said back in the chapter on outlines? Have the guts to finish and 'sign off' on drafts, too. You cannot be endlessly tinkering with the same drafts, year on year. You need to move on and prove your worth as a writer. As Lee Jessup writes in her excellent blog, 'Time is NOT on your side':

> *'You have to be developing ideas, developing new work, all the time. Not developing content at all times, in whichever format, is just not acceptable. Do not take your time. Do not sit on your laurels and wait to see what comes from the last screenplay you've put out. Quality is balanced by quantity in this game. So it doesn't matter if you did it once. Or, worse, if you did it once in 2009. The industry wants to see you producing content ALL THE TIME. A writer's job is to write.'*

Jessup is bang on the money. If you do not keep writing and developing new material, new writers will not only catch up, they will overtake you. So if you want to even so much as HAVE a career in screenwriting (never mind advance in it), you need to realise you have to let go of old work and literally write new stuff. That's just the way it is. So if you want to create your career and advance, you must:

- Come up with loglines for new ideas every single month (and get feedback on them – tweet them; email friends and contacts; see what sticks)
- Develop one-page pitches for the loglines that pique people's interest
- Write outlines for those one-page pitches
- Get feedback on those outlines and work out plot flaws and character problems
- Write a draft of a new project every 3–6 months

It may seem insurmountable, but it can be done. It all comes down to this: the writers I have seen advance, whatever that means, such as a contest win, gaining representation (and keeping it) or getting their work produced, do the above. If you want to join the ranks of the professional writer – or get back to it after a period away – then you need to do the same. Don't let the grass grow under your feet or allow your existing specs to distract you. New, polished material is ALWAYS the way forward. But how to get that all-important feedback?

GETTING FEEDBACK

Writers can get feedback from a variety of sources, but most obviously from peer review via social media, particularly Twitter and Facebook; and/or writers' groups (both online and in real life). Ideally, getting feedback via peer review means you should be able to avoid the customary traps. However, there are still the same mistakes and issues in the spec pile in terms of story, as outlined in previous chapters, especially when it comes to the first ten pages and cliché, but also the 'usual' characters and concepts, as well as structure. It is for this reason I feel peer review can only get a writer so far. Whilst I always suggest writers share their work, I think it's a good idea if a writer also shows their work to someone involved in the industry. A good shortcut is to employ a paid-for script reader, whose job it is to assess problems in scripts (and who should verbalise problematic areas and give suggestions on how to combat them, without taking over and insisting the writer rewrites to his/her vision).

Before approaching a paid-for reader, I would recommend finding out from your peers who have paid for coverage before, where they got it, and whether they thought it was worth the money; if they're willing to show you their notes or report, then even better. Alternatively, check out the reader's online presence via their Twitter and LinkedIn accounts, Facebook page or blog/website: do you agree with their worldview/persona? Do you think s/he seems to know what s/he's talking about? A good reader should be able to give a list of the people and places they have read for before, as well as testimonials and sample coverage on request.

However, some writers cannot afford a paid-for reader or else they believe one should not have to pay for feedback. In these situations it is helpful if you can find someone with more experience than yourself in writing and/or reading scripts. Several Bang2writers have reported good results with read throughs with actors. Sometimes competitions or initiatives will offer these as prizes to writers, but it's not difficult to organise one yourself if you put some thought into it and make sure you do not take advantage of people. In return for food and drink (and usually only for a short period of time, i.e. two hours), professional actors may be persuaded to read your screenplay or an extract of it aloud, then give feedback on what they think is working and not working, in terms of plot and character. Screenwriters frequently forget how valuable actors' input can be, which seems crazy when they are such an important part of the filmmaking process. Some are even writers themselves, giving them a unique ability to see both sides. It's worth remembering actors spend a lot of time with screenplays and have very strong opinions about what makes a good story and good characters. Actors are not merely meat puppets for screenwriters and filmmakers to control!

Another way of getting feedback is by finding yourself a mentor, who is probably a professional writer already rather than someone on the same level as you, who perhaps lacks the experience to verbalise the issues s/he sees in your work. Finding someone with the time and inclination to mentor your writing is difficult and frequently happens in an organic way – no two people's 'discovery' is the same – so it's hard to offer tips on how to find one. What I would suggest is being as open as possible and trying to meet people, online and in 'real life', whenever you can. Don't forget you will have skills other people need; if you have an opportunity to help someone, always try to. Many bloggers and tweeters have made useful contacts by helping professional writers promote or research, for example. The more people you meet and offer to help, the more likely you are to come across that mentor you seek.

USING FEEDBACK EFFECTIVELY

Whilst most writers know they should get feedback (by whatever means), few appear to know what to do, even with good notes. This is because utilising feedback in order to make one's drafts better is a skill in itself. Typically, one of two things might happen when I send notes to a writer who does not know how to use feedback effectively:

- **The writer loves the notes and rewrites immediately**. This becomes an issue when the writer does not give him/herself time to digest and work through the notes in his/her own mind. Often this writer will attempt to chuck in every single note I give, rather than use them as a springboard for his/her own ideas. As a result, the draft may become turgid or feel convoluted.
- **The writer despairs and grinds to a halt**. Often this will not be because of the notes themselves, but because the writer feels there's too much choice of where to go in the story, which makes the writer feel intimidated. The writer may feel s/he is going

around in circles, as I have made reference to issues s/he feels cannot be overcome in the draft, often because s/he's swung from one end of the spectrum to the other (i.e. with scene description – from 'too much black on the page' to too little).

Wherever you get your feedback, I would recommend considering the following in utilising it (or not, as the case may be):

- **Who is giving it?** Generally, the more experienced the person giving the feedback (in whatever field of the industry), the better the feedback will be. That said, just because someone is starting out doesn't mean their feedback is invalid. There are some very talented young writers, readers and agents' assistants who give excellent and insightful notes; it is a question of finding them and sticking with them. Conversely, not everyone is good at giving feedback (no matter how experienced as a writer they are). We all like to think we are completely objective when reviewing others' work, but this cannot be the case; we are not robots, but human beings with our own experiences, prejudices, ideals, etc. As a result, this may mean someone who is giving you feedback may not like your central concept for reasons best known to themselves. It does not pay to second guess why, as you will never please them. Other times, a reader may like your central concept SO MUCH they want to impose their own vision of how they would prefer it plays out. Try and recognise if a feedback-giver has their own agenda and, if they do, disregard or temper their feedback in your thoughts.
- **What do I lose?** We hear the phrase 'kill your darlings' a lot, but rarely what this truly means. Many of my Bang2writers over the years have ended up throwing the baby out with the bathwater on their drafts, because they think they need to get rid of everything and start again. Recognise there are bits of your work that are good. A feedback-giver should tell you which bits work for them: stick with those good bits, if they work for you too. Don't get rid for getting rid's sake. Very often, rewriting is about trimming fat and shaping your story, rather than chopping it to little pieces and grinding it all up again.

- **What do I gain?** Sometimes, getting rid of one thing means you have room for something far better and the transaction is a no-brainer. Other times, you must weigh up carefully what you gain if you chuck something else out in its favour. Give these potential substitutions the attention they deserve.
- **How do I use it?** A feedback-giver may be committed to helping you, but they cannot be as passionate or involved in your actual story as you are. As a result, any suggestion a feedback-giver makes might be good, but yours will be better. Using notes as a springboard for your own ideas is the ideal, rather than blindly following whatever the feedback-giver offers. That's not to say you can't choose to take what they give, but give it proper consideration – and, again, this takes time. Always give notes time to settle in your brain before rewriting.
- **Why should I use it?** You don't have to use all, or even any, of the notes you're given. Really! If it's a spec, it's your baby. You are the authority on your own work and you must write it as you see fit. If your screenplay is optioned or an agent gives you notes, then of course you should utilise some of the notes you're given – but you STILL don't have to use all of them. Industry people do not want to work with people who nod dumbly and try and incorporate everything that is said to them in script meetings! Industry people want to work with real, live writers with their own opinions and ideas of making a story work.

These five questions put a 'barrier' in place to ensure you are the authority on your own work, preventing what I call 'feedback fatigue'. It is very easy to get trapped in a vicious circle of rewriting; getting feedback; finding more issues; rewriting; finding more issues... And so it goes on. Equally, on the other end of the scale, those five questions keep one's own ego in check, too!

THE NEXT BIG THING

Knowing people in the industry – whether script readers/editors, actors, mentors or all three – has another useful side effect: getting the jump on 'The Next Big Thing'. It's important to note I am not advocating writing solely for the marketplace here: you can still write about the things and issues that concern you, just within perimeters that others want, too. It is another way of thinking, 'Why this story?', as outlined in Chapter One.

Like anything, scriptwriting follows fashion, and knowing what people want before they want it means you will not waste your time on a project that feels stale and past its prime when you come to send it out. Savvy writers ask industry people what they think will be popular in the years ahead. If certain genres, themes and elements keep making an appearance from these industry people, then there is a very strong chance scripts within those genres and carrying those themes and elements will be in demand soon (probably the next year or two).

The great news is that it's never been easier to ask industry people what they think will be The Next Big Thing. You can ask them directly at events such as film festivals, literary events or networking evenings; you can scour blogs, social media (particularly Twitter) and sites like InkTip, IMDB, Screen Daily and Done Deal. There is a plethora of information at your fingertips to ensure you can create the script that everyone will be looking for. In breaking down script leads and information, think about the following:

- **Who has bought/is making what?** I'm always staggered by how little people purporting to be screenwriters know about their own industry. Knowing the big sales of the moment is an absolute must, as is knowing which production companies are making what. What's more, it's not enough to know X Company is making a 'thriller': what TYPE of thriller is it? Who is in it? Who is distributing it? Knowing this information will help you make your own sales. You cannot know too much; you can only gain from such knowledge.

- **What are the concerns of our time?** Film Studies students believe it's possible to deconstruct the concerns of various decades and even individual years by the themes that appear in produced movies. It is, in part, true: producers and agents do actively look for scripts about the issues people are most concerned about in the here and now. For example, whilst 'End of the World' thrillers are always popular, they can peak in certain times – and often for a good reason. Consider the turn of the noughties. We were worried about the turn of the Millennium (remember the so-called 'Millennium Bug'?). In addition, the true impact of climate change was first being realised. Is it any wonder then we saw films like *Armageddon*, *Deep Impact*, *The Core* and *The Day After Tomorrow* around that time? In the same period, on a smaller scale, we saw many thrillers about the 'end of the world' on religious or personal scales, like *End of Days*, *Stigmata* or *28 Days Later*. Consider what the concerns of our times are NOW and tap into them: you may find your script gets loads of attention.
- **What elements are in demand?** Take a look at the thrillers you're seeing being made/coming out... What is missing? Back in late 2009, I looked at produced content and saw there were hardly any spec screenplays or produced content around with female protagonists, in ANY genre. On that basis, then, I started blogging in earnest about the lack of female protagonists I was seeing, prophesying that this element would be The Next Big Thing. Fast forward a decade and, suddenly, that's what everyone was asking for/talking about! So take a good look, see what's missing and make your prediction... Whatever that element is, there's a strong chance that is what people will want next.

It's never too late to rewrite. If you think you can realign your thriller screenplay to suit any of the three things above, do it. Don't be a martyr to the script you first conceived, sticking with it the way it's been from the beginning just 'because'. Agents and producers want work that feels fresh and relevant, from writers who know what they're doing. Too many writers are too self-focused rather than industry-focused, which means they try and get the industry to fit their story, rather than the other way round.

'PRE-SOLD' AND GENRE BUSTING

> *'Bemoaning sameiness misses point. As with sonnets/pop songs structural originality ain't the point. The magic is in the detail.'*
>
> **– Jared Kelly, screenwriter** (@twatterer)

So, as we know, it is not the execution that counts; it's the concepts that sell. What's more, human beings prize novelty and originality, but, at the same time, agents, producers and filmmakers are risk-averse, hence the hallowed notion of *'the same... but different'*. This can seem an impossible dichotomy to many writers, who frequently complain their highly original ideas are a hard sell in an industry that seemingly only wants safe options. Then other writers will claim that many big genre movies – particularly those that come out of Hollywood – are derivative anyway, expressing disbelief that their own idea (which is derivative) is not selling. What the hell is this industry's problem?!

The uncomfortable truth is that execs, agents and filmmakers know a good idea when they hear it. It's said that a great pitch makes its mark within 30 seconds. This has always been my experience, plus I've lost count of the number of pitching sessions I've witnessed where a writer sits down in front of a largely uninterested pitchee, only to grab them within one sentence. So it IS possible. But how to do this? Picking the 'right' idea should not be blind luck. Like everything in this industry – including the movies themselves – it should be a highly constructed thing. It's all very well bandying about the phrase 'the same... but different', but we need to know exactly what this means. So let's break it down:

> *It needs to be 'samey' enough that it's recognisable to an audience... but it needs to be 'different' enough to interest them – we DON'T want stories that have already been told.*

I think a much more useful notion than 'the same... but different' is the idea of 'pre-sold'. If we look this up in the dictionary, we find the definition:

> *'To condition (a potential customer) in advance for later purchase of a product.'*

Now consider stories, characters or even just ideas as products that your potential audience may be familiar with. Here's two that crop up in the spec pile a lot: vampires and time travel. Unless you've been living under a rock in outer space for the last 30 years, everyone knows what these two elements are: there have been countless representations of vampires and time travel in fiction, thus they are pre-sold to the public... and thus present an opportunity for filmmakers to have something that is 'the same' but to do something 'different' with them.

But that's where many writers come unstuck. Whilst there are countless spec thriller scripts in the pile about vampires and time travel, very few are different ENOUGH to attract an agent, exec or filmmaker's attention. We're hearing the same types of pitches involving vampires or time travel, day in, day out, such as the notion of vampirism as a metaphor for AIDS, cancer or drug addiction; or the rag-tag group of time-travelling friends who are up against some evil empire in the style of *Star Wars*, *Firefly* or *Dr Who*. But those stories have been told; we want something fresh and new, something so seemingly obvious about vampires or time travel that we go, *'Why hasn't someone pitched me this before?'* In other words, we want something that busts the genre wide open.

'Genre busting' is another term that gets chucked about at pitching events and script meetings, but again it's something few writers seem to really grasp and run with to their own advantages. To bust a genre is to take something pre-sold and do something with it that we do not expect. A genuine genre-busting concept excites EVERYONE, from the person you're pitching it to, to the audience member who sees the poster and goes, *'Wow. I've never seen THAT before!'* A genre-busting thriller screenplay is nearly always destined to become hot property and, more often than not, becomes (if nothing else) a cult hit when it's produced, if not a box-office success, because it treats the movie-going public to something other than just the 'usual'.

Consider a genre-busting thriller movie such as Netflix's *The Old Guard* (2020). On IMDB its logline reads, *'A covert team* **of** *immortal* *mercenaries is suddenly exposed and must now fight to keep their identity a secret just as* **an** *unexpected new member is discovered.'* We've had many, many stories now about immortal protectors of humanity and it's not difficult to see why many people refer to *The Old Guard* as being similar to the *Highlander* franchise... That said, it's not *exactly* the same, it's PRE-SOLD. The notion of the undying hero who must fight to the death for the final honour ('There can be only one!') is instead a ensemble cast headed up by female lead hero-for-hire Charlize Theron, along with strong LGBTQ commentary and diversity. It worked, too: the notoriously secretive Netflix boasted freely about how a whopping seventy-eight million households watched *The Old Guard* in its first four weeks on the platform, greenlighting a sequel.

Of course, being pre-sold does not guarantee success. *Eternals* (2021) mined the same kind of material, in the same sort of way as *The Old Guard*. Despite making nearly half a million worldwide at the box office, it's considered one of the MCU's few misfires. The key reason is likely because of its sameyness; it didn't offer enough about it that was 'different' to *The Old Guard* and all that has come before it.

So if you're going to try a pre-sold property like immortal soldiers, vampires, dinosaurs, robots, ghosts, haunted houses, time travel – be sure you know what you are doing by studying what has come before in minute detail.

SAMEY STORIES

Knowing people in the industry, plus checking out what's 'the same... but different', as well as trying to predict The Next Big Thing, helps writers avoid samey stories. Every year, I see a single story (sometimes several) come to the fore when reading scripts or hearing pitches. This SAME story will be written or pitched by DIFFERENT writers. Sometimes it's obvious how this has occurred: an anniversary is approaching or a particular news story, hit movie or TV series has influenced a bunch of writers, all at the same time. Samey stories may come about when a load of writers are simply writing the 'usual' stories, with the 'usual' characters, thus wandering into cliché territory; other times, there's no particular reason at all (though this happens infrequently in my experience).

Writers are typically resistant to the notion of their screenplays being samey stories. When faced with the knowledge their script is the same as any number of others, many will insist it's all pot luck anyway, or that tired old argument, 'It's execution that counts'. Remember: it is not the execution that counts. Concept sells in the first instance, whether it's to agents and filmmakers, or to your potential audience. In terms of luck, the odds are already against writers in getting their spec screenplays noticed; a samey story lengthens those odds even more. Samey stories make it extraordinarily difficult for individual writers to stand out above the crowd, because their concepts are the same as everyone else's (so why should yours get picked?). Also, it may well be that your execution is something never seen before in that story, but, if the actual premise is the same as everyone else's, your script may never get off the blocks because you will falter in the pitch.

I have already mentioned how I often see quite broad samey thrillers (non-linear detective mystery – missing wife; gangster – one character wants to leave but Mr Big stops him; supernatural thriller – woman is accused of a mental breakdown), but I can be even MORE specific about other samey stories I have seen:

- **In 2006, I got a run of 'Witchfinder General' thriller spec screenplays.** All were historical and involved the graphic torture of women, plus a sadistic representation of Matthew Hopkins, who was a real person tasked with finding witches between 1644 and 1647 in England. In most of the screenplays, a real witch dispatched him, though in reality he probably died of tuberculosis (according to Wikipedia, anyway). There was no anniversary that year, but throughout the decades movies set in medieval times (with and without witchcraft) have been generally quite popular. Around the time I saw a lot of witch-burning scripts there was a lot of focus on movies like *The Village* (2004), *Kingdom of Heaven* (2005) and, of course, the Harry Potter franchise.

- **In 2009, the spec thrillers of the year involved vigilante murders.** Vigilantes have always been popular in thriller, but it was not difficult to see why there was a sudden peak of these in 2009: it was because of *Harry Brown*, starring UK favourite Michael Caine, who was enjoying somewhat of a comeback in the thriller genre, after roles in *Children of Men* (2006) and *The Dark Knight* (2008).
- **In 2011, spec thrillers were science-based and most frequently involved cloning, particularly of internal organs/flesh.** Why 2011 was the 'year of the clone' is up for interpretation. Dolly the Sheep is, of course, the world's most famous clone (and born in the UK), but was created in 1997 and died in 2003, years before cloning hit scribes' thriller sights. A Google search reveals that, in January 2010, Reuters reported that 'many expect organ cloning could be routine by 2020', so perhaps this was the inspiration? Or perhaps it was thinking about Ridley Scott's *Alien* 'prequel', announced in 2010, which eventually became *Prometheus* (2012)? I suspect the latter.

Yet it's very easy to avoid samey stories: create something genre-busting and, suddenly, any worries about it being too samey vanish, because it is different enough to grab someone's interests. Alternatively, if you feel it is not possible for you to 'bust' the genre, then knowing what stories are 'doing the rounds' means you can put yours on the back burner and concentrate on something else; you can then bring it out again when there is not a plethora of similar stories on the marketplace. It may seem counter-intuitive, but NOT ignoring samey stories actually empowers you and gives you a better chance of getting the attention you want. Now what? It's time to double-check...

IS YOUR SPEC THRILLER SCREENPLAY READY?

First impressions count in the industry. Your thriller screenplay will not get a second chance; it's rare that agents and producers consider redrafts. John Yorke, producer, show runner and author of bestselling screenwriting book *Into The Woods* boils down whether your screenplay is 'ready' to just four questions:

1) Can you read it to the end without stopping?
2) Can you sum it up in a sentence?
3) Does it make a noise?
4) Is it sufficiently original, but sitting inside a recognised genre (such as thriller)

But how do we apply the above points to our own work? Before firing your submission off into cyberspace or pitching it at an event, double-check whether it's ready by asking yourself the following:

- **What is my concept (aka premise, controlling idea, seed of the story)?** Know exactly what you're dealing with here – too many writers in meetings simply look like rabbits in the headlights when asked about their premise. Be able to do it justice with your logline and one-pager, but also conversationally. Give producers and development execs a good idea of the characters and how an audience could relate to them and the story via those all-important '3 Cs'.

- **Why this story?** It's simple – there are so many spec scripts out there, so why should people pick yours? What's 'the same... but different' about yours? Do you know if the elements making up that story are 'pre-sold'? If they are, what is fresh and new about your take?

- **Why these characters?** And your answer: these characters are recognisable, but they're still surprising; they're not the same as all the rest. They're not bland – and they're not off the scale either.

- **What is my opening image and where do my characters begin?** Get visual. Avoid those clichés. There really is no excuse.

- **Do my first ten pages work?** Remember, you need to state your story's intent and introduce your characters hand in hand; don't make the reader wait for the story to start as you go about setting everything up. Do it together.

- **Do I know what The Next Big Thing is?** If you do, are you willing to rewrite with this in mind? Are there bits of your story you feel you really can't lose, else it will become something else? It pays to know in advance.
- **Is it 'pre-sold'?** Does it bust the genre? Remember, we want 'the same… but different' – but emphasis on the different. We don't want stories that have already been told; we want something fresh and new. The best ideas grab us, because they seem so *obvious*.
- **Is it a samey story?** Knowing there are other scripts out there like yours means you may have the opportunity to change this in order to stand out; or perhaps you should pitch this script at another time? Whatever the case, knowing whether your script is something that is seen frequently in the spec pile means you are empowered.

So now you've considered what has gone into your thriller screenplay and your approach to the industry. You're ready now to get your FINISHED work out there to agents, producers and filmmakers… so now you need some great pitch material.

SUMMING UP…

- Remember you are the authority on your own work.
- Don't act as if time is on your side. It's not. You need to sign off on drafts and move forward if you want to create a screenwriting career and advance in it.
- Utilising feedback is a skill: think about what losses and gains you make.
- Learn to recognise feedback with an agenda attached; don't let others impose their own vision on your work.
- Using paid-for readers is a great shortcut to getting industry-based information, as long as you pick the right one. But there are lots of ways to get free feedback: just do your homework and don't take advantage of people.

- Actors' skills and experience are frequently underestimated by spec screenwriters.
- Avoid samey stories wherever possible and remember it's concept that sells in the first instance.

GETTING YOUR WORK 'OUT THERE', PART 1: **PITCH MATERIAL**

'No executive has ever said after hearing a pitch, "I wish they talked longer."'

– Stephanie Palmer, pitching coach & author of 'Good In A Room'

ARE YOU READY?

I spend a lot of time talking to writers, so I frequently hear the same writers talking about the same scripts in their portfolio. I've known writers to hawk round the same screenplays over and over, for years at a time. During this time some of those scribes will perhaps tweak various elements, but largely leave them alone; alternatively, others may rewrite them over and over again. Whatever the case, the end result is still the same: those writers form such an attachment to their scripts that they effectively sabotage any effort to really get them out there and market them properly. Even those who have their screenplays requested may insist on rewriting them before sending them, meaning the agent or producer's interest has waned, or even moved on, by the time that scribe's script hits their inbox.

Timing is really important, especially if someone wants to read your thriller screenplay. Though everything generally moves at a snail's pace in the industry, you can guarantee that when a producer, agent or filmmaker wants your script, they want it YESTERDAY. So don't lose out by not being ready. If you are going to take advantage of someone's interest in you and your thriller screenplay, I recommend having the following ready to go at the very least:

- The thriller screenplay you are pitching, plus its one-page pitch doc and short treatment (sometimes referred to as a pitch deck, series bible or sizzler.) Don't pitch work you are not willing to send straightaway.
- Another feature screenplay, plus its one-pager (preferably another thriller, but low-budget horror and comedy are also frequently in demand).
- A selection of other one-pagers for features (minimum of three).

The idea is simple: if someone turns down your script after requesting it, you have another ready to go. Ask if they are interested in the script or at least its one-page pitch. A one-page pitch is exactly as it sounds: a single page selling your story 'off the page'. This means it needs to be as interesting as possible; you don't want your thriller to degenerate into *'And then... and then... and then...'!*

With this in mind then, I always suggest one-pagers do the following as basic minimum:

- Logline at the top (both of them if it's a TV pilot)
- Set Up (aka Act 1) – protagonist, antagonist, what they must do for what's at stake
- Jump straight to Act 3 and how it ends (yes, ALWAYS include the ending)
- Summary at the bottom of any relevant info, ie. if it won any contests, got favourable feedback from industry pros etc
- Don't forget to include your contact info!

(You can download a free one-page pitch reference guide from the B2W main site as well – scroll down to the PDF gallery at www.bang2write.com/resources).

If the industry pro is not interested, or reads it and turns that one down too, you suggest sending them a pitch. In other words, you create a relationship with this industry person, one step at a time... The more relationships you have with industry people, the more likely you are to 'break through'. It's a simple but effective strategy – just remember you are playing the long game.

ONE-PAGE PITCHES – ADVANCED

Like your killer logline, your one-pager should also follow those all-important 3 Cs. Broken down, they may look like this:

- **WHO** is this story about? Include protagonist and antagonist, plus any other characters that play a VITAL part in the story. Who is this story aimed at? (Know your audience.)
- **WHAT** is the antagonist's Evil Plan? How must the protagonist counter it?
- **WHERE** is this set? Time/place. Arena. Do your characters have specialist knowledge? Is this a fantasy world, etc?
- **WHEN** do we join the story? When does it end? Remember to include Act 1 (the SET UP) and Act 3 (the RESOLUTION) – omit Act 2 (the CONFLICT). This is what people mean when they give the advice to 'sell the sizzle, not the steak'. And never, ever end the pitch doc with a question instead of the ending. Many writers believe erroneously that being vague on the ending is somehow enticing – and maybe it is to them. But if you're a script reader, agent or producer reading one-pagers all the time, vague endings are annoying. We want to know what the set up is and what the resolution is – the 'skeleton', if you like; we'll read the screenplay for the meat of the story.
- **WHY** this story? The most neglected question, not only on pitch docs, but by writers themselves... Yet there's a very strong chance you'll get asked this question if you're asked in for a meeting. You need to know exactly *why* we need to be told this story and what's different about it to all the others.

Obviously you can do the above however you like; as long as it is interesting and entertaining! Just make sure the information is there, preferably in continuous prose. It is possible to write good profile-style one-pagers, though I haven't seen many.

'EMERGENCY' PITCHES

Of course, Sod's Law being what it is, sometimes you'll pitch your gleaming, FINISHED screenplay to someone at a pitchfest to be met with an uninterested 'meh' – and none of your other finished works lights their fire, either. It does not make sense then to sit there and twiddle your thumbs, especially when that person says, 'What else have you got?' If you have a great idea for a pitch, share it with them NOW. But be honest with them if they like it. Tell them it's just a pitch and what you have – an outline, a one-pager, a half-finished rough draft or even nothing but the logline you're telling them now. DO NOT tell them you have a finished, polished draft ready to go and then rush home and work like the clappers on it. Chances are, the draft will be half-arsed and they'll only end up thinking you're a bad writer. If you're honest about what you have, however, that person may want to work with you on that draft: it could become the 'in' you want to the industry. This may seem obvious, yet it's surprising how many writers tell outrageous fibs about the status of their work and hope they'll get away with it. They hardly ever do. Remember: producers, agents and filmmakers spend a huge chunk of their time reading scripts. This means they can tell the difference between a rushed early draft (even if it's had several passes) and a polished, gleaming one. So be honest and INVITE people to work with you. You may be surprised how many take you up on your offer.

THE TREATMENT

So, let's say you crafted a great logline and one-pager. You pitched it and a producer, agent or sales agent loved the sound of it. But they haven't got time to read a whole screenplay, they're going to film festivals and book fairs and all sorts in the next couple of weeks... Have you got a treatment they can read instead?

Treatments are frequently left out of screenwriters' arsenals and this is always a mistake in my opinion. Note the treatment I'm talking about here is NOT the same as that 'blueprint' personal outline I talk about back at the beginning of this book. The outline is for YOU, the writer: a 'note to self' on how you're going to tackle the story and characters in your thriller screenplay. In contrast, the treatment is a polished selling document, just like the one-page pitch, to send out to agents, filmmakers, etc. Sometimes the treatment is called an 'extended pitch' or 'scriptment' or, unhelpfully, an 'outline' too (if you're not certain what someone is asking you for, always ask).

If you have a polished treatment ready to go with your screenplay and one-page pitch, I'd venture you have significantly more chance of getting an option or finance deal in the long term. But what is expected in the treatment, aka extended pitch or scriptment? The treatment is a document that gives the reader a complete plot breakdown as it is IN THE SCRIPT. But it needs to be intriguing enough to sell your story OFF THE PAGE again – just like the one-pager. Oh, and it can't be too long... Those people requesting it haven't got all day, you know!

So, in other words, you need to:

- Include the title, your name and contact details (including email address).
- Put your killer logline at the top.
- Give a 'blow by blow' account of the plot, 'what happens' – but try to ensure it's not dull. Do so in an interesting way that hopefully matches the tone of your story (so, being a thriller, you need to strive to ensure your treatment is as thrilling as it can be: use short, snappy sentences and appropriate vocabulary).
- Try to break up your text where you can so it's not swathes of black. Do this any way you like, as long as it's interesting and doesn't create 'noise' in terms of preventing selling the story off the page. The most common way I've seen this as a script reader is by including fragments of dialogue from the screenplay that sum

up the characters' worldviews and/or plight in the story (hence the 'scriptment' idea).

- Avoid a huge page count… The best treatments are typically four to ten pages long; these days the closer to four, or even less, the better (agents and execs sometimes call them 'sizzlers', so make sure they totally rock and are interesting to read!). That's right… Not much space at all. But perfectly possible.

SUMMING UP…

- Be ready. Have a polished draft of your thriller screenplay and its one-pager ready to go. Have others, too, ready for when they hopefully ask, 'What else do you have?'
- Be honest. If you end up pitching something you haven't got a draft for, be honest about what you DO have. You never know, that producer or agent may want to develop your idea with you.
- Realise you are not locked out of the industry. You *can* get your work solicited.
- Have a brilliant one-pager to query with.
- Make sure you also have a treatment (aka extended pitch, scriptment or 'sizzler') ready to go that gives a breakdown of all the events in the screenplay as a further selling document.

GETTING YOUR WORK 'OUT THERE', PART 2: STRATEGY ROUTES AVAILABLE

As mentioned at the beginning of this book, there are two main routes available for spec thrillers (and, indeed, all screenplays): using them as samples to get work as a writer for hire or getting them sold and/or made yourself. And, although using your screenplays as samples is arguably the more straightforward route, it's actually as difficult as the alternative, albeit in a different way. First, though, you need to get yourself an online presence – and pronto.

ACCESSIBILITY, ACCOUNTABILITY, ENGAGEMENT

The various platforms and tools at your disposal, like blogs, Twitter, Facebook, Tumblr, YouTube, LinkedIn and beyond, can work for you or against you as a writer and/or filmmaking team. The notion of accessibility is key when it comes to a 'good' online persona, but so is accountability. Remember:

- People should be able to find you easily. Don't make it hard for them by choosing URLs or Twitter handles that hundreds of others have chosen.
- Keep your sites and profiles regularly updated. There's only one thing worse than a non-existent online persona and that's one that hasn't been touched in months.

- If your name is the same and/or easily confused with someone else's, consider using a professional name or pseudonym, but DON'T muddy the waters by making submissions with both your names. This drives assistants and contest administrators absolutely nuts. Stick to the pseudonym, including your actual email address.
- If you prefer, consider 'branding' yourself. My name is the same as historical figure the Countess of Carlisle, so it's impossible for me to win a Google contest on this, though, gratifyingly, I am FINALLY the second result now. But back in 2005, when I was about the 75th result for my own name, I decided to use a brand to easily identify me online. I ended up choosing Bang2write and the rest, as they say, is history: people can find me easily without the need for requesting a business card or even my full name at events. If you decide to brand yourself in this way, make sure your website, email and social media handles – especially Twitter – match.
- When you buy your domain name, make sure you buy its variations (such as the .com and .co.uk versions) so people don't buy them and piggy back on your brand.
- Remember that producers and agents Google names, so check out what turns up when your name is searched for on the Internet. Is it what you want/hope for? Remember you can change what comes up if you put some thought into it.
- Think about how you 'look' online. You wouldn't go into a crowded place and start ranting and raving randomly, would you? Yet people do this all the time on social media, especially writers it seems. Whilst you will always be able to find others to complain with, it's unlikely you will find others to work with if you do this. Writer Andrea Mann (@andreamann) echoes this sentiment: *'Try to keep your public persona on Twitter, Facebook, etc, fairly positive. If you talk about failure, you – and others – will start to believe it of you!'*

Never forget social media platforms and sites are your tools, and powerful ones at that. Use them to construct a 'shop window' that will enable others to see what a great writer you are; that you know what you're talking about; that you are good to work with. By using social media well, you can see your perceived value go up; use it badly and you will see your perceived value take a nosedive.

Besides accessibility and accountability, the third important element of a successful shop window via social media and the rest of the web is engagement. The most successful writers engage with others online. This may seem obvious – and it is – but is something too easily forgotten. Every day I am sent messages, tweets and emails by various writers, either pitching me or asking me to visit their website and check out their blogs, articles or screenplays. I rarely respond. Not because I don't care, but because there are only so many hours in the day and I prefer to spend that time TALKING to people about things that interest me. Imagine going to a party and people simply come over and talk AT you; you'd leave, right? Yet if people ASK you what you're working on and talk WITH you about subjects you find interesting... Suddenly you're all having a good time AND you all get what you want. Talk about a no-brainer. So, the key for engaging with others online is:

- **Conversation first, always.** The more people you meet and chat with, the more likely it is that you will create allies. The more allies you have, the more likely it is that you will find the people you need to advance in your career.
- **Give more than you take.** If you are generous with your time, resources and knowledge, that good karma will come back to you. It really is as simple as that. So write great content for your blog; share the leads and info you come across; help people further down the ladder whenever you can.
- **Build a following.** If you Google 'Bang2write Lucy V Hay', scanning the results you will find various keywords such as 'features'; 'characterisation'; 'Devon'; or 'helps writers' jumping out at you. My online persona is highly constructed. This does not mean it is a lie, far from it; it is all based on truth, but none of it is accidental. Decide in advance what you want out of your online presence and work towards that. If you're sensitive, never indulge in flame wars (unless, like B2W flaming doesn't bother you and you actually use

such threads to help build your following! Proceed with caution however). Otherwise, unfollow or block all dissenters – you're not 'afraid of discussion', you just don't have time for negativity. And try not to be negative yourself. Everybody's human and has off days, but if you have nothing but off days your perceived value will plummet.

THE SAMPLE SCREENPLAY ROUTE

A lot of screenwriters have little interest in production or do not have the time to pursue it (especially those writers who have family and/or other work commitments). As a result, these writers may decide instead to use their screenplays as samples in the hope of either selling their specs to the highest bidder or showing producers what they can do, so they gain paid work on others' productions as writers for hire. An agent is of course a lot of help in achieving this, but is not strictly necessary, plus many agents will not consider those writers just starting out on their journey, anyway. But, again, that's just the bad news. The good news is that there's plenty writers can do to persuade others – like prodcos and agents – their samples are worth looking at. Despite this, I often see the average spec writer approaching their samples in a haphazard way, writing and rewriting and firing off to all and sundry in short-lived and ill-focused bursts, rinsing and repeating *ad nauseam*. If you want your spec thriller screenplay to act as a sample to sell or get you noticed as a writer, you need a strategy, not only for your writing, but in using the tools at your disposal (like social media) effectively:

- **Check out all the paid-for screenwriting contests/schemes for the year ahead and plan accordingly**. It used to be that placing in the quarter-finals of any US screenwriting competition automatically meant agents and managers would look at your script, but there are so many contests now it's difficult to get the same attention. That said, the biggest paid-for screenwriting competitions can still offer very real opportunities and connections for their finalists and winners. Multiple placings in the quarter- and semi-finals of various contests do help writers access producers and agents. Try and budget so you can enter your spec thriller screenplay in at least three of the bigger contests; if it can place in one, there's a strong chance it can place in another – and that may be enough to persuade agents or producers to take a look at your script.

- **Enter your thriller screenplay in all the opportunities and schemes you can – again, look ahead and plan accordingly.** Most writers wait until these opportunities hit them in the face with just weeks or even days to go, so their submissions feel rushed. There is plenty you can do to plan ahead and ensure your submissions are ready ahead of the game. Throughout the year there are various script calls and opportunities such as screenwriters' schemes and initiatives. Many writers on social media share such opportunities, so try and look ahead and ensure you have stuff ready: ie. have a one-pager and your first ten pages already saved as one PDF file, ready to go.
- **Create buzz online about yourself...** If you want people to think of you when they want to find writers, you need to put yourself and your work out there ahead of the game. Having a social media presence, then, is a must, but, with so many writers on the likes of Twitter, you need to stand out. So, rather than just chat about writing online, have a speciality: talk about something in particular (and not just how great your work is!). The best bloggers and tweeters 'give' as much as they 'take': if you can offer something to people, then those people are more likely to feel goodwill towards you and will want to recommend or refer you when they hear of an opportunity.
- **...And about your work.** Lots of writers upload their screenplays to every site going and just as many hide theirs away. I think it's much more useful to have a balanced approach. Given that it is concept that sells above all else in screenwriting, I generally recommend uploading one-pagers to your various profiles, particularly on social media. This allows people to browse your portfolio and request your screenplays offline, should they choose.

- **Approach with caution.** Comedic and unusual approaches are rarely met with anything other than disdain, so beware of being quirky. Research all the people and places you want to approach and stick with their submission guidelines, if they have any. If their websites say 'no unsolicited material', query them anyway with a short and courteous email or letter. Always follow up politely after 6–8 weeks and let it go if you're hit with consistent radio silence. Never complain online about individual people or places being rude or unreasonable; it's more likely to come back on you than them.
- **Constantly review your approaches.** So many writers go through random phases of submitting, then sit on their work for the rest of the year. I recommend sending out loglines in short, considered bursts at various points throughout the year (avoiding summer and December, when everyone is away) and seeing which garner read requests. Usually a good query email or letter will get in the region of a 25 per cent take-up rate, with perhaps up to another 25 per cent response rate of 'thanks, but no thanks', with the remaining 50 per cent hit with radio silence. If you get no read requests or no responses, there's your answer: do not pester people. Instead, rewrite your logline and/or query letter or email.

Shortly, I'm going to look at finding producers and money for your project. First, though, it's time to get real.

WORKING FOR FREE: THE UNCOMFORTABLE TRUTH

> *'Writing spec scripts is by definition working for free. In LA people are very generous with their time and contacts, reading scripts, offering advice, helping you meet people. They all want to discover the next good writer, so it's in their interest. Time and work freely given opens doors and creates opportunities. Exploitation, on the other hand, is like pornography – you'll know it when you see it.'*
>
> **– Jonathan Turner, screenwriter**

Screenwriters have become more militant in recent years, defending their place in the industry with zeal. Frequently they may attack directors over the 'Film by...' credit or producers over free options or development, especially via online forums and social media. In fact, you name something filmmaking-related and you'll find swathes of screenwriters airing their grievances on some corner of the Internet! And if a director, producer or company is seeking to take advantage of those screenwriters, then good on the screenwriters for letting it be known 'dodgy' filmmakers and agents will not be allowed to get away with it.

That said, whilst screenwriters may tend to shout louder nowadays, they are often no more informed than they were a decade ago on the basics of money, especially when it comes to investment and distribution. This is quite ironic, since the matter of money usually comes down to this: *there isn't any*. Afraid so. When it comes to developing spec movie projects, most of the time you need a script in order to get the money to rewrite it and make the finished film. That's just the way it is. There's no big conspiracy to keep screenwriters downtrodden whilst producers and directors live it up. Of course there are charlatans and every produced screenwriter will have war wounds relating to somebody or another treating them badly (as will producers, about screenwriters). But, generally speaking, the average indie producer is no richer than your average spec screenwriter. To put it into context for you, even if a film is a so-called 'financial success' according to the likes of Wikipedia, that doesn't mean it actually made any money for the producers. Why? Because a film has to pay back its investors and distributors first, before it can even break even.

But it's not all doom and gloom: it's not a question of either being taken advantage of or being so high and mighty no one will touch you with a barge pole. As Seth Godin says in his brilliant blog article, 'Should You Work For Free?':

> *'...If you're busy doing free work because it's a good way to hide from the difficult job of getting paid for your work, stop. When you confuse busy for productive, you're sabotaging your ability to do important work in the future. On the other hand, if you're turning*

down free gigs because the exposure frightens you, the same is true… you're ducking behind the need to get paid as a way to hide your art.'

Godin is not only dead right, his article addresses all the nuances of what working for free truly means, which many of the most steadfast arguments about payment 'no matter what' refuse to recognise. Put simply, as I've said multiple times throughout this book, screenwriting is about balance and this element is no different.

THE SPECULATIVE WRITER VS THE COLLABORATIVE WRITER

'Your screenwriting career is not a Dali-esque delusion, but the result of hard work, talent, focus, sacrifice, patience and luck.'

– Mark Sanderson, writer & script consultant (@scriptcat)

When writing your own speculative screenplays (thriller or not), you are your own boss, and rightly so. It's your time and your effort, ergo you should be in charge. And there's a stronger than average chance your speculative thriller screenplay will come to nothing because it may not be produced (even if it is optioned and/or developed with someone). If you look up the word 'speculative' in the dictionary, you will see part of its definition is 'at high risk of loss'. So, yes, your time and effort may be 'lost'. That's just the way of the industry. Rather than let this depress you, switch it around. The loss may be literal – the screenplay in question is not produced into a movie – but, in an ideal world, during that time you will have created a relationship with an agent, filmmaker or producer and thus advanced in your career. This means you will have a better chance of getting your *next* speculative project produced.

In contrast, you may decide you are not a speculative writer, but a collaborative writer. You may decide that writing speculatively – plus its high risk of loss – is not what you want to do. On this basis, then, you will place contact making above the actual writing. You will need a sample screenplay to hook the interests of producers and filmmakers, but generally this is to show them you are a great writer, rather than to ask them to produce it for you. Instead you go to them and say, 'What can we write and make TOGETHER?' In short, you place collaboration at the heart of your dealings with the industry.

When talking with screenwriters about their projects, sometimes they will ask me what I am: speculative or collaborative? My answer: collaborative. I see no point in writing without an 'end point' in sight, whether it's a production or a contest deadline. That's just the way I am. And it's meant I've been able to attach to all kinds of projects, to all kinds of people, and thus done all sorts of things: I've produced movies; written books and novels; and organised and participated in events like London Screenwriters' Festival. But this is not a recommendation you do the same, just because it has worked out for me. There is no right or wrong strategy. Many writers will find themselves a bit of both: speculative and collaborative, dependent on which project they are doing. But I do believe it pays to know whether you are a speculative or collaborative writer at grassroots level, to stand your best chance of production in the long run.

TRANSMEDIA AS A ROUTE IN

Many writers have latched on to the notion of transmedia projects to create interest in their stories and characters. 'Transmedia' basically refers to the notion of storytelling across a variety of platforms, such as web series, mobile phones, novels, movies, TV, blogs, social media, and so on. For example, we have all read about various fictional characters on Twitter who have garnered X thousands of followers, and thus got a book, TV or movie deal. The Internet is fast becoming 'the' place to break new characters, stories and even writers, so it's very tempting to think you could create interest for your thriller screenplay this way. However, it's not simply a question of creating something, anything, and sticking it up online. If you want to utilise transmedia effectively, those three key elements of accessibility, accountability and engagement must come into play again. You must have a strategy: decide what you want from your thriller screenplay's transmedia project and how you want to achieve it – in advance, reviewing accordingly at given junctures. Otherwise you might as well be shouting into the wind, along with countless other ill-thought-out transmedia projects.

We can see this at work in the industry at the highest levels: Marvel is a clear contender, here. They have consistently packed-out cinemas in the past decade as part of its Marvel Cinematic Universe 'Phases 1-3', which began – out of order! – with *Iron Man* (2008) and officially ended with the post-*Endgame* action-adventure thriller, *Spider-Man: Far From Home* (2019).

The movies use serialised storytelling, easter eggs (secret moments fans can decode/recognise), teasers and crossovers to keep fans engaged. This is further backed up with transmedia output such as television series tie-ins, plus video games as well as the inaugural comic book source material.

Add to all that the fact there's so many superheroes of various different backgrounds, there's quite literally 'something for everyone' – the motto of the four-quadrant audience, in fact.

Any Marvel fan can tell you the movies, comic books, TV shows and other elements are part of a 'story universe'. This means everything we see and/or read are different narratives in different mediums, created within a shared story world, aka 'The Marvel Cinematic Universe'.

This mixing of mediums and story elements is known as 'transmedia'. It should not be confused with the term 'franchise', which refers to the exploitation of a single story via sequels and prequels (though certain transmedia story experiences may include multiple franchises within it, like The MCU does. ie. Multiple *Iron Man, Avengers* and *Spider Man* films).

It is necessary to establish a connection between the stories to create such a story universe. If you are a Disney+ subscriber, you can see this in action on your own TV screen. Though all the stories were released in 'the wrong order', with hindsight we can see where they fit in the timeline that takes us from phase 1 which begins in WWII (*Captain America: The First Avenger*) through to the beginning of phase 4 with *Doctor Strange in the Multiverse of Madness* which apparently takes place around 2024 (despite the fact it came out in the year 2022).

Another nifty element of transmedia is that the connection of each narrative is established by the incorporation of common elements. By adding new elements in this structure, new narratives can be created and the transmedia narrative can be expanded by including new narratives to the universe.

Did Marvel plan all of this from the beginning?? I reached out to various contacts who'd worked at Marvel to ask them: some said yes, others said no. No one was willing to go on record, which is very telling. I suspect no one other than Marvel Supremo Kevin Feige knows for definite.

It doesn't matter, anyway. Obviously $180 million budget blockbusters are outside the realm of possibility for 99.9% of us, but the creation of our own story universes are well within our reach thanks to a secret weapon in our back pocket: our phones.

We also live in an increasingly 'techy' world too, meaning our laptops are now capable of creating assets that look and sound both expert and professional. In creating our own 'story worlds', creator platforms and transmedia projects there's plenty we can access even if we have little money, time or others to help us, such as...

- **Websites and blogging.** It's possible to sign up and create a blog for free, dependent on which platform you use, though I am a big fan of self-hosted sites like the one at www.bang2write.com as it gives you many more options. What's more, it means anyone can find you via Google (as long as you pay attention to SEO 'search engine optimisation' via keywords and utilising headlines that score well). Having a site as a 'shop window' for your stories or your transmedia project is a must in the 2020s and you can expect to budget approximately £300-500 per year for hosting, paid-for plugins and any additional costs (such as fixes and repairs).

- **Podcasts and audiobooks.** Podcasts are super-popular in the 2020s. As we know, many podcasts have made the jump to television series including Netflix's *Dirty John* (2018) and *Gaslit* (StarzPlay in the UK, 2022). Sometimes audiobooks are adapted from TV and movie franchises, such as the hugely popular *Alien* series on Audible. Creatives can take advantage of this interest by creating their own podcasts and audiobooks utilising their phones and uploading to iTunes, Google, SoundCloud or one of the many other podcast sites. With competition so high, sound quality is paramount and your phone by itself probably won't cut it. Podcast equipment can be pricey, however it's often possible to buy it second hand, or in bundles from sites such as Amazon, so you can be sure you have what you need. Alternatively, if this feels beyond you, you may want to submit your audiobook pitch straight to Audible via their Audible Hub (details at the back of the book). There are other audiobook publishers too.

- **Social media.** This is a free resource most of us go on daily, yet don't use to its best ability. It can work especially for building our own 'brands' as creatives, but also an origin point for our story universes should we so desire. Video-based platforms such as TikTok and Instagram's 'reel' function can help us create clips or even whole series, especially now both support longer videos of three to ten minutes.
- **Paid-for subscription sites.** Websites such as Patreon or Substack allow people to subscribe to your content in return for 'first look' or exclusive rewards as part of your community. (These sites are different to crowdfunding campaigns like Kickstarter or Indiegogo which aim to hit a financial target within a given timeframe).
- **Free or cheap video editing and graphic design software.** There are multiple apps – both free and paid-for – that we can download for video editing, plus if you have a MacBook there's a strong chance it has iMovie built in already. When it comes to graphic design for book covers or social media assets, Photoshop is more expensive but a free alternative is Canva, which comes with handy templates built in (there's also a pro version of Canva, which is approximately $99 a year and has even more templates and stock photos etc built in).
- **There are many other useful, cheap programmes.** One such programme is Doodly, which helps you create short animations – I bought this on sale for approximately $47. There's also Designrr.io which creates eBooks for you in a variety of formats, PDF through

Kindle and Flipbook. One of the features I love most is you can upload blog posts or Microsoft Word documents, which means you can use it for making eye-catching pitch documents too such as treatments and pitch decks as well. I bought it for approximately $27. If you keep your eye out for sales and discount codes, you can find similar programmes at low prices.

- **Collaborations.** If writing a book or comic or creating a web series of Insta reels or TikToks sounds too much for you, you're not alone. Lots of screenwriters just want to write and feel frustrated at the thought of having to learn whole new skills just to get their stories 'out there'. This is where collaborations can come in handy. Pairing with a podcaster, or an author, or a graphic designer can really help all of you climb the ladder together. Just be sure you all know who owns the intellectual property (aka 'stuff you make with your mind' such as stories); this can also depend on what country you are in. Google 'intellectual property' and where you are. Your government will probably have details on how this works. If it's recommended you use a contract between you all, there are usually boilerplate contracts you can download for free from the internet that will protect all of you. Google keywords like 'Collaboration Agreement' to find some – if a law firm is offering the free download, even better.

INTERACTIVITY, GAMIFICATION AND STORYTELLING

Transmedia offers multiple opportunities for the spec screenwriter in the 2020s. As someone who has built a platform online via 'content marketing' (aka blogging and social media content) and utilising low-cost, low-risk strategies like email newsletters, I am super-interested in how writers can access opportunities from their phones and desktops.

One such modern marketing trend is 'gamification'. This is an online marketing technique to encourage engagement with a product or service. Now, gamification is not a new technique by any stretch of the imagination, but it is being harnessed in the online world in increasingly interesting ways.

One obvious way creatives can use gamification is within the narrative itself. An interactive thriller like Netflix's *Bandersnatch* (2018) invites viewers to make selections to 'steer' the character in various pre-determined directions. It follows the fates of a young programmer Stefan (Fionn Whitehead) in 1984, who starts to question reality while he adapts a mad writer's dark fantasy novel into a video game.

There are numerous possible endings to *Bandersnatch*, including Stefan fighting his therapist, only to discover he is on a film set and none of it was 'real'. Another set of choices leads to Stefan crossing through a mirror and time-travelling back to the accident that killed his mother, which in turn ends up killing him. In other scenarios, Stefan kills his father, dismembering and chopping up his body, only to be found out and go to jail.

This cross-pollination of video games and movies is obvious, but is it satisfying? After all, we already have interactive narratives – the games themselves. Is the future having interactive narratives on streamers like Netflix as well?

No, says Rhianna Pratchett, a video games writer and journalist: 'There were definitely certain quarters that seemed to think Netflix had invented the interactive narrative, but it only did what video games have been doing for decades. I don't think we're going to get many more *Bandersnatches*. Plus Netflix has its own games now (for iPhone and Android).'

So where else can we utilise gamification to get our stories out there? One such way may be indie games. Just as spec screenwriters can team up with self-published authors in collaborations, spec screenwriters can enter into collaborative partnerships with indie game designers.

'As the indie game scene has flourished as we've seen a lot of games on Kickstarter on Indiegogo. We're seeing more adventure games coming up,' says Rhianna.

With various technology and platforms coming out, indie games have the potential to access the mainstream. Mobile phones, iPads and desktop sites offer real opportunities for indie games designers to bring a real diversity of gameplay. But if you're not *au fait* with how video games design works, Rhianna explains.

'You've got the equivalent of big studios in Hollywood,' she says, 'then there's the indie games which are more like indie prodcos on the ladder. Then there's the individuals doing it for the love of it... So we have the big blockbuster games, then the thoughtful, more involved narrative indie games, then the one-offs that are like matching, colouring or learning games.'

Whilst most spec screenwriters do not have the money to option games from giants like Nintendo or Xbox, they may be able to enter into partnership with an indie games designer. This may be to adapt their existing game as a narrative on platforms such as TikTok or a web series released on YouTube or as Insta reels; or to create buzz and a following for a much bigger narrative project, such as a movie.

Many movies launch games apps to help create buzz for the film's release. I recall being in a meeting where this was discussed (back when everyone met in real life rather than Zoom all the time). One of the execs suggested the investors look into a game designed to create interest in shark movie *The Meg*. It was free to download and targeted at children, who would then tell their parents to take them to see the movie.

I returned home and asked my kids if they'd heard of the game. Unbeknownst to me, all three had downloaded the game to their devices that week. They then asked me to take them to see the movie. We all went that weekend and of course it was terrible, but fun. More importantly: the app had worked and done its job!

Again, the average spec screenwriter and indie game designer cannot hope to compete on a monetary level with a big studio with deep pockets. But there's still opportunity here: with technology and social media being so cheap and easily accessible in the 2020s, creating apps and 'gamifying' our narratives online is a very real possibility.

As *The Meg* game shows, when target audiences engage, they are willing to pay out money for the main event. Utilising gamification and creating a following online can demonstrate to production companies, development execs and investors your target audience is more than just theory and hope.

USING BOOKS TO SELL SCREENPLAYS

Not so long ago authors had as hard a time getting published as screenwriters getting produced. The only real way 'in' used to be making submissions to literary agents and crossing your fingers that your manuscript would make it out of the slush pile to the right person.

The Kindle turned the publishing landscape upside down. Now writers can self-publish for free and/or at a very low cost. Early commentators were of the opinion the kudos and prestige of traditional publishing contracts would mean only the 'worst of the worst' novels would be self-published.

Whilst the lack of barriers means there is indeed some awful self-published work, KDP has also seen the birth of the 'authorpreneur'. These are writers who treat their writing as a business, churning out multiple novels in a year. Bestselling thriller novelists such as JF Penn, Mark Dawson and LJ Ross have proven it's possible to write novels readers love AND 'stack and pack 'em'.

This means writing our thriller screenplays as novels first may prove our concept has an audience, something *Killing Eve's* author Luke Jennings has first-hand experience of.

For the uninitiated, *Killing Eve* is a British assassin thriller starring Sandra Oh and Jodie Comer that began on BBC1 in 2018. Its first series was a smash hit as soon as it hit screens. Phoebe Waller-Bridge was celebrated for helping create a TV series that was both relatable and infinitely 'queer', pointing to unrealised sexual tension between protagonist Eve and the psychopathic antagonist, Villanelle. Would the two women ever be together? (Sadly not, as season four revealed – despite the fact this deviated from the source material of three novels: *Killing Eve: Codename Villanelle*, 2014; *No Tomorrow*, 2018; *Die For Me*, 2020).

Whilst anyone can write and publish a book on KDP, Kindle Singles are specifically curated novellas. This means writers have to submit to Amazon for approval like they would a publisher, but if picked their titles have extra prestige and are marketed by Amazon. Kindle Singles are usually somewhere between five to thirty thousand words and were first released on Amazon in 2011.

So the book we now know as *Killing Eve: Codename Villanelle* was originally four novellas published as Kindle Singles in 2014. What is unusual about them is the author Luke Jennings had a particular goal in mind from the offset: he wanted his own TV series and wrote the Kindle Singles with this in mind.

> *'It was a long shot, but I knew if I could get the right people to read them, the characters could have a life beyond just the stories.' Luke says, 'The stories were about fifteen thousand words each, the right length for reading on a commute home in an hour, not a big ask.'*

The key in Luke's words are '*if I could get the right people to read them*'. Many writers publish to the Kindle or even with traditional publishers and simply hope producers might come across them by themselves.

Whilst this is possible, it's not probable: there's a whopping 33 million titles on Amazon alone! As a result, Luke had to research and send copies of his Kindle Singles to various prodcos until his *Killing Eve* novellas landed with Sid Gentle Films.

BOOKS AS SUBMISSIONS

The revelation authors have to submit their books like Luke Jennings often makes screenwriters throw up their hands and say, 'Well I might as well send the producer a screenplay, then!'

But those screenwriters miss a very important point: producers frequently don't like reading scripts. That's why they often outsource them to script readers like B2W. It's also the reason writers now need to jump through a variety of hoops like loglines, one-page pitches and treatments before producers will finally give in and read the damn script!

It's not that producers are lazy (sure, some are – but they usually don't get very far). Rather it's that there's SO MANY spec screenplays in circulation at any one time. That number is increasing, too. When I started as a script reader back in the early noughties, the first literary agent I ever read for estimated he got about 30 submissions per week. For the purposes of this new edition of the book, I rang him up and asked him what he thought his old agency got now (since he retired in 2017).

He didn't hesitate. '80 to 100 submissions, easy.'

Even allowing for exaggeration, I'd say he's probably in the right ballpark. I've been script reading for 20 years now for various agencies, investors, contests and schemes. If I were a betting woman I would put real money on the number of screenplay submissions trebling in the past two decades.

The fact these submissions are spec screenplays means it's difficult to stand out. Whilst scripts obviously can be brilliantly written, compared to a book it's still harder to grab and keep a reader's interest. This is because screenplays are essentially blueprints for a movie or TV series. In contrast, a book is 'the whole story'.

Bladerunner's Hampton Fancher told B2W that *'99% of scripts are intolerable'*. This is because the average spec screenplay is NOT brilliantly written. They may rehash various concepts we've seen before; have generic characters; lumpy structure or a plot that's all over the place; or lack visual potential and have chains and chains of dialogue instead.

All of these problems probably account for the fact most screenplay submissions result in a PASS verdict, meaning they are rejected because they're simply not ready or if they are, there's something else wrong. This can vary from being in the wrong place, to the wrong genre or something else totally avoidable.

Screenwriter of the thriller *Extracurricular Activities* (2019) Bob Saenz echoes Fancher's point, though drops a percentage point and says 98% of screenplays are bad. More importantly, he estimates that of the 2% that are good, *'Only 0.5% are useable.'*

Again, this sounds about right to me based on my script reading experience. There's a pyramid to script reader recommendations: PASS, CONSIDER, RECOMMEND.

As mentioned before, most spec screenplays get PASS. If we take Bob's estimation of only 2% of spec screenplays being good, then the 'useable' 0.5% are the RECOMMENDs. (Note that a 'Recommend' just means it gets passed up the chain to the producer to read, it does NOT mean a guarantee of production!).

This means only 1.5% get CONSIDER. 'Consider' generally means 'There's something *about* this worth a second look, BUT there's something craft-related in the way (usually structure, character or both)'.

Producers can be real hard-asses about CONSIDERs and even RECOMMENDs. As a script reader you can find yourself in hot water if you send a script up the chain that doesn't knock their socks off.

Similarly, if you recommend or even consider a script with substantial craft problems they may even decide you don't know what you're talking about and never hire you as a reader again. In short, it's just not worth the risk unless the reader is willing to go to bat for a script.

In contrast, producers often LOVE books. There's multiple reasons for this, but via my time as a script reader doing coverage on books, as well as a novelist myself, I'd wager it all boils to the following three things:

- **Producers can put their own stamp on books.** Everyone wants to be 'the one' who discovers The Next Big Thing. This is much easier if you're developing and adapting a book.
- **Books are 'pre-sold'.** If a book has a following and/or has sold a lot of units, then it has an audience built in. Whilst new screenwriters like to decry producers as being 'risk-averse', it's not hard to see why. Producers are loath to try out untested stories because the dent they may take to their finances or to their reputations if it's unsuccessful may literally mean they never work again... so is it any wonder they are 'risk-averse' and like books because of this?
- **Authors can deliver.** Many producers like authors because they've proven they can deliver a holistic story by virtue of writing the book in the first place. This means producers like to keep authors on as the screenwriter, or as a consultant. But even if the author doesn't write the screenplay for the adaptation, there is still a 'draft zero' source material for everyone to work from. In contrast, if it's an original script it's very easy to get lost in all the possibilities and end up in 'Development Hell'! This is because multiple returns to

page one often means everyone loses the thread of what excited them about the story in the first place.

So it makes sense to write a thriller novel and send that, rather than a screenplay in the 2020s. It's a good way of standing out in the spec pile, plus you have more chance of grabbing a producer's interest.

I should know: I did exactly the same as Luke Jennings with my crime thriller debut *The Other Twin*. I'd wanted to work with a particular producer for a long time, plus he did with me. He liked the scripts I sent him, but for one reason or another he never optioned them. We seemed destined to miss each other.

Then I wrote the book and sent him a copy (apparently my publisher gave him a copy too!). I didn't hear anything for a good while so chalked it up to yet another miss. Then he called me up, raving about my book and inviting me to a meeting. He not only wanted to option the book, he wanted me to write the series. Yes please!

At the time of writing this book it hasn't been made yet – a nightmare combo of Brexit and Covid got in our way – but even if it comes to nothing, that's the way of so many projects. It was a great experience and I earned money. Bar actually getting produced as well, you can't ask for much more.

A Discovery of Witches

With the above in mind, think of all the TV series and movies you've seen spring from books. Often they can be very different, swapping out various elements to keep them current and relatable for audiences.

A good example here would be the British television series *A Discovery of Witches*, which began in 2018. The book by Deborah Harkness was published in 2011 and at a whopping 688 pages, is a bit of a monster. Though the worldbuilding is fantastic, I found it a little unwieldy upfront: it feels like we're 'waiting' a long time for the 'real' story to kick off. I also found the novel rather languidly paced with the vast majority of action 'back-ended' to the resolution.

Television has no such luxury; it must hit the ground running. Screenwriting also eats plot: what takes the novel's author nearly two hundred pages to describe is done and dusted within the first ten minutes. They also have to 'solidify' what's possible in the story world regarding the 'unholy trinity' of Witches, Vampires and Daemons and why they are all under threat, whereas the book is sketchy about this as these answers come in the second and third books in the trilogy.

In addition, the characters are much more diverse than in the book. Vampires, Witches and Daemons can be any race, plus there is some LGBTQ characterisation as well. Whilst the latter appeared briefly in the book, there's no discussion of race beyond fantasy creatures.

Though only seven years passed between the book's publication and the TV series, it's not difficult to understand why this is the case. In the past five years in particular audiences have started to demand much more nuanced characterisation in general.

As mentioned in the *Black Widow* case study back in the earlier part of this book, there has been a steep and sudden demand for more diversity in screenwriting post–2009/10 by modern audiences, largely fuelled via social media. Just as we can see audience preferences changing how we 'binge' serials, we can see those same changing preferences fuel what types of character audiences want to see too.

In addition, there are some changes to the main characters too. Diana is much more capable in the TV series than the book. Diana is constantly called brave in the book, but I found her a little wet, rather like Bella from *Twilight*. Yet just like Stephenie Meyer's *Midnight Sun (2020)* which reimagines her from Edward's POV, I found its protagonist Diana (Teresa Palmer) in the TV version of *A Discovery of Witches* MUCH more rounded. She is understated but does indeed appear to be as brave as everyone says, taking on her new powers and the fact her life has been turned upside down.

Vampire lead Matthew (played by Matthew Goode) is much creepier in the book, plus he's also much more controlling of Diana. Again, his characterisation is very much 'of its time' in that 2011 we had such toxic male characters as Christian Grey from the *Fifty Shades* series. There's also some obvious influences from Edward Cullen in *Twilight* (which in turn influenced *Fifty Shades*!), with some of Matthew's beats literally identical to Edward's.

Harkness insists she never read the *Twilight* series or watched the movies. I actually believe her but would point to the fact that franchise made a huge cultural impact at the time of its release and beyond. It's almost impossible then for a writer to NOT absorb these influences unconsciously and ironically reproduce them without realising. This is why I always recommend writers 'immerse' themselves in stories LIKE their own so they can see what has gone before. I've already mentioned it's impossible to avoid rehashing stuff by accident otherwise and Harkness' book illustrates this perfectly.

SCREENPLAY OPTIONS

> *'Writing isn't about being locked alone in a dark room. It's about building a blueprint for collaboration, whilst simultaneously protecting a singular vision. That takes people skills as well as talent. That trifecta is rare, which is why when I find it in someone, I tend to work with them over and over.'*
>
> – **Arvind Ethan David, producer** (@ArvD)

Many screenwriters are asked to sign options on their screenplays by producers and filmmakers, yet many writers have no clue what these entail or what's normal. Basically, a screenplay option is:

- A contract between producer and screenwriter. Ever had a rental agreement on a flat or house? In much the same way, the option will list all the things the producer and screenwriter can/can't do, just as between landlord/tenant. Make sure you read the terms and conditions and that way you don't get any nasty surprises later down the line. If you've never seen an option agreement, visit the B2W FAQs (listed in the resources section at the back of this book) or Google 'example screenplay option agreement'. If you see anything in your option agreement that doesn't tally with the samples you find online or anything in particular concerns you, reach out and ask a professional writer his/her opinion. Most will be happy to answer your query if you are polite and to the point. Just remember to say 'thank you'!

- The producer pays a set fee for the option on the screenplay (anything between £0–500 is typical, though of course options can be far more).
- The screenwriter signs away his/her screenplay to the producer and/or the producer's company for a set time (anything between six months and five years normally, though I have seen longer).
- The option gives the producer the right to develop the screenplay with the writer – and provides the time the producer needs to raise the finance to make the movie. Essentially it's a way of producers reserving material they like with an *'IOU... one movie of your idea'!*
- The writer will work on the screenplay with the producer or filmmaker in that set time. If the producer is unable to raise the finance to make the movie, then the rights to the screenplay will revert to the writer again once the producer's set time is up.

It's worth remembering rights on options sometimes refer to the story, rather than just the screenplay. This means that if you want to write your thriller screenplay's story as a novel, for example, you will not be able to whilst it is optioned. It's also important to note that the option fee should not be confused with the writer's fee for the work, which is separate. Make sure you are up to speed with writers' rates by checking out the Writers' Guild of Great Britain and BECTU websites. Typical fees and deals for the writer may be a payment on signature of the option, a 'payment on delivery of the finished draft' and a third on 'first day of principal photography' of the shoot of the movie. Some options promise back-ended deals to the writer like 'payment when the film goes into profit' but beware of these deals, as many movies never go into profit officially.

IS IT 'WORTH' IT?

So next time a producer says they want to work with you, but they don't have any money for an option or development, think very carefully before you automatically say 'no'. Instead, consider the following:

- **Is the producer an individual or a company?** It goes without saying that big prodcos should pay their writers, and a good portion of them do. But if the former, chances are s/he is telling the truth when saying s/he does not have any money for development. However, even if s/he trades under a company name that does not automatically mean s/he is rolling in it, either – even if that company is VAT registered. Don't be afraid to ask that producer about the returns on his/her previous films: if the producer is telling the truth when s/he says there is no money, s/he will be able to put your mind at rest by saying whether his/her previous films broke even or ended up in the red.
- **Does the producer want a free option of your spec thriller screenplay or pitch material?** I'd hesitate to say you should never sign a free option, because they can work out for all the parties involved. So instead I would counsel caution: don't let a producer take a free option on your material for any longer than one to two years maximum and make sure they are serious about your script, rather than simply asking a bunch of writers to sign away their scripts to them and then putting them all on the back burner. If that producer wants the rights to your screenplay, s/he should be prepared to focus on it. You have every right to ask producers what their plans are in advance and how they will act on them. If you don't have an official agreement between you, don't forget you still own the screenplay, so can walk away with it if you feel it's not working out after all. Do remember, however, the producer could argue later s/he created various parts of it, like characters or plot threads, so, if you do part company, it's generally a good idea to chuck all the drafts the producer worked on with you and 'reset' to the last draft you wrote by yourself before approaching other people with it.
- **What is the producer offering you in return?** If that producer wants you to write or rewrite various elements with a budget in mind or to make the concept more marketable to potential investors, s/he should give you decent, clear notes on a good timescale. If you're working for free, then you've probably got a day job, so it's not reasonable of the producer to expect you to turn notes around within a period of time that does not suit you. If you've signed that free

option with the producer, then they should offer you a percentage of any profits, though remember there is a strong chance there may not be any profits once investors, distributors and marketing have been paid. I would also recommend setting up how many drafts the producer expects from you and by what date – in advance. That way you can both work to a schedule, and to an agreed pattern, and there are no unpleasant surprises for either of you.

- **What are the chances of this project coming to fruition?** If you're an unknown writer, teaming up with someone more experienced than yourself is a wise move as s/he can help you propel up the ranks. However, this is not always possible. With that in mind, then, consider who the producer is and how likely it is they can, a) get money to make your project, and b) make sure it gets made and distributed. Check out their IMDB, resumé or website, qualifications, even what their film-school lecturers and contemporaries think of them.

By understanding finance and investment and creating transmedia assets like novels, games, multi-platform storytelling on social media and characters from story 'universes', we can present industry pros with a no-brainer: our stories are 'pre-sold' and we can demonstrate we know what we're doing. We are no longer a risk, but an opportunity for industry pros.

FINDING PRODUCERS

Now you have a spec thriller screenplay and pitch material, if you want to see it produced it stands to reason you need to find yourself a producer. This is frequently where screenwriters come unstuck and say they are 'locked out' of the industry, as mentioned in Chapter Four when dealing with the subject of one-pagers. This is often because writers are making their approaches in the wrong way, such as:

- **They are querying producers who are unlikely to look at unknowns.** I'm a firm believer in the notion that 'anything that can happen', but if you're an unknown writer with no credits fresh off a screenwriting MA or similar, the likelihood of a massive thriller producer like Jerry Bruckheimer picking up your script without a big contest win or agent attached is not very high. So by all means query your favourite big producers and companies, but do it on the off-chance it *might* work, rather than as your main strategy, else you'll probably be destined for disappointment.

- **They are sending their pitches to the same producers and prodcos, over and over again**. I met a producer friend once for coffee who got a number of emails on her Blackberry whilst we were talking. When I asked her why she wasn't checking them, she replied she already knew who it was: it was the first Monday of the month, so a writer who always emailed that day would be contacting her! She explained this writer repackaged his loglines and re-pitched them every single month, even though she now rejected them without reading. Of course it's good to make contacts in the industry: if a production company does read your work, then it's a great idea to ask if they want to read your other stuff too so they might form a picture of the type of writer you are and hopefully ask you in for a meeting. However, if this does not happen and that producer or production company keeps rejecting you, there should come a point where you move on, unlike that writer who was basically stalking my friend. There's a thin line!

- **They are not following up on their submissions**. As with most things in the industry, there's an opposite end of the scale, too: writers don't follow up, believing that if a producer is *really* interested, s/he'll get in touch. But the reality is that a producer is usually busy with existing projects so, even if s/he is interested, they might forget about your submission. There's nothing wrong with following up – and, indeed, many a follow up has resulted in a deal. Just don't stalk them into it! Be sensible.

- **They are sending pitches at the 'wrong' times**. Timing is very important in the industry and there are two times of year when queries and pitches will often literally vanish into space, unnoticed: the summer (lots of people are away) and December (in the run up to Christmas). Similarly, when a particular producer or company is already shooting a movie, queries will take a back seat and may get ignored altogether. Knowing when is a good time and a bad time to send queries is important; it can make the difference between a producer or company showing interest – or not. So find out when is a good time. It's never been easier to find out when individual companies are shooting, thanks to Twitter in particular.

- **They are ignoring the producers right in front of them.** I've lost count of the number of screenwriters who have told me there are 'no' producers interested in their work... usually because they have only approached them using methods 1–4. The reality is, there are a huge number of new producers looking for great screenplays who are literally twiddling their thumbs. Lots of new producer friends tell me 'no one' has contacted them in months and asked them out for coffee – yet again, it's never been easier to find them online, thanks to social media. These producers may not be 'big' or 'cool', and they almost certainly have no money to pay you (or themselves!), but they are ready and willing to work with you on your spec thriller screenplay and get it to the screen. What's not to like?

So, whenever you find what looks like a good script lead and/or place to pitch, DO check the following:

- Have you heard of the person/place making the call?
- If you haven't, can you do a search on the company or person making the script call?
- Does the person have an IMDb listing or website or other online presence?
- Does the person or place making the script call respond to tweets or similar?
- Do you know anyone who has made a submission to this person or place? What was the outcome? Always do your due diligence.

If in doubt, be sure to Google them and check whether they turn up on the Writer Beware! Blog, which you can find at www.writerbeware.com and http://accrispin.blogspot.co.uk

Do remember: reputable agents and producers will NEVER ask you to pay for your own readers' reports or to pay them money to 'take your work to market'. So don't fall for this; it's a scam.

HOOKING UP

So, in terms of 'hooking up' with a producer or filmmaker via approach number five (above), and/or establishing a presence online, here are some things to consider:

- **Check out social media first...** Twitter, Instagram and LinkedIn are fast becoming the hubs for up-and-coming producers, with script calls and leads posted daily. Search terms like 'looking for screenplays' or 'looking for scripts'. Don't forget that people on social media are more likely to respond to conversation than pitches in the first instance; blindly tweeting pitches *at* people is likely to get you blocked or unfriended.
- **... But don't make a nuisance of yourself**. There's nothing wrong with posting your killer logline to social media, plus a link to your one-pager and asking for RTs or 'likes', *but don't spam people!* Let them come to you if they're interested. You may not get a reply straightaway, but don't lose heart; repost at *sensible* intervals and make sure you engage with your followers: don't just post the same thing over and over again, it's off-putting.
- **Query, query, query!** Screenplay hosting and evaluation sites like Inktip and The Black List can be very helpful, but they cost money and are not for everyone. Evaluate your logline and synopsis at least weekly. Look beyond 'no unsolicited material' and start querying – research industry pros and write them a short 2-3 line email with NO attachments. Try and aim for at least three replies a week here (not just producers, either; talk with other writers,

too, who express interest. The more people who know you and what you do, the more likely you will hook up with someone who will be able to take your work somewhere). If you get no interest at all, take another look at how your title, your logline, the way your prose, or even your online presence, comes across. Are you putting people off?

- **Know 'who is who' and 'who is making what'.** Make sure you know what individual companies' remits are. Check out the likes of IMDbPro and send query emails and letters to all the companies that you believe would be a good fit for your spec thriller screenplay. Don't send it to everyone blindly: there's no point sending your non-linear, female-led psychological thriller to a company whose output consists mainly of gangster films, for example. Get to know who is making what, with whom and approach the right people. Obvious stuff, perhaps, but again I've lost count of the number of producers who've told me they're frequently offered things outside their remit.

- **Go to events and meet as many producers as possible…** There are loads of events, paying and free, in 'meat space' and on Zoom, where you can find producers. If you're outside London, that's no reason to feel cut off: film and arts festivals are great places to meet producers and run everywhere, up and down the country, even in rural areas. Alternatively, why not set up your own free networking event? Use social media to connect with producers and writers and set up talks online or pick a 'halfway point' in reality everyone can get to.

- **… But make the most of it.** This is frequently where writers screw up their chances: in real-life events they may stay in their own little groups, rather than mingle; or they simply watch passively at online events and don't ask questions, *even when invited to*! Sometimes these writers demand producers read their script, especially via 'lovebombing' them on instant message first. Again – and I'm in danger of boring even myself on this point – *it's all about balance:* say hello, ask what they're working on. If you're able to slip your logline into the conversation – casually! – all the better. Follow up with any people you meet with a short, polite email or tweet, saying how nice it was to meet them. And maintain that contact: friend those people you've met on Facebook or add them to your LinkedIn contacts. You're more likely to get something made if you make and maintain a relationship with someone.

- **And remember fellow writers are your allies, not your competition.** Many writers make this mistake: they think fellow writers are not worth knowing when they're on the hunt for producers. The reality is, a referral from another writer is worth its weight in gold, especially if they garner respect, either for their own produced work or other 'standing' in the industry. So meet as many writers as you can and tell them what you're working on. Let writers who express interest in your work read it. Don't hide it away. The more people who read your work, the more likely your work will land on the desk of someone with the power to make it.

HOOK, LINE & SINKER

So let's say you have a producer's interest: s/he has responded to your logline and/or link to your one-pager, and hopefully your thriller screenplay too. You get an email or phone call: s/he wants to meet with you. But that doesn't mean you have to take the first producer who shows an interest. And don't be afraid to 'interview' them all and even take notes if several want to meet you. Here are some things you may want to consider in finding the right producer for your thriller screenplay:

- **Experience.** The producer you want should ideally have some previous experience in short film and/or at least one feature, either as a producer, line producer or similar; ideally that previous project made some money and/or attracted a named actor to star in it, plus some critical acclaim – or infamy!
- **Buzz.** S/he should know how to utilise online and offline marketing to create buzz about movies, so ideally you would have heard about the movie or him/her. If you haven't, that shouldn't put the

producer out of the running altogether. Google them and their movie and see what comes up.

- **Funding/Investment.** S/he should know how to negotiate public funding and private investment and have some understanding of casting and other related production issues like editing.
- **Contacts.** S/he should have a selection of useful contacts, either in the industry, such as with directors, or its ancillary markets, like equipment hire companies; ideally both.

And, most important: though s/he will inevitably have his/her own ideas about realising the screenplay as a finished movie, s/he should essentially be on the same page as you with regards to the concept and story behind your screenplay and what you want to achieve. So get out there and find the best man or woman for the job!

THE DIRECTOR

Oh, and one last thing: if you don't have one already, now is the time to find one if you are not an established writer/director. Generally speaking, producers will know directors, but it's possible to attract a director via the same route I've just outlined to find a producer. I've worked on just as many projects where the director brought the producer on board as vice versa. As with producers, the director should have some level of experience and be able to bring that experience to the project, thus adding value to it. If your director is a woman, or disabled, or part of an ethnic minority, it's worth remembering these three groups are wildly underrepresented in the industry, therefore you may be able to access extra pots of (usually) public money designed to help correct this. If you want to direct yourself, then go for it. However, if you have never directed before or have only done short films, be prepared for the eventuality you may get replaced at a later date, especially on the say-so of investors.

SUMMING UP...

- Whether you choose to use your thriller screenplay as a sample or decide to find a producer to make it, look ahead and plan for the next year; set yourself goals and be realistic.
- Remember your web presence is a 'shop window': it should be 'constructed' as well as being truthful, not accidental; recognise social media as a TOOL to help advance your career.
- Decide whether you want to be your own boss and write speculatively or to attach to a team with a producer and director and write collaboratively.
- Decide what you will and won't do in advance, especially when it comes to working for free, but also with reference to your web presence.
- Structure and review your approaches to the industry, especially if you're being met with consistent radio silence.
- Timing is all-important: avoid the times people will be away or shooting.
- Knowing what a producer is and does means you will, a) find the right one, and b) avoid the common pitfalls of development and production.

MONEY, MONEY, **MONEY**

'When the time comes for raising finance, a skillful filmmaker will do two things: firstly: de-risk the project as far as possible. In the UK it means using the very advantageous tax write-offs. It could also mean signing bankable stars… The second thing a producer needs to do is to make the additional investor benefits enticing.'

– Elliot Grove, founder of the Raindance Film Festival (@Raindance)

FILM AS A BUSINESS

It comes down to this: there is *always* money available for the 'right' project. A lot of writers express disbelief at this, especially if they have had no luck accessing funding via the 'usual' routes like screen agencies. But what is the 'right' project? Well, that's the million-pound question and one I'm going to attempt to crack open here. First, though, realise one thing: there is no mythical pot of gold at the end of the rainbow. Forget about art and think on this: your thriller screenplay is a *business opportunity*. Your producer must do a great job of persuading potential investors they want to put their cold, hard cash into that business opportunity.

WHAT MAKES A SCRIPT MARKETABLE?

There is one thing your producer needs from you to make the whole thing float and that's a marketable screenplay. So what is a marketable screenplay? To qualify, you need three things:

- A great story with a commercial hook
- Great characters that will attract bankable ('named') stars
- Be relatively cheap to make on a 'low' budget

Dealing first with number one, cast your mind back to the notion of premise outlined in Chapter Three. Premise works as the foundation of your thriller screenplay: it helped you to write it; it also helped you pitch (and nab) a producer and filmmakers to make it. And now it will come into its own for a third time, because it will help you potentially hook your audience. A commercial hook refers to an idea that grabs the potential viewer and makes them want to watch: the easier it is to boil down that idea, the better. Not because your potential audience is stupid, either, but because, generally speaking, people want to know what they're spending their money on. Fair enough, hey?

In addition, great characters are a must in your thriller screenplay. They are not an optional extra. Remember the antagonist drives the narrative of most thrillers and frequently a lone protagonist is literally forced to swim against the tide. The best thrillers do not sideline secondary characters, but equally they do not allow their secondaries to take over events, either. It's worth thinking about how characterisation works on a symbolic level to create 'layers' to your characterisation and produce fictional people different to the usual ones we see in spec thriller screenplays and produced content. In doing so, your thriller screenplay stands a better chance of standing out from the crowd, not only to producers and filmmakers, but to actors as well. We've all read accounts in *Variety* and *Screen Daily* where 'X Big Name Star loved the script so much s/he took a massive pay cut'. Invariably, what this really means is the star loved the CHARACTER in that script so much s/he was willing to be in a film s/he would not usually be in, regardless of the fact s/he was not paid as much, since that actor saw an opportunity to present a different side to the public.

And, finally, the notion of money: one of the most misunderstood aspects of filmmaking by writers. Some productions are 'micro budget', which usually means they cost in the region of £20–50,000, though some films are £10,000 and under, especially one-room horror films, which saw a roaring trade in the early noughties. 'Low budget' usually means in the range of £100–500,000 in the UK (with generally the lower end, budget-wise, for the less experienced filmmakers), with the bigger prodcos mastering budgets of £500,000+, though there are always exceptions.

MONEY'S TOO TIGHT TO MENTION

The savvy writer knows the notion of 'low budget' or 'microbudget' is key. Every single penny counts in indie film, but very often screenwriters believe their screenplays are low budget when they are in fact medium budget, or even beyond. It helps to know what budget constraints mean if you are to give producers and filmmakers what they need, so your spec thriller screenplay has its best chance in the marketplace. You need to consider:

- **Health and safety & risk assessment.** Writers frequently think this relates solely to stunts and explosions, but, in reality, health and safety is an important element of ALL film productions. Every producer and filmmaker must perform a risk assessment in order to get insurance. Thriller scripts often have a good chunk of action in, even if it's just running around. Basically, if your actors could potentially hurt themselves (even if it's just by falling over) or your crew have to do anything 'risky' (like run after the actors, whilst looking through a camera at the same time!), then the risk assessment will have to reflect this and the insurance on the film will be more expensive. That's not to say you should take out all your action sequences or stunts. A thriller sitting down most of the time, whilst not impossible (and, indeed, several adaptations of plays have worked in this way, like *Death and the Maiden*, 1994), is not necessarily desirable solely for budget reasons. Just make sure you know how health and safety impacts when your screenplay is rendered as image – and, most of all, what the alternatives are to those action sequences when your producer tells you they're too expensive and you need to rewrite.

- **Actors.** Big-name actors cost. Your lead actor/s will probably be paid in excess of three times as much as the secondaries, but it will be worth it, as they will not only bring a fan base with them, but haters too, who love to slag him/her off! What's more, a recognisable face will always add value to a project and bring viewers who may not watch otherwise. So, think of how this will reflect in your thriller screenplay, especially with reference to the protagonist and antagonist (the two roles named actors will generally be most interested in). The lead actors in your thriller screenplay will need to work the hardest for that money – it's only fair! Consider putting them in the most scenes, with the secondaries occupying less story space, so those lesser-named actors can do their parts in one or two days maximum, rather than hanging around for the whole shoot, which will cost the production more in terms of keeping them on time-wise, but also in terms of food, make-up, etc. Similarly, make those secondary characters hot property and you will instantly have more choice of actors to work with.
- **Children and animals.** It's said you should 'never work with children or animals' and this is certainly the case when it comes to low-budget film productions. There are all kinds of rules and regulations relating to kids and animals in terms of how much time they can work and when (which can depend on where you're shooting, too). In addition, children and animals must always be paid the going rate, in direct comparison to adult (human) actors who can decide whether they will work for less or on deferred payment. That said, I don't recommend avoiding children all together, especially if it's to the detriment of the story; if a child is best, then make it work. Otherwise, if a child is central to the story, use teenage characters: as soon as a teenager hits 18, s/he is counted as an adult and is not subject to the same laws any

longer, but handily the 'right' 18 year old can easily pass for 16, or even younger. Similarly, if you have to use animals, make sure they can be replaced easily with whatever the production assistant can get in for the day or the director of photography can film (in the case of wild animals)... In other words, don't make them central to the story.

- **Locations vs studio shooting.** Generally speaking, shooting on location is less expensive than shooting in a specially built set, but obviously this can depend on the type of story being told. So-called 'man in a box' or contained thrillers are obviously very cheap to make in studios, whereas an epic Bourne-type thriller made on location and racing through recognisable landmarks like Waterloo station is very expensive. The low-budget thriller, then, should preferably have five or six locations maximum; if you can make your thriller with less, or make one location *look* like more than one, then all the better. Try and avoid landmarks and crowds, because you will need permissions.

- **Permissions.** You need permission to shoot just about anywhere – even in the middle of nowhere! It usually works out *something* like this: the more people there are in a place, the more expensive it is to shoot there (though farms, secluded national parks and private estates can make filmmakers pay handsomely for the privilege of shooting on their land, too). So a low-budget screenplay does well to avoid having its characters in the middle of the street, on tubes and buses, and in places like cafés, universities, schools, etc... in daytime. That's right: all manner of places suddenly become open to filmmakers very easily at night and, given thriller's bent towards the 'deadline', setting your thriller screenplay in one night can really aid its production. Similarly, tourist towns often all but close down out of season, so can be open to having film crews come into the resort during winter. So take a good look at where your action plays out... and how it impacts on making it. Can you change it and make it more attractive to producers?

Obviously this is just a crash course in budget constraint. There are plenty of other elements that can cause logistical headaches for producers, often dependent on the story being told. But knowing the main ones can really help in assessing your thriller screenplay's chances of being considered 'low budget'. Screenwriters who know that it doesn't just finish with the page invariably have better chances in the marketplace.

WHERE TO GET MONEY

As mentioned previously, there is money available for the right project… but knowing where to get it and how to access it is a skill in itself. Breaking it down, there are three available routes for the indie producer:

PUBLIC FUNDING

The Film Council was set up in 2000 by the then-Labour government in order to help develop and promote British film, using funds from various sources including the National Lottery. In addition, each area had its own screen agency, made up of South West Screen; Screen South; Film London; EM Media (Midlands); Screen Yorkshire; Northern Film and Media; Northern Ireland Screen; The Film Agency for Wales; and Scottish Screen. The Conservative government announced the axing of the Film Council in 2010 and it ceased to exist in March 2011. The British Film Institute (BFI) took up the reins instead, with the screen agencies amalgamating into Creative England (with Film London & Northern Film and Media still acting separately for filmmakers in those areas); Creative Scotland; Northern Ireland Screen and the Wales Film Commission. It pays to be aware of the various schemes the BFI and its partners offer. iFeatures and Microwave are still the flagship schemes, both of which have developed and produced thrillers, such as *Shifty* (2008), *Ill Manors* (2012) and *In the Dark Half* (2012). So before attempting to access public money, consider:

- **Who has accessed this money before?** Knowing which projects were selected for what scheme, and whether they went on to be made (and how long that took and what reception the film got), will help inform your own choices on whether going for public money is right for you and your project. Sign up for all the newsletters and take a look at what has been funded before: Who was in it? What was the story? Who distributed it?

- **Who do I need to work with to access this money?** Writers usually cannot access public funding alone and producers usually have to have a registered company, though this is easily achieved online. It helps if you can find a producer who is already familiar with the various hoops teams have to jump through to qualify for public funding: if s/he has produced a short film for one of the many 'Digital Shorts' schemes run by the screen agencies in the past, then even better. Don't forget working with people currently underrepresented in the media means more potential access to public funding.
- **Is this route right for me and my project?** Remember, public funding means promoting British talent and the UK, so your project generally needs to be about UK life, featuring UK actors, created by UK crew. It may be worth rewriting, recasting or rehiring in order to qualify, or it may not. Only you can decide. Public funding is not the only route and it is not a good fit for all.

ABOUT FILM FINANCE

Film finance is frequently something that writers find rather dry, plus the mixing of art and commerce can often feel uncomfortable. This means writers don't really understand how it works, so they may insist that's the producer's job, or even say that it's 'selling out' to consider such things.

The irony is, the more you understand about film finance, as a writer – even if you're not interested in producing yourself! – the more likely you're going to write things that people will be able to make.

Enter Clive Frayne, development consultant and author of *The Process of Screenwriting*: 'I think a change in mindset would be useful for screenwriters to adopt when they're coming up with ideas. Instead of thinking of themselves as "artists", writers should bear in mind that what they're *really* doing is product design.'

Clive makes a brilliant point here. Though many of us like to think of films as art, we know deep down films are *also* products that need to be sold to the movie-going public. What's more, even a supposedly 'cheap' low-budget movie is very, very expensive.

'Let's say we're making a film on a budget of one hundred and fifty thousand pounds,' Clive says, 'too many writers reply, "Oh that's not very much money." I'm always taken aback by that kind of response. Where I live, you can buy a house for one hundred and fifty thousand!'

Once again, Clive is bang on. Framing the budget in those kind of terms is a reality-check for many of us. If people can buy actual homes for the same budget as a low-budget movie, then we can appreciate a film is an expensive, high-risk product.

'So, screenwriting is the design of a product. And not only that, it's the design of an expensive high-risk product,' Clive explains. 'We also need to remember people watch films for very specific reasons. And they have A LOT of choices.'

ALL ABOUT SALES AGENTS

Before a film can find its way to its target audience, it has to sell to a distributor via a sales agent. A sales agent is as their title suggests: they usually act on behalf of the producer to sell the rights to an independent film or TV drama to distributors. These distributors then release films on different platforms (cinema, TV, DVD and Blu-ray around the world, streaming platforms like Netflix or Amazon, terrestrial TV channels like BBC, ITV etc).

Sales agents need to make detailed assessments of the film's commercial value, as this will help them negotiate projected sales estimates with the distributors. They also take care of promotion, representing their films at festivals and film markets. They will invite distributors to screenings, hold premiere parties and send out screeners to critics.

Financing can depend on the types of deal a sales agent can broker. It's worth remembering that unknown directors often must make their film before they can engage a sales agent to sell it. In contrast, A-list or those directors with a lot of buzz (such as winning major awards) may be approached by a sales agent earlier in the process. This is because the sales agent may be able to sell the film to a distributor as a concept, draft screenplay or during shooting or post-production. Never has the old adage 'it's who you know' been more apt!

Sales agents tend to have three main questions then when they're approached to take on a project:

1. **Who's in it?** People have favourite actors and may watch literally anything that actor appears in. This of course is how 'star power' or 'bankable talent' works: there are actors out there who are so popular they can command huge pay-outs because their very presence in a movie puts bums on seats. (The Ryan Goslings, Margot Robbies, Chris Hemsworths, Sandra Bullocks and Dwayne Johnsons spring to mind here). However, I would venture we all have a favourite actor whom we adore because we believe their presence always elevates a story. For me, such character actors as Walton Goggins, CCH Pounder, Octavia Spencer, Oliver Platt, Jason Bateman and Laura Linney are always MORE than enough to make me tune into a thriller (movie or TV shows). That said, it's important to remember even these acclaimed character actors won't unlock finance by themselves unless the film is very low budget.

2. **Who's directing?** Just like actors, people have their favourite directors. There are of course the A-listers such as Steven Spielberg, Michael Bay, Christopher Nolan, Martin Scorsese and David Fincher that even laypeople not interested in filmmaking or screenwriting recognise straight out the gate. Then there are the award-winners that may do well in ceremonies such as the Oscars which in turn creates buzz about their movies. This may enable them to access the mainstream via higher-budget projects, such as Kathryn Bigelow, Jordan Peele or Chloé Zhao. (Outside of this depressingly small circle, it's very, very difficult to get people's interest in directors which has the knock-on effect of sales agents often not caring either. This means 'no one' really cares about

screenwriters either as directors always trump writers in the industry. We can howl into the void about how unfair this is, or we can accept it's just the way of things and get on with it).

3. **What's it about?** People in the industry like to say 'story is king' (or queen for us women... or monarch, for non-binary people). This is both true and untrue. On the one hand, great concepts are incredibly important for getting those bums on seats. That said, an awful lot of concepts are very similar to concepts that have gone before, plus 'pre-sold' elements that appeal to target audience familiarity will always do better than wholly original ideas. This is why genre is so important and why thriller is one of the most malleable types. It's significantly easier to find a pre-sold element such as aliens, serial killers, vampires or time travel and put an original twist on it because target audiences want 'the same... but different'. This means producers want this too because that's exactly what sales agents are looking for.

A USEFUL ANALOGY FOR FILM FINANCE

Feeling a little freaked out by film finance? Not sure how to get a handle on how this system works? Clive has a useful analogy for you.

'You have to kind of think about every new film is you going on *Dragon's Den* or *Shark Tank* and saying, "I'd like to raise X amount of money to make this new product",' Clive says. 'On those shows the product creator has to demonstrate that if they ask for fifty thousand pounds, that investor will at least see that fifty thousand back.'

Of course, on *Dragon's Den* or *Shark Tank*, creators are rarely asking for anything like one hundred and fifty thousand pounds or above. It's usually something in the region of fifty thousand pounds. Unless that creator can demonstrate that the Dragons can get a return on it, then they won't get the money.

It's the same with film investment... only a LOT more money is involved.

THE PROBLEM OF ££££$$

Lots of spec screenwriters who love thrillers want to be able to step straight into the top 1% of the industry and write big-budget blockbuster pictures. This is similar in television too: writers may want to go straight in at the top of television networks and studios, working at the highest level.

It's understandable why: most of us will have grown up on such fare; maybe a particular TV show or blockbuster even inspired us to be screenwriters in the first place.

The problem is – yet again! – money.

'My question for those writers who want the budgets of fifty million plus is again, "What is it about you that makes you think that what you're doing, is worth that much of anyone's investment, regardless of how good you are?"' says Clive.

It should be noted Clive doesn't say this to put writers off. I often find myself saying this to writers myself. I'm not being rhetorical: I really want to know!

Too often these writers reply with generic stuff like 'because this story means so much to me'. But we have to be realistic. Would YOU want to gamble literally millions of pounds on someone ELSE's dream, especially when it could mean you tank your own career?

Yet a smaller budget is not all plain sailing, as Clive points out.

'I always ask this: "What is it that gives you the brass-necked belief that what you've written on a page is worth one hundred and fifty thousand pounds' worth of someone's investment, the equivalent of somebody putting *an entire house* into the words that you've put on the page?" Clive says, "Seriously, what makes you so confident that somebody should do that?" Once you start to look at it in that way, I think people's attitude about screenwriting and money changes. You realise that any time somebody puts even the slightest amount of money into production, they are taking a huge risk on a lot of the time on unknown talent.'

Of course, there are certain disclaimers to the above. If a writer has a close connection with a star, an A-list director or studio executive, then the playing field suddenly looks very different.

Also, ironically *because* writers are not automatically required by sales agents to have a track record like directors, producers and actors, it is possible for a relatively unknown writer to break through on a very high-budget production. That said, not that many big-budget features are made – period. This means the likelihood of being one of those few newcomers to break through on a high-budget movie is still very slim.

THE SEIS TAX CREDITS SCHEME FOR FILMMAKING

SEIS stands for 'Seed Enterprise Investment Scheme'. This is a British government scheme set up by the HMRC ('His Majesty's Revenue & Customs'). SEIS is designed to help a company raise money when it's starting up. (Other countries and areas – such as states – have their own schemes, so if you are not in Britain, make sure you check out what's available).

SEIS is a tax relief scheme that allows investors to invest in high-risk endeavours – like film and TV – and get 50 per cent tax relief on their investment, plus other benefits.

'So the maximum amount you can have on this scheme is one hundred and fifty thousand pounds,' Clive says, 'Which is the reason that one hundred and fifty thousand pound budget has been the gold standard for independent films.'

SEIS does all this by offering tax relief to individual investors who buy shares in the company (or film). Producers can receive a maximum of £150,000 through SEIS investments. There are various rules that must be followed so investors can claim and keep SEIS tax reliefs relating to their shares.

'Basically what this all means is, is you are incentivising rich people to put money into film,' Clive says.

'Let's say you're in the top end tax bracket and you put fifty thousand pounds' investment into a company. You immediately get 50 per cent tax relief on that, which is 25,000 pounds. Now in the magical, mystical unicorn world where the film goes into profit, you don't pay any capital gains tax on the profit. So that means that from a fifty-thousand-pound investment, you get 25,000 pounds in tax relief but you could make a potential £75,000 in profit tax-free.'

Clive continues. 'So what that means is, this is high reward, low risk, because you're only risking half of the amount. But actually, it's even less than that. Because if there are any losses, you can claim another percentage of that back in tax relief again.'

FILM TAX CREDIT RELIEF

There was a time in which lots of projects qualified for SEIS. In the 2020s however, SEIS is much, much harder to get. This is because there was lots of abuse of the system: not illegal stuff either, just – shall we say – 'creative accounting'.

Nowadays, film tax credit relief is the more recognisable system and is used most often. Most countries have one. You may even have seen such schemes listed in the credits of your favourite movies and TV shows. (If you haven't, watch the credits right to the end and see – chances are you'll find some).

Tax credit relief is awarded when a production satisfies various criteria. In the UK, this is usually handled by the British Film Institute in conjunction with HMRC. The money producers can raise for film tax credit is unlimited, in contrast to SEIS which was capped at one hundred and fifty thousand pounds.

In direct contrast to SEIS as well, Film Tax Relief does NOT offer tax breaks to the individual investors. This means film and TV is not as attractive to private investors as it once was. Under SEIS, single projects were eligible so producers would make each film a company in its own right – this would protect individuals if the film failed. This is no longer allowed.

Instead, producers must demonstrate how the SEIS money is helping them build and develop their company as a whole. This – plus the death of DVD to streaming – means it's MUCH harder for producers to get a movie off the ground in the 2020s.

Under Film Tax Relief however, producers can qualify for a cash rebate of 25 per cent covering up to 80 per cent of film expenditure. In addition, the film must qualify as 'British' via a cultural test. It's a points-based system and films and television series must score 18 out of 35 possible points to be counted as a British work.

British co-productions also come under this banner. At the time of writing, the UK has co-production agreements with Australia, Canada, China, France, India, Israel, Jamaica, Morocco, New Zealand, Occupied Palestinian Territories, and South Africa. Of these, Australia, Canada, New Zealand, Israel and the Occupied Palestinian Territories also allow for television programmes.

These co-productions are all subject to various cultural and financial conditions too. For example, films usually must be intended for theatrical release in cinemas, plus at least a minimum of ten per cent of the film's core expenditure must be in the UK. There are similar conditions for high-end television tax relief, which can be found on the UK government website, simply search 'TV tax relief'.

UTILISING EXISTING RESOURCES

Another important part is who the investors are doing business with. The producers who can leverage SEIS or film tax credits well are usually part of production companies who have lots of equipment and contacts. They're usually making corporate and music videos, as well as commercials. They have cameras, cinematic lenses, lighting rigs and everything needed to make films already. They know Directors of Photography, Steadicam operators, film directors already because they've worked with them before.

'They'll say to these people, "Are you sick of doing commercials? Do you fancy coming out for a couple of weeks to do some narrative drama?"' Clive says, 'This means they can leverage the budget into three times' worth of resources. So that initial budget film trebles in real terms too.'

But that's not all. Clive continues: 'Another thing you need is a business plan. This is something else we can see at work in *Dragon's Den* or *Shark Tank:* you say "If you give me X amount of money, I will do this and sell products to Harrods and we will make [THIS AMOUNT] of money."

'It's exactly the same in the film industry. So what producers have to do is describe what the product is, and how it fits the distribution market. Because that's where the money comes back from. And these days, a lot of that money in independent film is coming from deals with streamers, from international sales, from TV sales, or international TV sales, via sales agents, and all of these kinds of things.'

From there, producers have to take the film – aka the product – and negotiate with the sales agents. Where they can go with that product affects how much projected £££$$$ they can make. For example, certain territories love or hate certain types of things. China tends to love the more adult action thrillers but dislike ghost stories for example; Americans love action-adventure thrillers for the whole family – the 'four quadrants' – but tend to dislike film with subtitles.

'All creative decisions all have impacts, like the idea for the story, the genre, the kind of cast you can attract, where you can sell it,' Clive says. 'Writers need to understand that they might write the most brilliantly crafted script in the world, but it's absolutely no use to the producer because they can't sell it anywhere, which means they can't get investment.'

'Writing a clever, well-written movie that you can shoot for one hundred and fifty thousand pounds is probably the most difficult task a screenwriter has to take on. And you can only do it if you understand what the money gets spent on.'

But what does it get spent on? Well, that can vary country to country too. Unfortunately, there are lots of things that don't qualify for Film Tax Relief in the UK, such as development, publicity, the option fee on the book for adaptations, or E&O insurance ('Errors and Omissions' – this covers filmmakers from various mistakes not covered by public liability insurance and can be very, very expensive, sometimes as much as ten to twelve per cent of the final budget).

THE PRICE OF DOING BUSINESS

So, how do producers make Film Tax Credit Relief work for their production? First off, it's worth knowing there's LOTS of competition from various places to grab this kind of financial assistance. This means Film Tax Credit Relief tends to work a lot better in poorer countries than the UK, where wages and prices are lower.

For example, though the UK's tax rebate is 25% of the 80% of allowed expenditure and Hungary's is 30%, that extra 5% in Hungary goes a LOT further. Put simply, filmmakers get a lot more 'bang for their buck' abroad.

Let's break it down and apply all this in a simple way. You are a producer and your production company has £500K to shoot a film. In the UK, you would get approximately £125K back in film tax relief, so in real terms you have £625K to make your movie.

The movie is mostly shot on location in the middle of woodland in Devon, which means your heads of department (who are probably from London) will have to be put up at local guesthouses.

Some local crew are driving or taking trains each day from other areas of the West Country and must be compensated for this on top of their wages. A local food truck is doing the catering and has agreed to a lesser cost because it's not peak summer and it's guaranteed work and mouths to feed for a ten-day shoot.

You have also managed to negotiate with some students from the local theatre college to do the make-up and hair. You've found some runners have been recruited from Exeter University. They're working all for free, but need their expenses paid, especially accommodation.

Now let's imagine your production company takes £500K to Hungary. Thirty per cent of £500K is £150K, so that five per cent extra in tax relief equals another 25 grand straight out the gate.

That might not seem great shakes at first when you consider you have to pay for plane tickets, and accommodation etc for cast, some crew and yourself, but there are still major savings to be made.

The cost of living is markedly cheaper in Hungary than the United Kingdom, which means hiring some crew and support staff (caterers, runners, drivers, etc) can be made within Hungary. Hotels and AirBnBs are often much cheaper there too. Similarly the hiring of equipment, buildings or technicians for some post-production (such as CGI) is markedly cheaper as well.

Let's not forget either the exchange rate from pounds to Euros makes the filmmakers better off. At the time of writing, five hundred thousand pounds to Euros is five hundred and eighty-seven thousand euros, almost a hundred grand more for doing nothing other than moving country.

In short, other countries have the jump on the United Kingdom, not only on low-budget films, but big-budget films too. Consider a behemoth like *The Expendables* (2010–2023) franchise. It's been shot all over the world – Bulgaria, Brazil, Greece etc – not only for its global appeal and target audience, but because it literally saves money and ups potential profits. It is good business.

SO, WHAT DO SCREENWRITERS NEED?

- **Investors.** To get investors on board, we need to understand how tax schemes like SEIS work and what investors can get out putting money into our films. This is harder to do in the 2020s because SEIS is so hard to get.
- **Film tax relief.** Understanding how this works in your country is super-important. Don't leave money on the table by being unaware what is available. Also make sure you contrast what you can get in other countries and how much more you can get for your production if you film in another territory.
- **A producer with a business plan.** You also probably need one who has access to equipment and people, either via their own production company or because they are excellent at schmoozing, have a ton of goodwill and know everyone.
- **A kick-ass script.** It needs a clear genre like thriller, a fantastic concept that rolls off the tongue and characters with discernible role functions that can attract actors of high calibre. (What's more,

if you want stars to take a pay cut, you need to be able to offer them a role that will help them make a comeback or redefine how we 'see' them – ie. a previously comedic actor can show off his/her serious acting chops).

- **Can be shot abroad.** Ensuring your story has global appeal can help sales agents sell it, plus ensures it can take advantage of various tax relief deals. Write scripts that can be shot in other countries easily.
- **Can be shot in a short timeframe.** Ten to fourteen days is optimum for indie film. This doesn't mean you have to be all in one location (though that can help), but you need to cut down on the time it takes to pack up and set up in various locations. This means having locations that are geographically close can really help. Alternatively, if you can shoot in a studio at low or no cost – maybe because your producer's company has their own – even better.
- **Understanding of what sales agents want.** Sales agents think in the terms target audiences pick their next film to watch. Being able to provide stars or actors audiences like (rather than tolerate), a director with some kind of 'buzz' and a strong sense of what the movie is about from the title and concept is key.

Lastly, you need the brass-neck belief your project is worth the money. If you have all the above, you're a contender.

ALL ABOUT CROWDFUNDING

Crowdfunding your thriller may seem like a no-brainer to some; it bypasses the difficulties of film finance and private investment, plus it potentially places audiences in the driving seat of the stories they want to see. What's not to like? Quite a bit, to be honest: many crowdfunding campaigns run aground thanks to one or more of the following:

- **They are not realistic**. Many projects set funding targets that are beyond them. It's improbable you will generate all of the money you need. Whilst it is possible to generate a lot of money via crowdfunding, unless you have a large following online already or your project has a specific focus or message people actively want to buy into (such as anti-racism or anti-bullying), generating a huge wad of cash is unlikely. Be realistic about what you can achieve and you're more likely to achieve it.
- **They lose their momentum**. The longer you crowdfund for, the less interested people become. That's just part of the human condition. It's no accident that many of the most successful campaigns have been 30 days or less. Momentum is key in a crowdfunding campaign. Make people think they may miss out if they don't invest, there and then. It is possible.
- **They are annoying**! Most filmmakers' crowdfunding strategy appears to consist of just three things: stick up the funding page; offer all kinds of dubious perks for various amounts of money; then spam the hell out of everyone via Instagram, Twitter and Facebook, especially people who have large followings online.

The key in avoiding the above is reframing the concept of crowdfunding. Lots of creatives I have worked with see it as a kind of legitimised begging and treat it as such. As a result they are more likely to annoy people on social media and also less likely to hit their target. Yet as director Chris Jones points out, *'Offer people the chance to contribute. No one wants to donate. Subtle but important difference.'* But how to do this? Try these things:

- **Think of all your crowdfunders as potential audience members.** This is so basic, yet something I see screenwriters and filmmakers miss time and time again. Instead they will send out missives asking for £££$$$ saying 'Please help, because this means so much to me.' Whilst that might get your mum or work colleagues to donate, it's unlikely to motivate people you've never met online. However if you reframe the campaign from that potential audience member's POV and make them want to SEE your thriller?? Suddenly they're more willing to part with their cash.

- **Know who your target audience is – and where they hang out!** Work out who would want to watch your thriller and why – not just in terms of human elements like age group, but also what would make your thriller appealing to them. For example, if you're crowd funding a sci-fi thriller, identify those sci-fi blogs, sites, newsletters, events etc that may help you get the word out about your campaign to their readers and patrons.
- **Understand timing is EVERYTHING in crowdfunding.** As mentioned, 30 days or less is optimum for your campaign. Always make sure that you have the end of the month in your crowdfunding, because that's when the most people get paid. Similarly, avoid running crowdfunding campaigns around Christmas because people tend to be all tapped out. The summer holidays can have an impact as well: fewer people are paying attention to their phones and social media when it's sunny and/or they're off work too.
- **Understand the impact of 'interested parties' versus random posting.** One of the reasons crowdfunding campaigns have such a bad reputation on social media is because those running campaigns tend to spam groups and timelines, even tagging people they've never met before. Sometimes they repeat the same message again and again and again. This will get you blocked and unfriended. It's far, far better to have a posting strategy about your film, highlighting issues or elements of your story and intriguing people, who can then choose to engage. In addition, social media moves FAST and people rarely see much of what gets posted on it. This is why marketing gurus are still of the opinion the best online marketing strategy in the 2020s is the email newsletter. Sending updates and interesting tidbits about the project to someone's inbox is far, far, far more likely to hit the 'bull's eye'. Learn all you can about newsletters to make the most of this opportunity – the average email software will allow you the first thousand subscribers for free, too.
- **Give yourself enough 'lead time'.** Having 'champions' who will help you roll out your crowdfunding campaign is important, but you need

to identify them early. Every week I get pitched guest posts for www.bang2write.com from creatives doing crowdfunding campaigns. B2W gets many thousands of eyes on it per month so I like to support as many campaigns as possible, but unfortunately I have to turn the vast majority down. Why? Because the crowdfunders don't leave enough 'lead time': they want me to post their guest post that week or the week after, before their campaign ends. Yet I plan content on the B2W main site and on its social media at least two weeks in advance, which means the crowdfunders have to wait... and frequently that means they have to take the guest post elsewhere. So if you want a big site that gets a lot of hits to help get the word out about your campaign, it pays to plan in advance and get them to agree to this BEFORE your campaign begins.

- **Pick rewards that won't sacrifice the integrity of your project.** If your campaign goes well, then it's worth remembering the vast majority of your crowdfunders probably won't be part of the film industry. Sometimes crowdfunding campaigns offer up an 'exec producer' credit as a reward for anyone who donates a significant amount of cash. Exec Producers are typically big industry names who bolster a project when trying to get private investment, tax credits, an Oscar run or so on. This begs the question: do you REALLY want people you don't know and have never met listed as 'exec producer' on your project? Similarly, beware of offering up a physical copy of the film as a download or DVD. When piracy is so commonplace, those crowdfunders may put it on YouTube for free (or similar). Obviously crowdfunders should see the finished product they contribute to, but it's better to offer real-life screenings and/or online viewing that's password-protected and can't be downloaded.

- **Be transparent.** Be prepared to answer questions, such as *'Why are you making this film if you don't have the money?'* Some people will need to be won over and that's fair enough. Be prepared to tell them the routes you have tried already (if applicable), plus why you are crowdfunding. There's a lot of bullshit in this industry, but if you are transparent you are more likely to find those who believe in you and your project.

You need to treat your crowd-sourced thriller as a business opportunity. Think of the people who hand over the money as your investors. Have the screenplay available for them to read, so they can make an informed decision on whether they want to get behind your thriller. Talk online about making the film, involving your potential investors and your 'champions' wherever possible. Also, understand you're FAR more likely to reach people who sign up for updates on Kickstarter, Indiegogo etc or via your website's newsletter than randoms on social media.

Most of all, be professional at all times. Don't just have endless countdowns, retweets, regrams or reposts either: talk about the message and purpose of the film: WHY you are making it. Talk about who is in it; who the crew is; what your influences are and so on. Bring people to you and create buzz online and you're far less likely to annoy people and much more likely to reach your funding target when you run your campaign.

SUMMING UP...

- Your film is a business opportunity. Realising this is key in accessing money/getting it made/crowd-sourcing money.
- Knowing what production logistics can impact on filmmaking can aid rewrites.
- Knowing the various routes and what they entail will aid your chances in getting your script produced.
- Do your research: know what money is available, where and how it works.
- Read books on film financing and/or consider doing a course, or see panels on the subject at festivals in real life or on Zoom.
- Don't think it's all up to the producer – you can only gain from this knowledge.

PACKAGING & ATTACHMENTS

WHAT IS PACKAGING?

Never forget: we all respond to packaging, whether it's washing powder, or a trailer in the cinema or on Netflix. This means your movie must be packaged in order to, a) get the money to make it, and b) sell it to the people that matter. The people that matter are varied, but include actors and money men (and women) or the people who get the movie to your target audience. So you need to know what you're doing when it comes to packaging – and why. In general, the people holding the purse strings for movie money (whether public funding or private investment) do not read scripts, at least in the first instance. There isn't the time. Instead, they will look at 'packages' to determine whether the script is worth consideration.

In recent years, I've noted 'packages' for projects approaching production tend to get called different things now: they may be referred to as 'pitch decks', 'series bibles' (for TV) or just 'treatments'. Whatever you call them, these packages usually run to between five and ten pages and consist of the following for your project:

- **A short pitch.** Of the packages I've seen, this is usually the logline and runs between 25 and 60 words. Occasionally it's longer and written in the style of the blurb on the back of a DVD box, with quotes from various reputable producers or script consultants who may have read it before when the screenplay was in development.

Here is also the place to put the names of those involved in the project: the writer, director and producer.

- **An extended pitch**. Your one-pager, usually. Sometimes that polished treatment is included; more often not.
- **A short budget breakdown.** This page is usually written by the producer. S/he will give the budget, how much they're seeking in private investment as well as what avenues they will be exploring in terms of tax credits, leaseback, what they have 'in kind' (deals they have struck with people in getting equipment, people's time, etc, for free or at reduced rates).
- **Casting suggestions**. Ideally these should be for actors who have agreed, or who are attached to your film via a reputable casting director. However, I have seen some packages with 'wish lists' of casts.
- **A director's vision**. What, no writer's vision? Nope! How your script will be made is an important point and one screenwriters frequently underestimate, yet it's how your audience will perceive the end product. What's more, sales agents never ask, 'Who wrote it?', but they DO ask, 'Who's directing?' If you don't like this, go back to film school and study directing so you can become a writer/director!
- **Concept art/mood boards.** If your thriller screenplay is set in a surreal or future world, or features a new take on a monster or alien, it's a really good idea to pay an artist to draw up some concept art for you so potential investors can see where you're coming from. Otherwise it's perfectly acceptable to use stock photos to give an idea of the tone/look of your thriller screenplay and how it will be rendered as image. It's NOT a good idea, however, to use photos from existing movies to do this; you don't want to create 'noise' in the potential investors' minds when considering your thriller.

Sometimes public-funding bodies insist on various additions, like CVs and references, but the above will satisfy most potential private investors. You will usually attach the screenplay at the same time as applying for public money, but generally not if going for private investment. If potential private investors like your package, they will usually request the script next.

In the case of both, whether they read it themselves or farm it out to a script reader will depend on the place: production companies tend to do the former; private investment companies (especially those specialising in investing in movies and entertainment) and public-funding bodies, like screen agencies, tend to do the latter. If they do farm out the script to a reader, the reader will be asked to provide a synopsis of the script, which gives a blow-by-blow account of what happens. Then the reader will be asked to rate certain characteristics of the script, including the obvious things such as characterisation, structure and dialogue, but also things like health and safety; how easy it would be to film; what audience it would appeal to; what opportunities could the film take advantage of (i.e. a female protagonist, in a thriller with a theme about women's rights? Release the film on International Women's Day) and so on.

Whether your thriller script even gets read tends to rely on the attractiveness of your package, but I have seen so many that are rushed or undersold. It pays to make yours as appealing as possible. Just like your screenplay, then, get feedback – from whatever source – on your package before you send it out. And if you're crowd-sourcing the money for your movie? It still pays to package your project professionally: the more people know about your thriller and what is going into it, the better. Again, treat Joe Public as potential investors, not donors. Remember, if people aren't giving to their friends and family, they want to invest in projects they can believe in. How can they know whether your project is the 'right' one, out of the thousands listed on Indiegogo, Kickstarter et al? Tell them! Create a website for your project with your package on it. Keep it professional, like a real business opportunity. Upload a copy of the script as a PDF so potential investors can read it at their leisure – and share it if they want to. The easier you make the process of investing in your thriller, the more likely it is that you will get the investment you seek.

PRE-SALES AND ADDED VALUE

Sometimes you will be able to use the package for pre-sales, and, by this, I generally mean attract a sales agent. Sales agents handle things like working out the market value of your project; where it will be sold in the various territories (Europe, USA, Asia, etc) and how, i.e. theatrical run, straight to streaming services as 'Amazon Originals' etc, and so on. If you can get a sales agent BEFORE making the project, this immediately means your movie has added value because it won't be languishing in the can. This also means you're far more likely to find the investment to make the film. However, it can become a bit of a catch-22, as sales agents generally like to know whether you've got the investment to make the film too.

Sales agents are easy to find online, but can be slippery eels in terms of holding their attention. However, a shiny, well-developed package can work wonders in getting you through the door, especially as so many packages are ill-conceived or scrappy. More often than not, sales agents are most concerned with those all-important three questions mentioned in the previous chapter from any package:

- **Who's in it?** This is where the notion of 'bankable stars' really comes into its own. The short version: if you have a named star, you're far more likely to garner interest from a sales agent.
- **Who's directing it?** That's right, the director can have pulling power too. Remember, no one really cares who wrote it, I'm afraid, which is either depressing or liberating, depending on your viewpoint (the latter, surely? It means 'anyone' can write it!).
- **What's it about?** This is where your fantastic central concept and killer logline come into play. Remember that all-important notion of a 'great story with great characters'. Grab those sales agents by the short and curlies, make their eyes light up!

So take another look at your package. Does it address these three, all-important questions? If it doesn't, it might be wise to have another pass before sending it out to sales agents.

STRINGS ATTACHED

As Clive Frayne posited, the investors in *Dragon's Den* or *Shark Tank* on TV will frequently offer investment in people's ideas for products or services, with various conditions attached. The Dragons usually want a higher stake in that person's company than is offered, or they may say they want to bring someone else on board, or chuck one of the original team off. We've seen the same in talent shows like *The X Factor* and *Britain* or *America's Got Talent*: two people or a group will come on stage and perform; the judging panel may say there's one person they like more than the rest, or one person they think is bringing the rest down. There will be many tearful close-ups as the people in all the scenarios consider what the Dragons or Judging Panel have to say, complete with tense music and perhaps the odd recrimination and bout of pleading. Decision made, the person in the Den or the people on stage will accept or reject the proposals and the show will go on.

It's often the same with getting the money to make your film. Production companies and private investors rarely offer money for feature films and TV series with no conditions attached whatsoever. Common conditions include:

- **Producer credit.** Money moguls are typically awarded an 'Executive' or 'Associate' producer credit anyway, but they may want a 'Producer' credit as well and also to be involved in the shoot or various production decisions. Whether that's a good idea depends how much input that investor wants, not to mention who your investor is and how much they know about production.

- **Director attachment.** As mentioned previously, if the director is inexperienced, investors may insist s/he is replaced, especially if they know or have an 'in' with the 'right' director. Named directors, especially ones with previous major commercial or critical successes, bring value to a project almost as much as the stars in them. It is a wise move to let your investors replace you, especially if you have never directed a feature before. You will have more clout once your thriller screenplay is produced and you can try again another time. But if you stick to your guns, you may scare investors off and not get that added clout next time, as your thriller screenplay will stay on your desktop instead.

- **Script rewrites.** Sometimes an investor will want the script rewritten if they are to part with their cash. I have worked on projects where these demands have been as small as changing a character's age or name, through to larger changes like gender or ethnicity; through to changing the set up or ending; to even keeping the premise and going back to page one and starting over. As with most things scriptwriting-related, it is a question of balance: don't say no automatically, but don't be too eager to please, either. You don't want to end up with a completely different film.
- **Location.** Sometimes an investor has a preferred place they want to shoot movies. This might be because it helps them access other money (particularly public funding, but producing partners of their own, too) or because production is typically cheaper in that area, i.e. in Eastern Europe or the Isle of Man. The investor may stipulate you must shoot in that preferred location if you are to get their money, so you must weigh this up carefully.
- **Distribution.** There are many different channels of distribution now that bring their own opportunities and threats. On the one hand, the plethora of platforms, especially online, means well-conceived, well-made genre movies with strong hooks rarely languish in the can for years like they once did. But, on the other, piracy is an even bigger issue than it once was: thieves can steal your movie virtually and have it streaming on various sites within hours of it being released. Because of this, investors may want to know your plans for protecting your thriller from piracy, such as a reduced theatrical run, with a streaming release weeks, rather than months, afterwards; or a multi-platform launch across all formats – cinema, online – on the same day.
- **Star attachment.** Sometimes investors, especially big prodcos, will have agreements with stars to be in a certain number of movies. On this basis, then, the investor will give you the money for your thriller *as long as* that star who 'owes' them is in it. You must then decide if that star is the 'right' one. Other times, you may have

your own star attached and the investor gives you the money *as long as* that star does not drop out. Occasionally, the investor will tell you s/he likes the script but doesn't like the star and wants them replaced with someone else. In all these cases, you must work out how you can keep the star (or substitute someone else for him or her) and the money, because star power is a massive draw when it comes to thrillers.

STAR POWER AKA BANKABLE TALENT

Casting is one element of the package that can speak for itself, especially if you have a named star attached to the project. I have read some genuinely appalling screenplays over the years with big names attached that have gone on to be made… and done reasonable, or even great, business at the box office. Why? Because of star power. Screenwriters can stick doggedly to the notion that it's 'only' story that counts, and maybe it does to fellow writers and filmmakers. But most of your potential audience are NOT your fellow writers and filmmakers, and it pays to remember that.

This is how star power works: my tween daughter is looking for something to watch. Even though she is my child, she takes after her father and is more interested in science than screenwriting. She is not a creative and doesn't care how movies and TV are made: why would she? Remember, just like approximately 90 per cent of your audience, she 'just' wants to be entertained. So imagine this scene: like so many kids, she loves Netflix. She tells me she has finished bingeing the latest TV series and is wondering what to watch next. Knowing she enjoys action adventure, I suggest a movie in which four teens are sucked into a video game. I'm of course talking about *Jumanji: Welcome To The Jungle* (2017), the remake of the classic 1995 Disney movie starring Robin Williams. My daughter is not interested; she is not a gamer and it doesn't sound like her type of thing, she says. Then I say five words that grab her attention: *'The Rock is in it.'* Her eyes light up. *'Oh I like him. I'll watch it.'* Boom! Done.

Never underestimate the importance of star power. Your thriller is for laypeople like my child, not fellow writers and filmmakers.

Laypeople don't always care what your movie is about, but they nearly always care who is in it: it can mean the difference between them seeing the film or not. So whilst star power can be a risk – they may hate the actor, thus not see it – it's one that usually pays off, since all big-name actors have a fanbase, even ones who are as equally reviled... That's why they're big-name actors. Attaching such an actor to your script, then, can only be a good thing.

THE PROBLEM OF BANKABLE TALENT

The fact there's so much more money and more choices now means there's a reliance on star power to not only get potential viewers' attention, but financiers' and studio too in getting low-budget movies in particular greenlit in the first place.

Financiers need to 'de-risk' their investment in a production. Star power was traditionally one way of doing this: if an audience like a particular star, they're more likely to watch a movie (even eclipsing other important things like character and story!).

Investors often call this 'bankable talent'. With streaming literally grabbing up all the bankable stars by the bucketload for series then, they can be at a premium for all but the biggest of movie franchises such as the Marvel Cinematic Universe (MCU).

After all, if the bankable star you want for your low-budget movie may get literally double or even treble their fee in a television serial AND guarantee they're a) seen internationally and b) get months or even years of work (rather than a few weeks), why would they bother? It's a no-brainer.

This has led to some redrawing of what constitutes 'star power' and 'bankable talent' in the 2020s, as I've witnessed in various movie deals, especially in the past five years.

It's even affected A-list producers such as Jerry Bruckheimer, who's responsible for some of the biggest thrillers of the last 40 years: *Top Gun, Beverley Hills Cop, Bad Boys, Con Air, Armageddon* (to name just a few). Speaking to the *Telegraph* newspaper in the UK in 2022, Bruckheimer said:

> *'I still get the same list of men studios want in a movie. You get Tom, Leonardo, Brad. Get one of those big names and you've got a good shot of getting a movie made.'*

It's surprising how few male actors have broken through in the same way as Cruise, DiCaprio or Pitt in the past 30 to 40 years. Though Bruckheimer conceded in the interview that Chris Hemsworth has made it to A-list status, he also admitted female stars do not have as strong a position as their male counterparts. (Whether this is because their careers are shorter due to Hollywood ageism or just as standard Bruckheimer did not say).

But if it's affecting a big hitter like Bruckheimer like this, you can bet it's rippling all the way from the top of the industry down to the bottom.

As an example, it *was* accepted wisdom in the past that actors could use soap operas as springboards for their careers. In the 2020s this tried-and-tested route seems less certain. Some investors even veto soap actors for low-budget movies because they're apparently 'not famous enough'.

This seems a shame given soap operas have launched the careers of Hollywood stars like Guy Pearce (who started on *Neighbours*); or the aforementioned A-lister Chris Hemsworth (he started in Aussie soap *Home And Away*). British TV drama favourites like Suranne Jones, Katherine Kelly and Sarah Lancashire, to name just a few, also started in *Coronation Street*, another soap opera.

In addition, this has trickled down the scale to affect *non*-stars too. Whereas once established and popular character actors could be enough to greenlight a low-budget production, this is not always the case in the 2020s.

I am reminded of one particular production that I cannot name that had a fantastic central premise, a killer script and some brilliant roles for the female lead and the male antagonist.

A well-known character actor had promised to sign on for the male lead. The filmmakers were thrilled, especially as that particular actor had just completed a variety of prestigious TV roles for which he'd garnered across-the-board acclaim.

Best of all, he'd starred in an indie film in the similar ballpark as the one on the table just three years before. The film had done exceptionally well, impressing critics and audiences alike and selling well across the world.

What a difference those 36 months made, unfortunately. Despite that actor's attachment and the success of that previous movie, investors ended up in gridlock. They didn't feel the actor could carry the movie on his own name; he was not 'bankable enough'. Before long, the project had collapsed.

HOW ACTORS CAN MAKE POWERFUL CONTACTS

This does mean having a prior relationship with an actor (who then becomes a star in their own right) can pay dividends. The British star Tom Hardy is well-known in the thriller space in the 2020s, having garnered critical acclaim in the UK and Hollywood, for roles as varied as Alfie Solomons in the BBC's *Peaky Blinders* (2013–2022) and Max Rockatansky in *Mad Max: Fury Road* (2015).

Hardy is also Eddie Brock in the *Venom* movies. Though not technically part of the MCU (due to various legal wranglings which means the Venom character belongs to Sony), he has made a considerable splash in the superhero/antihero subgenre. He even shares a 'story by' credit on *Venom: Let There Be Carnage* (2021) with screenwriter Kelly Marcel, who explains how it came about:

'Tom and I have been friends and collaborators for a very long time. We started way back in a little theatre space where actors would gather to workshop scenes. I was working in the DVD shop across the road from the theatre. Then when he was doing Bronson *(2008) I came in to rewrite for him and we established a way of working on that film that has stuck on the various projects we've done together.*

'Tom's very involved with every aspect of whatever he's working, he's not an actor that's just going to show up and say lines you've handed to him. He wants to talk about the who's and what's and why's of a scene long before we get to shooting it. It was a natural and fair progression to have him get a story by credit because he has always been involved in the creation. He's brilliant to work with, his brain works so fast, he churns out ideas for hours and selfishly, writing can get lonely, so it's a bonus to be able to collaborate with my mate!'

Some of the spec screenwriters I have worked with seem to regard actors as 'meat puppets' who just roll up and perform lines. These writers may even guard their dialogue or scenarios so jealously they put up unintentional roadblocks around their work and stop actors' interest in the script or them. This is a serious own goal.

Though obviously the average actor won't go on to become a mover and shaker like Tom Hardy, it is worth writers collaborating with them. If nothing else, workshopping scenes and understanding how actors see their characters and the situations they find themselves in can be a real masterclass. Writers have nothing to lose and everything to gain, so look into opportunities to workshop pages or do readthroughs wherever you can (details at the back of the book).

ATTACHING STARS

Thriller is not like horror or drama, which can get an audience even with a cast of unknowns. Thriller usually needs a star to drive it. The average audience member wants to see a face s/he recognises at the heart of the thriller: this is why we see so many stars in this genre. But it's not a question of grabbing someone, anyone with a 'name'... You need to find the right one. But how? Consider these questions:

- **Who's right for the role?** A good producer or director will ask you who you feel is right for the roles in your thriller screenplay, so consider this question carefully in advance. Remember that notion of writing 'for' actors... but don't be too specific, either. Try and think of three to five actors who would be suitable for EACH of your characters. No fewer.
- **Who wants it?** Very often, big-name stars get bored of playing the same kinds of roles and are very vocal about it, either in filmmaking circles or on social media. This is hardly surprising; it's so they can get offered new roles to consider. As mentioned, big-name stars have even been known to accept substantial pay cuts to their normal fees if they like the script enough. So find out which

big-name star you like is looking for something different and see if your screenplay is something they might consider.

- **Where do you have an 'in'?** As Kelly Marcel discovered, the filmmaking world is very small. If you know someone who is making major inroads into the acting world, all the better. If not, find out if you know someone who knows, has worked with, or even goes to the same gym as the big-name star you want in your film. Ask everyone you know, but DON'T send blanket emails. Write a personal email – even two short lines is better than a blanket, non-personal one. If someone can introduce you to a big-name star and offers to introduce you (if only via email), brilliant. If not, find out who the star's agent is and call him/her on the phone. Introduce yourself and say that you know their client 'is interested in roles about…' (and make sure s/he actually is!). Ask if you can send your screenplay for his/her consideration? You never know, you may get lucky.

It bears repeating that it pays to build relationships with actors whenever you can – even those who are not stars. Producer Arvind Ethan David has some further wisdom on this: *'Actors become famous in unexpected ways and the chap who the agent was begging you to meet with one month, will be the toast of Hollywood the next. If you took the first meeting, then maybe you'll get your calls returned or your script read after they hit it big. Maybe. But if you didn't build the relationship from early doors, you'll need the pile of cash to hook their interest next time.'*

But if you don't have any time, luck or a pile of cash, don't panic. There's still another avenue, and one you may want to go straight to, especially if your contacts in the media world are lacking: casting directors.

ATTACHING CASTING DIRECTORS

Casting directors are what their name suggests: they are paid to cast actors and actresses in projects, usually for producers. Their role may vary from auditioning lesser-known actors to meeting with big-name stars (who tend not to audition, since their more prolific body of work usually speaks for their abilities). If the casting director is good, s/he will know how to get hold of just about any actor or actress a director or producer wants.

A casting director is the indie filmmaker's ally, yet is frequently overlooked, especially in this age of online actors' casting websites. As casting agent Caley Powell points out: *'The best way to get me as casting director interested in your project is to have a strong script with well-rounded characters, with a great script. That way ideas will bounce into my head as I am reading and I can begin compiling lists of the best actors for the parts.'*

So knowing a casting director and making friends with him/her really can make all the difference in getting your thriller screenplay in front of the 'right' people, attracting bankable stars or directors and producers. Having a specific casting director attached to your project gives it value, since it shows investors you have the ability to reach the actors you want; your list isn't just a wish list.

Casting directors are often very sociable people and frequent all the 'in' places, especially events where actors will be; find actors and you will find casting directors. A new casting director may be open to collaborating with you and/or your team, but be aware it is unlikely an established one will work on deferred payment. An established casting director may also only consider your screenplay if a producer is attached already. That said, nothing ventured, nothing gained: even established casting directors have dry spells, so may be glad to work with you in getting your thriller screenplay in front of actors. As with all approaches, avoid being quirky or weird and never pitch 'at' them. Engage them in conversation in the first instance and see what happens. Even if they are not interested, they may know someone who might be... Remember, the more people who know about you and your thriller screenplay, the more likely it is to get produced. This is echoed by producer Zahra Zomorrodian (@fnafilms), who gives me a run for my money with this VERY no-nonsense advice for writers: *'Leave your comfort zone, meet people, don't be a wanker and don't be mad.'* Simple, eh?

SUMMING UP...

- The right package brings investment – whether from public-funding bodies, private investors or crowd-sourcing.
- Investors frequently offer money with conditions attached. Work out in advance what are deal-breakers and what you will compromise on.
- Never compromise on the screenplay's story quality.
- Recognise the importance of star power, but don't take just anyone; choose the 'right' star.
- Most of your audience don't always care what your film is about, but they nearly always care who is in it, especially if it's a dramatic hook.
- Get to the 'right' stars by hook or by crook – and remember the casting director is your friend.
- Get out there and do it!

But there's just one more thing, lieutenant...

ADDENDUM

DEAL-BREAKERS & ARTISTIC INTEGRITY

Many writers tell me they don't write 'for' the marketplace and would rather pass up the opportunity of getting their screenplay produced than sacrifice their artistic integrity. Others tell me such writers are crazy and the industry is one big sausage factory that will grind them and their work up anyway, so they might as well 'sell out'. But, yet again, it's about finding the middle ground. Commerce is the driving force behind the industry, but that's not to say there is no room for art at all. It's perfectly possible to compromise, giving investors what they want and retaining your artistic integrity, but you DO have to figure out in advance what a complete deal-breaker would be. So don't get caught on the hop. Have a plan. And never, ever, let someone else change your work beyond your recognition, even if it is for a stack of cash. Otherwise, what's the point of making it?

Similarly, there will be times you will wonder why you are bothering. There are jaded writers, producers and filmmakers around who proclaim it is 'impossible' to make a decent, low-budget film, and they will cite any number of supposedly 'awful' films to make their point. Add to that the number of both bona fide and self-appointed film critics (especially online via social media) and it may feel as if you are swimming against the tide. So don't do it: change direction. Ignore these negative people, block or unfriend them if necessary. You know you are doing the best you can, with the materials, people and money available to you. What else is there? It's very easy to criticise; much harder to create. But those who actually work in the industry know this. If others point the finger about the quality of your writing or film, they are exposing themselves as the amateurs they are. Filmmaking is a learning curve; move forwards with your head held high.

NEVER FORGET: CONCEPT IS KEY

Again: there is no more important element than concept in selling your thriller screenplay 'off the page' to agents and filmmakers. A producer friend lamented to me once: *'The spec pile can be divided into two: the great ideas, written badly, and the bad ideas, written well.'* Absorbing this, I enquired: 'And which one is preferable?' To which she answered without hesitation: *'The great ideas, written badly.'* That's right! *Your brilliant writing will fall by the wayside* if your central concept is wanting. Why? Because the better the idea behind the script, the more producers and agents can do with it; they can teach you to get better at writing, if necessary, or buy the script for the idea and replace you with another writer for the rewrite. On the flipside, however good the writing is, if the central concept sucks, what's the point? As the classic saying goes, you 'cannot make a silk purse with a sow's ear'.

So forget about pardoning yourself with comfortable phrases like 'originality is overrated' or 'it's the execution that counts' because, in the spec market, that is simply not true. We want original; we want to be grabbed; we want to say, 'Why didn't I think of that?' Because that's the beauty of a truly great concept: it seems OBVIOUS. So get working on those concepts. A great philosopher once said, 'What's the worst that can happen?' Okay, it was Dr Pepper. But she/he/it was right!

FINAL NOTE: THE ONES THAT 'MAKE IT'

Now that you have a polished thriller screenplay with a great concept and are in the market for finding producers and filmmakers and beyond, I feel I should address 'making it' – not just in terms of actually producing the movie, but that mythical notion of being a 'professional writer'. Writers email, message and tweet me all the time: how come some writers 'make it' and others don't? Is it just luck? Or some other secret ingredient the professionals discover and greedily keep to themselves? Nope. There's *no* secret ingredient to 'making it'. That's the bad news… But, again, it's also the good news. Why? Because there is *absolutely nothing* standing in your way of getting out there and doing it, too. No matter who you are, where you're from, or what you want to write about, thriller screenplay or not.

It comes down to this: all (!) you need is that marketable screenplay with a clear central concept and a strong hook… And the balls to get it out there. Agents, producers and filmmakers are always looking for strong projects, so make yours the one they pick… or even fight over. Anything is possible, so go for it.

And the final word goes to Mark Sanderson, aka @scriptcat:

> *'Attack your screenwriting dreams with a zeal and passion for your craft. Once you light your creative flame, only you can extinguish it. So always keep writing and keep the faith.'*

Good luck!

RESOURCES

FIRST, A 'THANK YOU'

I have tried to list as many writers' resources and useful sites as possible but will inevitably forget some, so first of all: thanks to all the writers, publishers, filmmakers, script consultants, competitions, services, trainers, readers, agents and assistants who endeavour to share their insights on the web with students of the craft. We salute you! It can seem like a thankless task sometimes, but you are more appreciated and have made more of a difference than you know. Kudos!

GRAB YOUR FREE STUFF FROM B2W

First things first, DO grab your free stuff! You will find free downloads such as the B2W plotting worksheet, one-page pitch guide, logline cheat sheet, in the PDF gallery as well as free ebooks and links to the most popular articles at www.bang2write.com/resources.

B2W's Frequently Asked Questions (FAQs) can be found here >> https://bang2write.com/b2w-faqs-your-questions-answered. It covers the most common questions the B2Wers have asked, ranging from writing craft, through to submissions, recommendations networking, self belief and more.

You can also find B2W's FREE online, on-demand masterclass 'The Foundations of Writing Craft' on the resources page or at http://

bang2write.teachable.com. (There's also a range of other paid-for on-demand courses from B2W there too).

Don't forget either you're welcome to ask me a questions via social media:

- Instagram: www.instagram.com/Bang2write
- Twitter: www.twitter.com/Bang2write
- Facebook: www.facebook.com/Bang2writers

I also run various challenges, livestreams etc on social media too. Do come and join us by following me or signing up for the newsletter at www.bang2write.com.

USEFUL LINKS

I ripped all of these from my own favourites. These sites are useful for research and finding script leads. Note: some are fee-paying, plus do remember that if a site is free, it may go out of date quickly. Always double-check!

- Screen Daily – film, television and streamer news world-wide (subscription fees apply, though you can get some free articles): https://www.screendaily.com.
- Broadcast – UK-centric info about television and streamers, scripted & unscripted: https://www.broadcastnow.co.uk.
- IMDBPro – database of films & TV, PLUS everything in production & development (fee applies): https://pro.imdb.com/.
- Done Deal Pro – Film and TV script sales and deals (US-centric, fees apply): https://www.donedealpro.com/.
- The Film Catalogue – info about film productions and distribution (free newsletter): https://www.thefilmcatalogue.com/
- The Bookseller – publishing news in the UK and around the world (subscription fee applies, thought you can get some free articles): https://www.thebookseller.com
- Publishers Weekly – publishing news in the USA and around the world: https://www.publishersweekly.com.

- Lit Rejections – info plus free database of agents world-wide: http://www.litrejections.com.
- Selling Your Screenplay – info on how to sell yours: http://www.sellingyourscreenplay.com.
- The Big List of UK Writing Competitions (Neon Books): https://www.neonbooks.org.uk/big-list-writing-competitions/.
- Reedsy's US List of writing competitions: https://blog.reedsy.com/writing-contests/.
- Moviebytes List of Screenwriting Competitions: https://www.moviebytes.com.
- Writer Beware – great site to check bogus agents, publishers and practices out: https://writerbeware.blog.
- Inktip – Script hosting site for writers seeking producers (fees apply): https://www.inktip.com.
- BBC Writersroom – Runs several submissions cycles a year (UK writers only): https://www.bbc.co.uk/writersroom.
- The Black List – Script hosting site for writers seeking producers (fees apply): https://blcklst.com.
- Virtual Pitchfest – Writers can pitch to industry pros via this site, for a fee: https://www.virtualpitchfest.com.
- Roadmap Writers – Connects writers to industry pros, for a fee: https://www.roadmapwriters.com.
- Screencraft – writing competitions and talent discovery: https://screencraft.org.
- Shore Scripts – competitions include the prestigious Short Film Fund: https://www.shorescripts.com/.
- Coverfly – submissions portal & showcase for screenwriters: https://www.coverfly.com.
- Film Freeway – Film festivals and screenplay competitions submissions portal: https://filmfreeway.com.
- BAFTA Rocliffe New Writing Competition – runs several contests a year: https://www.bafta.org/supporting-talent/rocliffe.
- BFI National Film and Television Archive – as its name suggests! https://www.bfi.org.uk.
- The Bill Douglas Cinema Museum – check out its archives: https://www.bdcmuseum.org.uk.
- Short of the Week – watch short films of various genres online:

https://www.shortoftheweek.com.

- Authors Publish – information about publishers, as well as submission calls: https://authorspublish.com.
- The Fiction Desk – short story publishers: https://www.thefictiondesk.com.
- Jane Friedman's The Hot Sheet – newsletter about publishing: https://hotsheetpub.com.
- The WGA – The Writers' Guild of America: https://www.wga.org.
- The WGGB – The Writer's Guild of Great Britain: https://writersguild.org.uk.
- WFTV – Women In Film & Television: https://www.wftv.org.uk.
- The Script Vault – copyright registration: https://www.thescriptvault.com.
- CopyrightsWorld – another copyright registration service: https://copyrightsworld.com.
- Go Into The Story – VERY useful screenwriting blog: https://gointothestory.blcklst.com.
- StudioBinder – useful articles and resources: https://www.studiobinder.com/category/scriptwriting/writing/.
- The Script Lab – script downloads & useful articles: https://thescriptlab.com.
- Indie Film Hustle – podcast, blog & other useful resources: https://indiefilmhustle.com.
- No Film School – super useful site with plenty of resources, including script downloads: https://nofilmschool.com.
- Film Courage – fantastic YouTube channel and site about writing: https://filmcourage.com.
- Internet Movie Script Database – comprehensive listings of screenplays: https://imsdb.com.
- Simply Scripts – another great screenplay database: https://www.simplyscripts.com.
- Script Notes – podcast and resources from Hollywood screenwriters John August and Craig Mazin: https://scriptnotes.net.
- On The Page – podcast and info from Pilar Alessandra: https://www.onthepage.tv/on-the-page-podcast/.
- Festival Formula – company which helps filmmakers with the festival circuit: https://www.festivalformula.com.

- Smart Blogger – free downloads, info and advice on blogging: https://smartblogger.com.
- Social Media Just For Writers – advice on how to utilise social media properly as a writer: https://socialmediajustforwriters.com.
- Writer's Digest – good craft and career info: https://www.writersdigest.com
- Writers & Artists – advice and info, plus the annual yearbook: https://www.writersandartists.co.uk.
- Jerry Jenkins – fantastic writing advice from a 21 *New York Times* bestselling author https://jerryjenkins.com.
- Nanowrimo – yearly writing challenge, plus advice: https://nanowrimo.org.
- The Write Life – great info and advice on freelance writing & novel writing: https://thewritelife.com.
- Writers Helping Writers – brilliant writing craft advice: https://writershelpingwriters.net.
- Make A Living Writing – advice on earning money as a writer: https://makealivingwriting.com.
- Seth's Blog – Seth Godin's blog on self-belief, marketing and respect: https://seths.blog.
- The Creative Penn – advice on writing, publishing & marketing: http://thecreativepenn.com.
- Kindlepreneur – all about book marketing: https://kindlepreneur.com.
- The Self Publisher with CS Lakin – self-publishing advice and resources: http://theselfpublisher.com.
- Self Publishing School with Chandler Bolt – more self-publishing advice https://self-publishingschool.com.
- Publishizer – crowdfund a book deal: https://publishizer.com.
- Inkshares – build a readership, sell pre-sales of your book: https://www.inkshares.com.
- Unbound – another crowdfunding publisher: https://unbound.com.
- Wattpad – build your readership: https://www.wattpad.com.
- Kindle Direct Publishing – publish your book for free: https://kdp.amazon.com/.
- Audible – submit your book for the chance of an audio deal:

https://www.audiblehub.com/submit.
- WF Howes – another audiobook company: https://www.wfhowes.co.uk.
- Kickstarter – crowdfund your book or film: https://www.kickstarter.com.
- Substack – start a paid newsletter: https://substack.com.
- Patreon – monthly membership site for fans of your writing: https://www.patreon.com.

And many, many thanks to the countless writers, readers, filmmakers and fans who conversed with me, RT'd my requests and answered my questions about their favourite thrillers whilst I was writing this book. You rock!

Lucy V. Hay, February 2023

INDEX

OLDCASTLE BOOKS

POSSIBLY THE UK'S SMALLEST INDEPENDENT PUBLISHING GROUP

Oldcastle Books is an independent publishing company formed in 1985 dedicated to providing an eclectic range of titles with a nod to the popular culture of the day.

Imprints vary from the award winning crime fiction list, NO EXIT PRESS (now part of Bedford Square Publishers), to lists about the film industry, KAMERA BOOKS & CREATIVE ESSENTIALS. We have dabbled in the classics, with PULP! THE CLASSICS, taken a punt on gambling books with HIGH STAKES, provided in-depth overviews with POCKET ESSENTIALS and covered a wide range in the eponymous OLDCASTLE BOOKS list. Most recently we have welcomed two new sister imprints with THE CRIME & MYSTERY CLUB and VERVE, home to great, original, page-turning fiction.

oldcastlebooks.com

kamera BOOKS creative ESSENTIALS

HIGH STAKES

| OLDCASTLE BOOKS
| POCKET ESSENTIALS
| NO EXIT PRESS
| KAMERA BOOKS
| CREATIVE ESSENTIALS
| PULP! THE CLASSICS
| HIGHSTAKES PUBLISHING
| THE CRIME & MYSTERY CLUB
| VERVE BOOKS